Morton Feldman

Morton Feldman

Friendship and Mourning in the New York Avant-Garde

Ryan Dohoney

BLOOMSBURY ACADEMIC
NEW YORK • LONDON • OXFORD • NEW DELHI • SYDNEY

BLOOMSBURY ACADEMIC
Bloomsbury Publishing Inc
1385 Broadway, New York, NY 10018, USA
50 Bedford Square, London, WC1B 3DP, UK
29 Earlsfort Terrace, Dublin 2, Ireland

BLOOMSBURY, BLOOMSBURY ACADEMIC and the Diana logo are trademarks of Bloomsbury Publishing Plc

First published in the United States of America 2022

Copyright © Ryan Dohoney, 2022

For legal purposes the Acknowledgments on pp. 195–7 constitute an extension of this copyright page.

Cover design: Louise Dugdale
Cover image © Renate Ponsold, "Morton Feldman in Philip Guston's Studio" (1965) courtesy of the Paul Sacher Foundation.

All rights reserved. No part of this publication may be reproduced or transmitted in any form or by any means, electronic or mechanical, including photocopying, recording, or any information storage or retrieval system, without prior permission in writing from the publishers.

Bloomsbury Publishing Inc does not have any control over, or responsibility for, any third-party websites referred to or in this book. All internet addresses given in this book were correct at the time of going to press. The author and publisher regret any inconvenience caused if addresses have changed or sites have ceased to exist, but can accept no responsibility for any such changes.

A catalog record for this book is available from the Library of Congress.

ISBN: HB: 978-1-5013-4546-3
PB: 978-1-5013-4545-6
ePDF: 978-1-5013-4548-7
eBook: 978-1-5013-4547-0

Typeset by Deanta Global Publishing Services, Chennai, India

To find out more about our authors and books visit www.bloomsbury.com and sign up for our newsletters.

For Sheila Hall

Contents

List of Figures	viii
Introduction	1
1　Spontaneity, Intimacy, and Friendship in the 1950s	17
2　"*Élan vital* . . . and how to fake it"	53
Intermission: The Necessary Other	93
3　The Elegiac Science	107
4　"We broke up because of style"	143
Conclusion: Friendship's Silence	185
Acknowledgments	195
Bibliography	198
Index	209

Figures

0.1	Howard Kanovitz, *The New Yorkers II* (1966)	2
1.1	*Projection 2* (page 1) by Morton Feldman	25
1.2	*Intersection* (page 1) by Morton Feldman	29
1.3	*Marginal Intersection* (page 1) by Morton Feldman	33
1.4	Philip Guston, *Head–Double View*, 1958	41
2.1	Morton Feldman, *Intermission 6*, first version	61
2.2	Merle Marsicano	62
2.3	Morton Feldman, *Figure of Memory* (reconstruction by Edwin Hymovitz)	64
2.4	*Works of Calder*, directed by Herbert Matter, 1950	70
2.5	*Jackson Pollock 51*, directed by Hans Namuth, 1951	76
2.6	*Jackson Pollock 51*, directed by Hans Namuth, 1951	78
2.7	*Sculpture by Lipton*, directed by Nathan Boxer, 1954	82
I.1	William Lovelace. L to R: Nicholas Zumbro, Morton Feldman, Edgard Varèse, Frederic Rzweski, Charlotte Moorman	94
I.2	*Projection 1* (page 1) by Morton Feldman with Charlotte Moorman's realization	97
3.1	Morton Feldman, "Give My Regards to Eighth Street," working copy of *Three Clarinets, Cello, and Piano*	115
3.2	Morton Feldman, "In Memory of My Feelings," working copy of *For Frank O'Hara*	117
3.3	Paula Court. Joan La Barbara	126
4.1	Renate Ponsold. Morton Feldman and Philip Guston	144
4.2	Philip Guston, *Last Piece*, 1958	149
4.3	Philip Guston, *Attar*, 1953	150
4.4	Philip Guston, *Friend—To M.F.*, 1978	163
4.5	Philip Guston, *The Coat II*, 1977	165
4.6	Philip Guston, *Back View*, 1977	166

Introduction

In Howard Kanovitz's *The New Yorkers II* (1965, Figure 0.1), Morton Feldman sits in the painter's Second Avenue studio. He is shown on the far left in profile, eyes downcast, a cigarette in his hand. Others in the painting seem similarly distracted. Larry Rivers, back and to Feldman's left, also gazes downward. Sam Hunter, in front of Rivers, stares at the back wall of the studio. Next to the window, Kanovitz himself prepares to take a drag while looking past Alex Katz, who stands in the foreground with his back to us. An unidentified man in the foreground also gazes down. Positioned between Kanovitz and Katz, B. H. Friedman looks to the far left, past Feldman. Our focus is drawn to the center of the canvas, where poet and critic Frank O'Hara, with louche countenance and limp wrist, exudes camp glamour.

Along with being a signature photorealist work of the 1960s, *The New Yorkers II* is a curious social text. It portrays a group of close friends, all extensively involved in the midcentury avant-garde and each other's work. Frank O'Hara wrote poems and essays about Feldman and Rivers.[1] His great long poem "Second Avenue" was written in Kanovitz's studio that the painting depicts. Friedman edited Feldman's collected writings.[2] Kanovitz's photo portrait of Feldman appeared on the cover for the composer's 1968 LP, *The Early Years* (itself a reissue of a record from 1959 with liner notes by O'Hara).[3] Katz and Feldman served together on the faculty of Mercedes Matter's Studio School.[4] Rivers and Kanovitz played jazz together in the Village and Feldman arranged tunes for them.[5] Hunter wrote the foundational *Modern American Painting and Sculpture*, which positioned the New York avant-garde within the broader arc of modernism and which Feldman taught in his classes at the University of Buffalo.[6] Yet, despite all this intimacy, these men can't seem to face one another. O'Hara is radiant, of course, but no one can fix eyes on him. If this is an example of what Lytle Shaw would call coterie art, what do these deferrals of vision say about this community of friends? Connection and communication

Figure 0.1 Howard Kanovitz, *The New Yorkers II* (1966). © 2020 Artists Rights Society (ARS), New York / VG Bild-Kunst, Bonn.

are denied. Feldman and company are estranged from, or at least indifferent to, one another. Shaw has noted that "the term friends would often seem to designate an almost accidental social formation, stripped of intentionality and form."[7] It indubitably does here. The men appear to have run into one another in the studio and have nothing to talk about. But, as my account of this group's ties indicates, they were deeply intertwined. With cutting irony, Kanovitz's *New Yorkers II* dramatizes a fundamental, even agonistic tension within this world—a state of affairs to which Morton Feldman was hardly immune.

Unlike those depicted in *The New Yorkers II*, I don't know Morton Feldman. And after more than twenty years of listening and fifteen of research and writing, I'm not convinced I even *can* know him. This is the case even though I feel very close to his music. My recognition of this absent presence keeps certain questions in my mind as I write: What would he make of my work? Would he receive these words as gestures of friendship? What would he make of my interpretations, my imputations of agency, my attempts at recapturing his inner life, my invasive pilfering through his letters, diaries, and composition notebooks? Are these things friends do? The work of history does not necessarily depend on the bonds of friendship. Prying open archives, I've seen traces not meant for my eyes. My interpretations of Feldman's friendships presume to speak for the dead on which I had no claim in life. Along with Michel de Certeau, I ask, "What about the bizarre relation I am keeping with current society and, through the intermediately of my technical activities, with death?"[8]

"Friends, there are no friends."[9] In this writing, my travels to archives, my puzzling over Feldman's—I want to say "Morty's"—barely decipherable handwriting, I am no friend. My actions, while intimately bound up with Feldman's life, have impure motives. They contribute to my name as a scholar (whatever that might be), they made a case for my tenure, and they give me an audience. My gestures, made in the spirit if not the name of friendship, appeal across the chasm of death. *O friend, I am no friend.* But within this entanglement of intimacy, distance, and loss, an impertinent question sticks in my mind: What kind of friend was Feldman? It is a query he would probably prefer I didn't ask, but I will argue that it matters immensely for our understanding of his music. For all its austerity, fragility, and abstraction, Feldman's music is bound up with human relationships. One only need at glance at the titles of his works—*For Franz Kline, For Frank O'Hara, For John Cage, For Christian Wolff, For Philip Guston, For Bunita Marcus, For Samuel Beckett, For Stefan Wolpe.* A litany of dedications, and a partial necrology.

In what follows, I explore expressions of friendship and mourning across Feldman's authorship. Along with bringing fresh insight into his music and aesthetics, I hope to draw friendship forward as a matter of concern for music studies. I also advance the claim that music is a special mode through which friendship is performed—as dedicatory act and means of group formation. Musical friendship is constituted through acts of performance, listening, and artistic response—acts that cut across Feldman's history. A heady collaborative sensibility animated his artistic community, that bohemian demimonde of painters, dancers, poets, and musicians we call "The New York School." As I argue in Chapter 1, friendship's intimacies fed the aesthetic-creative value of spontaneity at midcentury. Spontaneity was hardly medium-specific and was valued in music and painting as much as in poetry and dance. Working with and against mid-twentieth-century aesthetic discourses—particularly Clement Greenberg's formalism—I advance the claim across these chapters that the most important medium within the New York School was friendship. To be more explicit: friendship—as a way of life and a practice of art—was the condition of possibility for the New York School.

Morton Feldman: Friendship and Mourning is an attempt to generalize certain claims in my previous book, *Saving Abstraction*.[10] There, I focused on Feldman's friendship with Mark Rothko and their patrons, John and Dominique de Menil. Together, these actors worked together to establish the Rothko Chapel, with Feldman giving it a musical identity with his piece *Rothko Chapel*. This handful of relationships was inflected by economic and spiritual forces that trouble the egalitarianism we usually associate with friendship. Opening up these agonistic tensions allowed me to tell a story about the entanglement of experimental music, abstract art, Catholic modernism, and petroleum-fueled patronage in Houston, Texas. As I argue in this book, Feldman's friends, collaborators, patrons, and nemeses have further insights to offer us. While *Saving Abstraction* focused primarily on cross-domain engagements between music and painting in a ritualized space, the chapters that comprise this book track Feldman's friendships and collaborations across a range of disciplines, including visual art, film, dance, poetry, and, naturally, music. Uniting my investigations into the bounty of aesthetic artifacts I explore is an aesthetics of affection, reciprocity, and friendship.

In taking up friendship as an analytic, I insist on its multivalent capacities. I am in sympathy with Anne Dewey and Libbie Rifkin, who define friendships as "intimate relationships—erotic or platonic, same sex and different, dyadic and nondyadic—often but not necessarily ones of affection or mutual support."[11] Friendships are pluralistic, mutable, and powerful for the way they cut across and reshape extant kinship structures. My theorization of friendship has been deeply impacted by religious studies scholar Brenna Moore, whose work on the French Catholic Revival bore directly on *Saving Abstraction*. She, like Dewey and Rifkin, sees friendship a wide-open concept. She writes, "If we take seriously friendship as a category of analysis, it must understood as expansively and capaciously as possible," including such things as "imagined intimacy," "memories of love," "posthumous presence," and "betrayal." "All of this enables a capacious, multivalent [use] of the term friendship and an essential way to fully understand the formation of the . . . subject."[12] The friendships discussed herein take all of these forms, though I focus especially on posthumous presence (Frank O'Hara, Philip Guston) and betrayal (John Cage, Charlotte Moorman, Guston).

With her emphasis on negative affects like betrayal, Moore is explicit in her belief that friendships are hardly idealized or utopian social relationships:

> As I have come to see it, friendship is no safe haven from other kinds of power, no magic circle protected haven from race, gender, and class, but intimacy and friendship have their own *specific* . . . power within these broader societal forces in ways that can never be fully disentangled. If we take seriously interpersonal relationships, we cannot neglect an analysis of power and politics; but it keeps our studies of structure tethered to people's experiences, and offers a crucial matrix for analyzing that intermediary realm between the individual and society. . . . Just as friendship as a category of analysis cannot exclude other kinds of disciplinary powers, neither can it occlude hatred, betrayal, and inevitable ruptures in bonds, the disappointments that can overwhelm them.[13]

I've suggested that these fraught dimensions of friendship subtend Kanovitz's *New Yorkers II* and throughout this book I emphasize the precariousness of Feldman's social ties. Moreover, I argue that Feldman's music is especially well-disposed to an analytic grounded in friendship. As the ephemeral performance of community, music—no less than friendship itself—is subject to myriad disciplinary powers. Disciplinary, yes, but also liberating and invigorating energies. One of friendships' affordances that recurs throughout this book is *permission*. Friendships within the New York School allowed these artists and musicians to do their work, to take aesthetic risks, and to make art a way of life. A letter from Feldman to David Tudor in the early 1950s gives us a sense of what this felt like:

> When M.C. [Richards] came over to June's the other evening, I realized for the fiftieth time this year how much I have taken your friendship and desperately (yes desperately) needed devotion to my work. Hardly a day passes when I don't think of you in either some connection with my work which you helped me make permissible for me to do, or the humanness of

just our lonely selves. Needless to say, I am just saturated with sentimentality as I write this short note.

The work goes on and the months ahead have exactly the same blackness as the kind of music I would like to write—a music like violently boiling water in some monstrous kettle. But I can't seem to get the water hot enough or the kettle large enough to do it. The last INTERSECTION, which I wrote for you, is just an unrealized hint of what is to come.

This past year! I know you know some of my troubles: THE LOUDEST SECRET LIFE IN THE WORLD—all that along with my continual nagging about a bronchial condition which is, at last, waning.[14]

Feldman's vulnerability is bracing. The sheer intensity of his and Tudor's friendship is charged with desperation, devotion, and—as noted earlier—permission. Tudor's commitment as a musical friend is what makes Feldman's work possible *at all* in the situation of privation they find their "lonely selves" in. Feldman calls back to *Intersection 3*, a piano solo for Tudor written in graph notation. It prophesied what Feldman hoped would come artistically thanks to the pianist's permission: violent, boiling sounds. Permission was something Feldman needed from his friends, including Cage—who gave him "early permissions to have confidence in [his] instincts"—and from Guston, who provided similar sustenance.[15]

Mutual support was not limited to encouragement, but encouragement was required for music to come into being. As I discuss in Chapter 1 and the Intermission, Feldman's graph music required the collaboration and goodwill of musicians. These *necessary others* (as I call them) provided essential contributions to the graph works' realizations.[16] Notated on graph paper and without indications of specific pitch beyond broad ranges, Feldman's *Intersections* and *Projections* required deep creative engagement on the part of their performers. The musicians complete the work either spontaneously, in the moment of performance, or with careful co-compositional collaboration. For musicians like David Tudor—as well as for Charlotte Moorman after him—co-compositional work consisted of transforming Feldman's graphs into fully notated and repeatable scores.[17] In his study of Tudor's realization of Feldman's *Intersections*, John Holzaepfel has beautifully captured their inherently social character.[18] He shows how the aesthetic sensibility of *Intersection 3*—its violent, boiling virtuosity—resulted from the deployment of Tudor's masterful technique in dialog with Feldman's subtle control of sonic texture and density. Open, indeterminate compositions like *Intermission 3* exemplify something fundamental about music: that it is always already a performance of plurality. As a pluralist practice, it is dependent upon communal effort. Such effort—emphasized in, but by no means limited to, avant-garde work—depends as much upon "sentimentality" as it does performing ability. It is the work of the chapters that follow to track these sentimental performances across Feldman's interdisciplinary collaborations.

My sense of music as a potent window onto friendship (and vice versa) grew out of a long engagement with the thought of Hannah Arendt. While she might at first blush seem an unusual interlocutor for Feldman, she was herself on the periphery of the New York School.[19] Arendt counted the critic Harold Rosenberg as a close friend and worked closely with Christian Wolff's parents at Pantheon Books.[20] Wolff considered her a friend. Arendt also lectured at the Eighth Street Artists Club, where she likely would have encountered Feldman, O'Hara, Guston, and Cage. Beyond these personal ties, her investigations into political action, natality, and plurality have stark aesthetic implications. She noted the important work that cultural goods—including artworks—do to help others build a common world. She writes that the world

> is related . . . to the human artifact, the fabrication of human hands, as well as to affairs which go on among those who inhabit the man-made world together. To live together in the world means essentially that a world of things is between those who have it in common as a table is located between those who sit around it.[21]

In my account of Kanovitz's *The New Yorkers II*, I noted how a slew of creative artifacts linked the group of men portrayed—including the painting itself. *Intersection 3* functions similarly: it brought Feldman and Tudor together into a mutually creative relationship that resulted in a public, world-making performance. Works of art come to fill the space between others—bringing them into relation while also respecting their uniqueness. Or as O'Hara put it, in rather Arendtian fashion, "The poem is at last between two persons instead of two pages."[22]

My engagement with Arendt's thought on aesthetics has been greatly aided by philosopher Cecilia Sjöholm, who has gone further than most in disclosing the political theorist's relevancy for artistic analysis. Building on Arendt, Sjöholm argues that "through its sensible qualities, [art] makes public space a product of aesthesis, implying an invisible web of forms of being that help produce our perception. When the public sphere is minimized and exploited, art escapes more and more into intimate details. At the same time, these details are made public."[23] Sjöholm insightfully draws out the tensions between public and private meaning in artworks—tensions to which Arendt is sensitive and that I myself have had to attend to in documenting the importance of friendship to Feldman's music.

If anything, Feldman relished intimate details and preferred performances between friends. He was explicit about the tension he felt between friendship and publicity, speaking in Toronto in 1982:

> So I really want you as my confidante, I want you all as my friends, but I don't want you as my audience. Because the problem is, is that, if music is to be an art form, it has to exist at least six weeks. Give us six weeks without an audience, and maybe something else could happen. So that's what I'm plea-ing for. Accept my goodwill. And my good nature. And feel that maybe the role of the composer and the audience has to, will, must, and possibly could, change.[24]

I explore in Chapter 1 how the tension between publicity and privacy plays out in Feldman's music in the 1950s, but it's clear that it was regularly on his mind: he often expressed an overwhelming nostalgia for his group of friends—those "lonely selves" who, without the intrusion of the world, could make art that mattered. Feldman's efforts resonate with Jon Nixon's powerful reading of Arendt. He finds in her life's work an ongoing "hermeneutics of friendship"—that is, persistent reciprocity and negotiation between oneself and the world, a practice deepened and made meaningful by one's relation to others.[25]

Along with insights from Arendtian aesthetics, I build on work from within literary studies that has thematized friendship in New York School modernism. Andrew Epstein notes a veritable "obsession with friendship" in postwar American poetry and convincingly argues that "aesthetic and cultural forms cannot be fully understood through the study of individual authors in isolation or solely as manifestations of external sociopolitical conditions, but rather should be seen as a product of densely interwoven cultural, intertextual, interpersonal spaces."[26] He deftly shows how the friendship of Frank O'Hara, John Ashbery, and Amiri Baraka provide one such space for the investigation of a mutually resonant but contested poetics.

Frank O'Hara also serves as a protagonist in Lytle Shaw's groundbreaking work on the "poetics of coterie." Where Epstein keeps his trenchant insights focused on poetry, Shaw shows how O'Hara's writing provides significant insight across disciplines (specifically literature and visual art) as well as how texts and artistic artifacts provide ways of reading kinship structures such as coterie and friendship. Shaw's analysis of coterie homes in on O'Hara's use of proper names in his poetry. These names—of friends, lovers, and so on—mediate between audiences, family structures, and literary history.[27] In one sense—a sense that Feldman himself privileges—coterie can be used to describe an avant-garde prior to its dissemination, when its art and music are known only to a select few. As discussed earlier, Feldman's eventual success and wide dissemination did not sit easily with him, and he nostalgically insisted on numerous occasions that he would rather be in Cage's loft or settled in at Guston's studio than in a concert hall.

Feldman expressed this desire throughout his writings and, like O'Hara, made frequent reference to specific friends. As he reflected in "Give My Regards to Eighth Street," "The fifties have to do with names, names, names. That's why they're worth writing about."[28] Feldman emphasized proper names in his essays and in the titles of his compositions; doing so, he shares a rhetorical strategy with O'Hara, for whom names are

> recalcitrant matter—designating identities from which we . . . are held at a careful distance. To universalize them is not adequate; instead, they are strategic remainders that block our easy identification. The effect of these names depends upon a version of the contextual loss—at the double levels of the speaker and the reader. . . . Though O'Hara is continually supplying context, he seems to be interested in what happens when it breaks down, when we encounter markers of identity that we cannot recuperate.[29]

Feldman's logic is similar. The emphasis across his authorship with "names, names, names" estranges us from his intimate community while at the same time highlighting what Shaw calls "contextual loss." This loss is dramatized and most pronounced as something Feldman experiences himself—hence his interest in transforming anonymous audience members into friends. He mourns coterie as his lost context, especially in his elegies for O'Hara and Guston, which I address in Chapters 3 and 4, respectively. Shaw's insight into O'Hara's poetics—that he is interested in what happens when context breaks down—finds a compelling analogy in Feldman's later, long works in which various musical contexts are supplied, ingratiated to us, and then unceremoniously withdrawn. While this is not the same as O'Hara's textual play, the fact that these profound moments of loss are often experienced in Feldman's elegiac works (including *Three Voices* and *For Philip Guston*) suggests affective resonances between their aesthetics. I explore these resonances in depth in Chapter 3.

Shaw is critical of a historicism that treats coterie "as a determinate 'context' that allows one to ground textual valences in specific historical conditions" because it tends "to hypostasize context."[30] Despite this, I remain committed to a historicist, archival approach, largely because empirical work brings to light conflicting intentions that, instead of hypostatizing context, result in their proliferation. My dilemma as a historian of Feldman's world has been how to respect the brute fact of contextual loss while productively speculating on what is recoverable.

I've been fortunate that there are recent models for this sort of inquiry within musicology. Ellen Harris's recent biography of George Frideric Handel argues for the revelatory power approaching a musician's life through their friends. Through her narration of Handel's friendship networks, Harris shows the composer's struggle to negotiate public and private personae—struggles not dissimilar to Feldman's own resistance to his increasing popularity in the late twentieth century.[31] Her historiographical approach—a triangulation of Handel's life and works through his intimate relations—serves as a model for my own. Edward Klorman, for his part, has shown friendship's potential use in our work as music analysts. Taking as his archive W. A. Mozart's chamber music, Klorman finds a sociability cutting across the music, impacting not only its scenes of performance but also its form. While out of courtesy to my interdisciplinary audience I have largely avoided technical musical discussion, Klorman's work shows us how friendship affects musical expression down to the smallest compositional detail.[32] Paul Berry, in turn, working from Johannes Brahms's circle of friends, looks beyond the oeuvre of a single musician and argues that patterns of allusion, nostalgia, and grief are shared across authorships.[33] Such intertextual interpenetration between the music of Brahms and others—including Clara Wieck Schumann and Joseph Joachim—shows how music can provide the basis for friendship. It sustains memory and revivifies our feelings for one another.

Berry's insights are particularly salient to the work that I undertake in the chapters that follow. But where he excavates resonances between musical works, I trace rhetorics of allusion and intertextuality across artforms—including music, dance, poetry, painting, sculpture, and film. Such inter-art translations are always approximate to some extent, but their reception reveals much about how New York School modernism gained a sense of social and emotional—if not aesthetic—coherence. In this book, I am particularly interested in what philosopher Adriana Cavarero calls *narrative reciprocity* as a form of intertextuality.[34] Building on Arendt's concern for "the web of human relationships and enacted stories," Cavarero describes friendship as a relationship woven from the mutual exchange of life stories.[35] These exchanges enliven the scene of our *narrative selves*: "The scene consists in the intersection of autobiographical narrations, which make sure of the result of the reciprocal biographical activity. Put simply, I tell you my story in order to make you tell it to me. At work, therefore, is a mechanism of reciprocity."[36] For Cavarero, friends are distinguished from acquaintances by virtue of the former's ability to tell the story of the other: "friendship is a specific horizon where this narratability can be meaningfully translated in the act of a reciprocal narration."[37] Cavarero's idea of narratability focuses largely on quotidian acts of female friendship, but she does recognize the role that artworks play in reciprocal narration—her prime example being Gertrude Stein's *The Autobiography of Alice B. Toklas*. In the Intermission, I connect Cavarero's reading of Stein to Moorman's realization of Feldman's graph music.

As I noted with regard to Kanovitz's *New Yorkers II*, the friends of the New York School told stories about each other. Feldman took the role of narrator seriously, as did O'Hara and Guston. Indeed, we might think of Guston's need late in life to tell stories through a return to figuration as a confirmation of this powerful impulse to offer narratives to his friends. I've already mentioned O'Hara's sleeve notes for Feldman's 1959 LP; he also wrote about Guston's painting. In offering narratives of both of his friends, O'Hara made their abstractions intelligible for audiences.[38] With Bill Berkson, he composed "St. Bridget's Hymn to Philip Guston," a sterling example of a poem being "between people" rather than pages.[39] Feldman, too, wrote on Guston and eulogized O'Hara following his tragic death on Fire Island in 1966. Guston, in a series of late works from 1977 to 1979, told stories about Feldman that attempted to keep the memory of a friendship alive after it had frayed. These acts of reciprocal narration are complicated by their status as public documents that purport to say something meaningful to both the artist and their audiences. Throughout Feldman's life, the public performance of private relationships returns as problem—one he bristled against even as he actively participated in it.

Several times in his life, Feldman found himself in a situation where narrative reciprocity became impossible. O'Hara's death was once such instance; his periodic disagreements with Cage another (Chapter 1); the collapse of his friendship with Guston another still. These events evince another aspect of friendship that I track through Feldman's friendship in the New York School: that of its *shared estrangement*. Tom Roach, building on the late work of Michel Foucault, has eloquently elaborated on this dimension of friendship. In sharing our estrangement with others, we recognize that that death is always already present. Being-toward-death positions friendships between production and negation. With Feldman's friendships, we see how negation can flare up as death (in the case of O'Hara) or as destructive aesthetic disagreement (with Guston). Feldman was at pains to recognize and develop the aspect of his and his friends' art that was *like death*. He recognized it in O'Hara's poetry, which conveyed affects of *sudden death*. Guston too, felt tremendous sympathy with Feldman's equation of creation and death (see Chapter 4). Feldman himself wanted his music—like Socratic philosophy—to be preparation for death.[40]

Near the end of his life, Feldman was asked by a stranger, "Do you compose only for friends or for yourself?" He responded,

> Friends? Most of my friends are now dead. If you had asked me that question thirty-five years ago I would have said: "Yes, I think I do." And there used to be a lot of them. You see here the last of a certain species. I am one of the last of the kind of character that you saw in New York thirty years ago. I am at the end of the line.

In the chapters that follow, I take Feldman at his word and show just how entangled with friendship his music and writing are. Chapter 1, "Spontaneity, Intimacy, and Friendship in the 1950s," takes a synoptic view of the 1950s, showing the power of Feldman's friendships to engender the creative spontaneity that was the hallmark of New York School modernism. Guston, Cage, and O'Hara figure prominently, and I track their role in narrating Feldman's work for his nascent public. Chapter 2, "'*Élan vital* . . . and how to fake it,'" documents Feldman's collaborations with dancer and choreographer Merle Marsicano and his soundtracks for films featuring his friends Jackson Pollock and Seymour Lipton. I show how these inter-art events drew upon vitalism as vernacular metaphysics that, like spontaneity, was a shared value among the New York School. This chapter reevaluates scholars' claims on Cage's estrangement from Abstract Expressionism, suggesting that vitalism provided more common ground than has been previously recognized. A brief Intermission, "The Necessary Other," focuses on Charlotte Moorman's performance of Feldman's graph score *Projection 1* and Earle Brown's *Synergy*, and in doing so, examines the reception the New York School's music in the 1960s. Moorman, through her alternately rigorous and irreverent performance practice, shows the ambiguous inheritance of the revolution of the 1950s.

With Chapters 3 ("The Elegiac Science") and 4 ("'We broke up because of style'"), my focus turns to mourning and shared estrangement. Chapter 3 looks in greater detail at the historical record of Feldman and O'Hara's friendship. I look for traces of O'Hara in Feldman's work following the poet's death and find the composer mourning him in his music throughout the 1970s and into the 1980s. I close the chapter with an extended discussion of Feldman's *Three Voices* and the role of composer-vocalist Joan La Barbara in its realization. Chapter

4 narrates the arc of Feldman and Guston's relationship and emphasizes the importance of dedication, mutual support, and reciprocal narration to it. I show how, following the demise of their friendship, each undertook projects that moved between mourning and melancholia—the latter experienced most prominently in Feldman's *For Philip Guston*. The conclusion turns to Hannah Arendt's work to reflect further on Feldman and Guston and the importance of silence to the maintenance of friendship. Taken as a whole, these chapters work with and through Arendt's and Feldman's styles of thought; they attempt to describe a shared sensibility, which, as Susan Sontag noted long ago, is particularly difficult.[41] More ruminative and speculative than *Saving Abstraction*, these studies of Feldman and his world are an attempt to capture something of what it felt like to be among his coterie at a moment when "nobody understood art."[42]

Notes

1. Frank O'Hara, "New Directions in Music," in Morton Feldman, *Give My Regards to Eighth Street*, ed. B. H. Friedman (Cambridge, MA: Exact Change, 2000), 211–17 and Frank O'Hara, "Larry Rivers: Why I Paint as I Do," in *Art Chronicles, 1954–1966* (New York: G. Braziller, 1975), 106–20.
2. Feldman, *Give My Regards to Eighth Street*.
3. Morton Feldman, *The Early Years*. LP. Columbia Odyssey 32160302. 1968.
4. For more on Matter and the Studio School, see Chapter 4.
5. See Kanovitz's prefatory note to Kurt Weill, "Alabama Song," arr. Morton Feldman (London: Universal Edition, 2004). UE 32423.
6. Sam Hunter, *Modern American Painting and Sculpture* (New York: Dell, 1959).
7. Lytle Shaw, *Frank O'Hara: The Poetics of Coterie* (Iowa City: University of Iowa Press, 2006), 235.
8. Michel de Certeau, "The Historiographical Operation," in *The Writing of History*, trans. Tom Cooley (New York: Columbia University Press, 1988), 56.
9. Friedrich Nietzsche, *Human, All Too Human*, trans. R. J. Hollingdale (Cambridge: Cambridge University Press, 1996), 149.
10. Ryan Dohoney, *Saving Abstraction: Morton Feldman, the de Menils, and the Rothko Chapel* (New York: Oxford University Press, 2019).

11 Anne Dewey and Libbie Rifkin, "Introduction," in *Among Friends*, ed. Dewey and Rifkin (Iowa City: University of Iowa Press, 2013), 5.
12 Brenna Moore, "Friendship and the Cultivation of Religious Sensibilities," *Journal of the American Academy of Religio* 83, no. 2 (2015): 437–63, 457.
13 Ibid., 439.
14 Feldman sent this letter to Tudor at Black Mountain College. Morton Feldman. Letter to David Tudor. June 15, 1953. David Tudor Papers. Box 53, folder 7. Getty Research Institute. Los Angeles, California.
15 Morton Feldman, "Liner Notes," in *Give My Regards to Eighth Street*, 5. For more on Guston's support, see Chapter 4.
16 I borrow the concept of "the necessary other" from Adriana Cavarero. See Adriana Cavarero, *Relating Narratives: Storytelling and Selfhood*, trans. Paul A. Kottman (New York: Routledge, 2000), 81–93.
17 The compositional nuances of Feldman's graphs have been extensively and insightfully detailed by David Cline. See David Cline, *The Graph Music of Morton Feldman* (Cambridge: Cambridge University Press, 2016).
18 John Holzaepfel, "The *Intersections* of Morton Feldman and David Tudor," in *The New York Schools of Music and Visual Art*, ed. Stephen Johnson (New York: Routledge, 2002), 159–72.
19 Brigid Cohen has done important work to bring Arendt's thought into dialog with music studies. See Cohen, *Stefan Wolpe and the Avant-Garde Diaspora* (Cambridge: Cambridge University Press, 2012), and Cohen, "Ono in Opera: A Politics of Art and Action, 1960–1962," *ASCAP / Journal* 3, no. 1 (2018): 41–66. Arendt spoke at the Artists Club on March 23, 1951, on the topic of "The European Intellectual." See Philip Pavia, *Club without Walls*, ed. Natalie Edgar (New York: Midmarch Arts Press, 2007), 162.
20 Christian Wolff, interview with the author, January 18, 2018.
21 Hannah Arendt, *The Human Condition* (Chicago, IL: University of Chicago Press, 1998), 52.
22 Frank O'Hara, "Personism," in *The Collected Poems of Frank O'Hara*, ed. Donald Allen (Berkley, CA: University of California Press, 1995), 499.
23 Cecilia Sjöholm, *Doing Aesthetics with Arendt: How to See Things* (New York: Columbia University Press, 2015), 12.
24 Morton Feldman, "Toronto Lecture," in *Morton Feldman Says*, ed. Chris Villars (London: Hyphen, 2006), 140.
25 Jon Nixon, *Hannah Arendt and the Politics of Friendship* (New York: Bloomsbury, 2015), 159–74.

26 Andrew Epstein, *Beautiful Enemies: Friendship and Postwar American Poetry* (New York: Oxford University Press, 2006), 1, 5.
27 Shaw, *Frank O'Hara*, 21.
28 Morton Feldman, "Give My Regards to Eighth Street," in *Give My Regards to Eighth Street*, 93.
29 Shaw, *Frank O'Hara*, 33.
30 Ibid., 20.
31 Ellen T. Harris, *George Frederic Handel: A Life with Friends* (New York: Norton, 2014).
32 Edward Klorman, *Mozart's Music of Friends: Social Interplay in the Chamber Works* (Cambridge: Cambridge University Press, 2016).
33 Paul Berry, *Brahms Among Friends: Listening, Performance, and the Rhetoric of Allusion* (New York: Oxford University Press, 2014).
34 Cavarero, *Relating Narratives*, 83.
35 Arendt, *The Human Condition*, 181.
36 Cavarero, *Relating Narratives*, 62–3.
37 Ibid., 63.
38 Frank O'Hara, "Growth and Guston," in *Art Chronicles*, 134–41.
39 Bill Berkson and Frank O'Hara, "St. Bridget's Hymn to Philip Guston," in *Hymns of St. Bridget and Other Writings* (Woodacre, CA: Owl Press, 2001), 28–38.
40 On this point, see Chapter 1 of Dohoney, *Saving Abstraction*.
41 "A sensibility (as distinct from an idea) is one of the hardest things to talk about." Susan Sontag, "Notes on Camp," in *Against Interpretation* (New York: Picador, 1966), 275.
42 Feldman, "Give My Regards to Eighth Street," 101.

1

Spontaneity, Intimacy, and Friendship in the 1950s

For J. Michelle Molina

The problem of music, of course, is that it is, by its very nature, a public art . . . Yet somehow there is something demeaning in the fact that there is no other dimension for music than this public one.[1]

Morton Feldman, "The Anxiety of Art"

Morton Feldman became a full-time composer at the age of forty. He had worked in the family business—a children's coat factory near LaGuardia Airport in New York City—since his early twenties and been disparaged by Pierre Boulez as a dilettante because of it.[2] In the spring of 1966, Feldman wrote to John Cage that the business "went kaput, and now I'm blessed with total insecurity."[3] His insecurity was hardly total. Through a chance meeting that year following a performance of Merce Cunningham's *Summerspace*—accompanied by his graph piece *Ixion*—Feldman established a long-lasting patronage relationship with Dominique de Menil.[4] Feted by a Guggenheim Fellowship as well, Feldman lectured in the UK, where his music was recorded and broadcast on BBC Radio. He also extended his avant-garde network within the United States, strengthening ties with musicians in California. Feldman at last seemed to be receiving public recognition. Yet all was not well. In a lecture given in early 1967 at Mercedes Matter's New York Studio School, Feldman cast a backward glance over his dissolving artistic community:

> When one begins to work—until that unlucky time when it is no longer involved with just a few friends, admirers, complainers—there is no separation between what you do and what you are. I don't mean that you

hope that what you are doing is real or right. That is not the question. You work. The work leads to a concept of music that draws attention. You soon find yourself in the world. Maybe not for the right reason—but you find yourself in the world.

Yet there was that other "world"—of conversation—of anonymity—of seeing the paintings in the intimacy of the studio and not in a museum—of playing a new work on the piano in your home and not in the concert hall—of the hours spent walking, eating and talking with John Cage and not wondering if I should fly to Paris from London in order to spend a few hours with him in arrogant crowds of people. Nothing lasts.[5]

Even with his burgeoning success, Feldman longed for the past. Publicity yielded estrangement. In Feldman's retrospection, home and the studio, not the concert hall, proffered security. There he felt the unity of who he was and what he did—whether sitting at his piano, watching Philip Guston paint, or having lunch with Mark Rothko. Intimacy arose from his experience of art and music within the private sphere.

It is ironic then that such intimate spaces were offered up for public consumption and became part of the general meaning of New York School modernism as the product of lonely men working in private. Hans Namuth's photographs of Jackson Pollock are the most famous example circulating in the mass media. As Caroline A. Jones has argued, artist films—like Namuth's of Pollock and Willem de Kooning, both soundtracked by Feldman—idealized the solipsistic creative vibrancy of studio spaces.[6] Even Feldman's home on the Lower East Side was offered up for prurient delectation in the middlebrow pages of *Harper's Baazar* in a 1952. The "Bozza Mansion," as Feldman and Cage christened it in honor of their landlord, was promoted as a far-out artists' colony: "Fresh, seemingly capricious winds in music, sculpture and painting come from an ancient ramshackle structure . . . at 326 Monroe Street in New York, in the shadow of the Williamsburg Bridge. There, in a neighborhood of grime and garlic, four friends—experimental, even stratospheric artists—have established three uncluttered studios with a spectacular view of the East River."[7] Accompanied by a photo of Cage at his piano and another of Feldman, Cage, and two other friends—Richard Lippold and Ray Johnson—sitting in Lippold's "de luxe hearse," the *Harper's* vignette grounds their off-center artistic practices in domestic creativity replete with the fresh air of American innovation. The "anonymous world" Feldman idealized was agonistically private and public, its primal scenes of creative spontaneity commodified in popular media.

Using Feldman's friendships within the New York School—with Guston, Cage, and Frank O'Hara—I explore tensions arising between intimate artistic production and its subsequent public circulation. In what follows, I elucidate intimacy's relationship to another affect of midcentury modernism—spontaneity. Whether achieved though "chance music," à la Feldman and Cage, or as "action painting," in Harold Rosenberg's formulation, spontaneity was, as Daniel Belgrad has argued, a cultural phenomenon at midcentury.[8] I take Belgrad's insights as axiomatic, but am more keen to track the gradations of meaning that shade spontaneity as it circulates from the private space of the artist's studio and musician's home into the public sphere. Risks accompany this movement, and spontaneity's heretofore unrecognized connection to intimacy is particularly audible in the music of New York School modernism. As a collective action produced by communities of varying degrees of familiarity, music dramatizes the ephemerality of spontaneity more than painting or poetry—the other arts I explore along with Feldman's compositions.

Following a brief theorization of intimacy and spontaneity in New York School modernism, I track their appearance through three interrelated events: Cage's promotion of Feldman's graph music at the Eighth Street Artists Club, the premiere of Feldman's orchestral graph piece *Marginal Intersection*, and the release of Feldman's first LP record, with liner notes by O'Hara. Each event raises questions about the proper place for the production of spontaneity. Is it within the confines of a close-knit group of friends? Can it survive wider circulation and, in the case of Feldman's LP, commodification? The question is ultimately a political one that highlights a fundamental tension between spontaneity's troubled relationship to both coterie and collective politics. For Feldman, spontaneity was lost the very moment it became a popular ideal. Feldman instead argues for a music of intimate autonomy resistant to the political demands of spontaneity. This palpable feeling of foreclosure becomes the lodestone for Feldman's post-1960 body of work, in which the improvisatory aspects of his music—especially the performer's role in determining pitch content—were curtailed.

Theorizing Spontaneity and Intimacy in New York School Modernism

But how were spontaneity and intimacy conceptualized in New York School modernism more broadly? If spontaneity was a desirable affective result of New York School praxis, how and where was it sustained? Despite the studio's mythologized status as a solipsistic zone of creation, it was hardly that. Guston, for instance, recalled his need for Feldman's friendship to continue his work: "Would Van Gogh have painted if he'd been all alone, if he had nobody to support him? And I answered that he couldn't have done. He had to have Theo, his brother. . . . So I had Morty. . . . I need Feldman to tell me I'm not insane."[9] He continued with an anecdote that elaborated on the chiasmatic relationship of friendship and creative action:

> I remember one time when I was beside myself—I'd destroyed a painting I don't know how many times. He lived at that time near me, a block away. And I was practically in tears and I called him. He said, "I'll be right over." And he came over and he looked at the painting. He didn't say anything. It was a painting I had destroyed a lot of. I'd been going on it for weeks, and in desperation I'd done some things, very spontaneous things, almost automatic, like you do when you destroy a painting. And so I told him all my troubles, and we went out and ate and saw a movie on Forty-second Street. And then he went home, and I went back to the studio and painted all night and did it.[10]

Of Guston's painting, Dore Ashton commented: "spontaneity occurs in brief flourishes, the winging strokes that he sometimes places in the atmosphere to set it vibrating. Or it is read in the assurance of a single, broad sweep of the brush, overriding the strokes beneath it. In other words, spontaneity is used artfully as another element that can express multiplicity in experience."[11] In Guston's reminiscence, spontaneous, "almost automatic" strokes no longer set things vibrating, and his overriding, destructive gestures no longer energized his creative practice. Only an encounter with his trusted friend restored him to a condition where action and spontaneity could again foster creativity.

Guston was not the only New York School modernist to note intimacy's role in sustaining spontaneity. Take, for instance, two manifestos: Meyer Schapiro's "The Liberating Quality of Avant-Garde Art" and Paul Goodman's "Advance-Guard Writing." Schapiro noted that

> The consciousness of the personal and spontaneous in the painting and sculpture stimulates the artist to invent devices of handling, processing, surfacing, which confer to the utmost degree the aspect of the freely made. Hence the great importance of the mark, the stroke, the brush, the drip, the quality of the substance of the paint itself, and the surface of the canvas as a texture and field of operation.[12]

The recognition of this spontaneous character depended upon communal reception grounded in intimacy: "The painting symbolizes an individual who realizes freedom and deep engagement of the self with his work. It is addressed to others who will cherish it, if it gives them joy, and who will recognize in it an irreplaceable quality and will be attentive to every mark of the maker's imagination and feeling." Schapiro, writing in the wake of Rosenberg's romantic anti-capitalism, envisions liberation emerging from an intimate exchange of mutual recognition. This recognition responds to the artwork's demand that it be approached tenderly and with joyful attention. The liberation proffered by avant-garde work is achieved through an erotics in which viewer, painter, and work cherish one another in a relational affective circuit. As the mediator of this affection, artworks bind a community together with a kind of social agency. Feldman described this agency as the sensation that "we are not looking at the painting, but the painting is looking at us."[13]

The idea that artworks could enable the spontaneous production of community was recognized earlier in Goodman's manifesto "Advance-Guard Writing," and he, more than Schapiro, explicitly associated avant-garde cultural production with community-formation. Like Rosenberg, Schapiro, and Feldman, Goodman sought an answer to the existential dilemma faced by the avant-garde's experimental world-making: "The essential present-day advance-guard is the physical reestablishment of community."[14] Affection is central to his avant-garde praxis, as much as cherishing is to Schapiro's: "the persons are estranged from themselves, from one another, and from their artist; he takes the initiative precisely by putting his arms around them and drawing them together."[15] Like Schapiro, Goodman sees the artwork as a mediator channeling intimate energies, beginning with "the artist's primary friends." As Lytle Shaw has shown, Goodman's work was an early influence on O'Hara, who later remarked in his own camp manifesto, "Personism," that "[t]he poem is at last between two persons instead of two pages."[16] Artworks knit groups together. Goodman notes that "community comes to exist by having *its* culture; the artist makes this culture."[17] Feldman echoed Goodman later in life when he quipped that the work of his community was "folk art" and that his own music was "like a new culture."[18]

Despite the importance of Feldman, Cage, and other musicians to New York School modernism, there is no equivalent *musical* manifesto to Goodman's and Schapiro's calls for spontaneity animated by intimacy. This is likely the case for two reasons. First, Cage was the primary musical manifesto writer in the 1950s and his Zen-inflected vitalism—though shared with others at the Club, as Valerie Hellstein has noted—emphasized an anti-subjective, anti-expressive position.[19] Cage, with his music of chance, and—as it was known by 1958—"indeterminacy," does not emphasize intersubjectivity as Schapiro and Goodman do. As Feldman's primary spokesperson in the 1950s, Cage identified his younger friend's music as a prime example of a non-relational spontaneity that accepted "whatever sounds come along." The second reason for the lack of a musical manifesto along these lines is that Feldman, with Cage's boosterism, barely wrote at all about his music in the 1950s. What is remarkably consistent in Feldman's writings post-1960, though, is his sustained lamentation over the loss of his community. A sense of thwarted intimacy suffuses these writings, lectures, and interviews.

Taking my cue from Schapiro and Goodman, I argue that Feldman's music sheds special light on problems of intimacy, spontaneity, and publicity. Music, as Antoine Hennion has insisted, is "the art of mediation itself," and simply because Cage did not describe Feldman's music in relational terms does not mean that it did not build communities.[20] (What, after all, is musical performance if not the ephemeral establishment of community?) I should, however, be clear that what emerges in my account of Feldman's music in the 1950s is not an egalitarian model of inter-art collaboration.[21] As Brenna Moore insists, "friendship is no safe haven from other kinds of power."[22] Substituting aesthetics for her focus on religious sensibilities, I follow her insight that "intimacy and friendship have their own *specific* religious power within these broader societal forces in ways that can never be fully disentangled."[23] Goodman himself noted that the continuation of community was no given: "To the extent then that this advance-guard does *not* succeed in welding a community, secure enough to bear criticism and anxiety . . . the sanctions against it are absolute and terrible."[24] Feldman's music often failed to forge an operable community in the eyes and ears of Cage as well as a broader public—even his deep friendship with Guston broke down in 1970 and never recovered. These private and public tensions shaped the varied meanings attributed to spontaneity in the 1950s and the ways in which Feldman's music was often misunderstood or unrealized in performance and audition. Feldman's spontaneity only conditionally overcame "the alienation of [his] art"—a desire he expressed privately in the early 1950s.[25] He did so most successfully only in the private sphere of trusted friends and collaborators including Guston, Rothko, O'Hara, and pianist-composer David Tudor. Feldman's spontaneity does not allow, as Joel Nickels argues of modernists poets such as William Carlos Williams, access to a self-actualizing multitude.[26] Nor does it produce—as Hannah Arendt, an occasional lecturer at the Eighth Street Artists Club, theorized—a spontaneous "space of appearances" congenial to the working out of politics.[27] Instead, Feldman idealizes a monadic intimacy that sidesteps the world to take refuge in friendship. This affectionate autonomy, Feldman concludes, is achieved only by reining in chance music's performative spontaneity, of which, as Cage noted, he was the originator.

Early Meanings of Spontaneity in Feldman's Chance Music

Cage and Feldman were merely acquaintances in the late 1940s. Both attended house concerts and salons at the Upper West Side home of Feldman's teacher, Stefan Wolpe and the poet Hilda Moorley Wolpe.[28] Feldman remembered that "the most significant composer that I knew was my teacher, Stefan Wolpe. It was actually through Wolpe that I met Cage. To some degree, though, I met him later in a more glamorous context."[29] The "more glamorous context," which circulates as the origin story of their meeting, was a performance of Anton Webern's *Symphonie, Op. 21*, conducted by Dmitri Mitropolous at Carnegie Hall in late January of 1950.[30] Cage arrived at the concert in the company of other gay modernists of varied aesthetic commitments—Virgil Thomson, Lou Harrison, and Ben Weber—but was alone when he encountered Feldman and his wife in the lobby following the performance of Webern's music. They had not deigned to remain in the hall for the performance of Sergei Rachmoninoff's *Symphonic Dances* that followed. Cage and Feldman's mutual love of Viennese modernism and antipathy for the romantic sentimentality of an "irrelevant genius" cemented their friendship.[31] Feldman, moreover, characterized their bond as a kind of modernist kinship: "Cage and I, we are the illegitimate sons of Webern."[32]

Despite Cage's greater popular reputation as the evangelist of indeterminacy, the composer credited Feldman as the originator of chance music, or, as Cage described it later, "[music] indeterminate with respect to its performance."[33] In their "Radio Happenings" conversations from the mid-1960s, Cage remembered,

> Isn't this true, that once when we had one of those conversations—I'm sure each of us so remembers—, walking through the streets of the Lower East Side and the Village and whatnot until late hours at night, I think I expressed once the idea that you had discovered a world, a musical world—because it was your music, really, that opened up everything.[34]

What Feldman had opened up were the notational strictures of the Euro-American classical tradition, which, especially with the extension of Arnold Schoenberg's twelve-tone music by Boulez and others, had become for both Feldman and Cage overly rigid and creatively stultifying. In late 1950, Feldman began a series of pieces composed on graph paper. He kept the main symbolic aspects of traditional musical notation: movement from left to right on the x-axis indicating progression through time and the y-axis indicating timbre, articulation, and frequency. Feldman's compositional invention was to prescribe only the broad range—high, middle, low—from which a particular pitch should be selected by the performers. On January 21, 1951, in what was the first public performance of one of the "graph pieces"—*Projection 2* (see Figure 1.1), for flute, trumpet, violin, cello, and piano—Feldman provided in the program notes the earliest extant conceptualization of his graphic notation:

> The title of this work refers to the projection of sounds into space. What particular sounds these are is left to the choice of the musicians at the moment of playing. The composer has indicated only timbre, register and time values. Since each performance of this composition is different, yet essentially the same, it will be played twice in succession.[35]

Here, in sharp contrast to his later statements, Feldman indicates that the performance of his graphic scores was meant to be realized "at the moment of playing" and not composed out by performers in advance, though Tudor took this latter approach.[36] This is the closest we come in Feldman's own words to the "improvisatory collaboration" with the composer that O'Hara described as one of the virtues of the graph music.[37] Spontaneity is here figured as decisions made in the flow of performance. That real-time music making was expected as a performance practice is indicated by the decision to play the piece twice, so that the changes might be apparent. Yet Feldman's insistence on

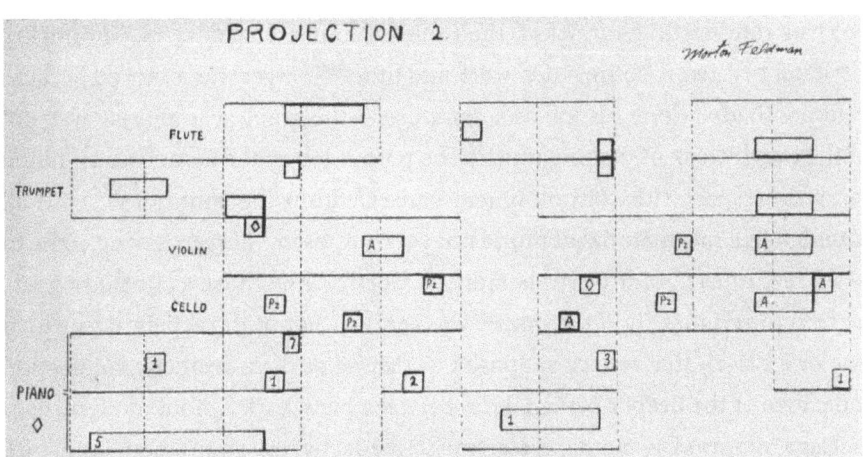

Figure 1.1 *Projection 2* (page 1) by Morton Feldman © 1962 by C.F. Peters Corporation. All rights reserved.

the different performances' essential sameness was justified by his interest in what he called "weight"—the particular combination and density of specific instrumental timbres at a given moment. Feldman expanded on this in a statement published in 1952—his only published commentary on his music of the 1950s: "Weight for me does not have its source in the manipulation of dynamics or tensions but rather resulting [sic] from a visual-aural response to sound as an image gone inward creating a general synthesis."[38] His elliptical elaboration, with its talk of responses and images, suggests that his version of spontaneity was inflected by the vitalism that he, along with Cage, encountered among members of the Eighth Street Artists Club.

Such metaphysical attributions did not endear Feldman's music to listeners. Early performances of Feldman's graph music raised many questions about its appropriateness for public audiences and even its status as music. The composer-critic Arthur Berger was among the first, if not the first, to apply the description of "chance" to this music and noted that Feldman "seems to have started the whole childish trend with his gimmick of indicating merely the note-lengths and ranges (high, low, medium) and allowing the players otherwise to choose any notes, within these broad limits, according to the caprice of the moment. The result was not even amusing."[39]

Berger's frustration with Feldman hinges on his view of graphic notation's incorporation of spontaneity as a "gimmick." As Sianne Ngai has argued, part of our frustration with gimmicks is their role as labor-saving devices. Gimmickry "irritates because it 'abbreviates' work and time."[40] Berger was annoyed because Feldman hadn't done his job as a composer—the graph was an easy way out of the tough work of making music. The proper job of the composer is "filling out a time span with continuity and pauses within the continuity. . . . It all sounded like raw material of music not yet composed." Berger, having come to hear "real music," didn't get his money's worth. Though, as a concluding jab, he recognized that "[a]ll this music was reminiscent of those paintings with a line or a blotch that we are supposed to marvel at"—an aesthetic connection indicative of the deeper personal ties between New York School modernists.[41]

Cage reported a similar assessment made by an anonymous audience member in his "Lecture on Something," given at the Eighth Street Artists Club on February 9, 1951, just a few weeks after the concert:

Someone said the other day, in reference to the performance of Feldman's music at Merce Cunningham's recent recital: "That kind of music if you call it music should not be played in a public hall, because many people do not understand it and they start talking or tittering and the result is that you can't hear the music be-cause of all these extraneous sounds." Going on, that someone said, "The music could be played and possibly appreciated, in a home where, not having paid to be entertained, those listening might listen and not have the impulse to titter or having it out of decorum squelch it and besides in a home it is more comfortable and quiet: there would be a better chance to hear it."[42]

Naturally, Cage disagreed with these comments and at more than sixty years remove it is quite easy to side with him. But in returning to the controversy over Feldman's music, the dilemma of the proper place for the production of spontaneity is opened up again. So too is the status of experimental music as a commodity form—its viability as a public art people will pay for. The critique of art economics and commodification is precisely Cage's point. The "new world" opened up by Feldman's music succeeds—in Cage's view—in demolishing the distinctions between public and private, between art and life. Cage's "Lecture on Something" was a dialogic exercise that echoed, developed, and put pressure on many of the ideas discussed at the Club. My reading of the lecture extends Hellstein's insights into its sympathetic resonances with abstract expressionist discourse. Moreover, I take "Lecture on Something" not only as Hellstein does—as evidence of a shared vitalist aesthetics common to Cage, Feldman, Rosenberg, and the painters—but also as a gesture of friendship on Cage's part offered to Feldman. Building on their intense creative exchange, Cage midwifed Feldman's initiation into the Club and made his music intelligible to it.

Near the opening of "Lecture on Something," Cage explores the problem of artistic production in relation to issues of gimmickry and commodification raised by the performance of Feldman's *Projection 2*:

[S]omeone said, "Art should come from within; then it is profound." But it seems to me Art goes within, and I don't see the need for "should" or "then" or "it" or "pro-found." When Art comes from within, which is what it was for so long doing, it be-came a thing which seemed to elevate the man who made it a–bove those who observed it or heard it and the artists was considered a genius or given a rating: First, Second, No Good, until finally riding in a bus or subway: so proudly he signs his work like a manufacturer.[43]

Cage's rhetoric is clearly contrary to a vulgar "expressionist" model of artistic production that insists upon a hierarchy of genius; but as Hellstein notes, few if any of the Club's members espoused such a view. For Cage, as well as other members of the Club, art "goes within"—a metaphysical transformation of the artist from the role of mass-producer to one who accepts without intentionality. Resistance to commodification and automation was a going concern for the members of the Club (of which Cage was an "honorary member"). The sole issue of *Possibilities* (1948), jointly edited by Rosenberg, Motherwell, and Cage, is shot through with this theme. Take for instance Andrea Caffi's "On Mythology," which noted, "The efforts of 'Taylorism' and other modes of 'rationalizing' work, so successful in a certain sense, show clearly enough that even the iron laws of 'technico-economic determinism' are unable to secure for 'praxis' a complete victory over the psychological caprices which engender gratuitous gestures."[44] Rosenberg consistently spoke of the need to resist the stultifying effects of commodification, most famously in "The American Action Painters," in which he warned of the risks faced by the new US painting once absorbed into capitalist exchange.[45] Even though, as Arendt claimed for music and poetry, the "reification and the workmanship it demands are kept to a minimum," Cage noted that the risks for music's absorption into commodity were quite real, and his comments on Feldman's music aligned him with the struggle of the painters.[46] Cage's interpretation of Feldman did not denigrate some unitary and universalizing "abstract expressionist ego," as Jones has called it, but elaborated a larger difficulty shared with friends.[47] The production of a radically communal art was a goal shared by Rothko as much as Cage: "It is really a matter of ending this silence and solitude [of modern life and art], of breaching and stretching one's arms again."[48]

Within this romantic anticapitalist discourse, Cage's interpretation of Feldman's music as an exemplary form of communal art would have resonated with a number of audience members. Cage first likens Feldman to the protagonist of *Finnegans Wake*, H.C.E. ("Here Comes Everybody"), and announces the coming community brought about through his music:

> That is: starting finitely everything's different but in going in it all becomes the same. H.C.E. Which is what Morton Feldman had in mind when he called the music he's now writing *Intersection*. Feldman speaks of no sounds, and takes within broad limits the first ones that come along. He has changed the responsibility of the composer from making to accepting. To accept whatever comes re-gardless of the consequences is to be unafraid to be full of that love which comes from a sense of at-one-ness with whatever.[49]

The piece Cage mentions, *Intersection* for orchestra (see Figure 1.2), was Feldman's first graph composition for full orchestra. In addition to the choice of pitch within specific ranges, the performers were given the added liberty to choose the exact moment of playing within the beats specified. The same principle governing pitch now governs rhythm. Performers are given some freedom, but not too much. Feldman remained "agnostic"—as David Cline puts it—about performers' decisions, but only to a point, as the graphs for orchestra were often failures—as in the case of *Marginal Intersection*, discussed later.[50] Cage interpreted this agnosticism as ego-less acceptance, though we might also read it in a similar light as Pollock's statement in *Possibilities* where he recognizes his openness to the agency of the artwork, "because a painting has a life of its own, I try to let it come through."

Feldman's own unpublished comments from around this time are a similar mixture of ideas encountered at the Club. In them, he longs to overcome his

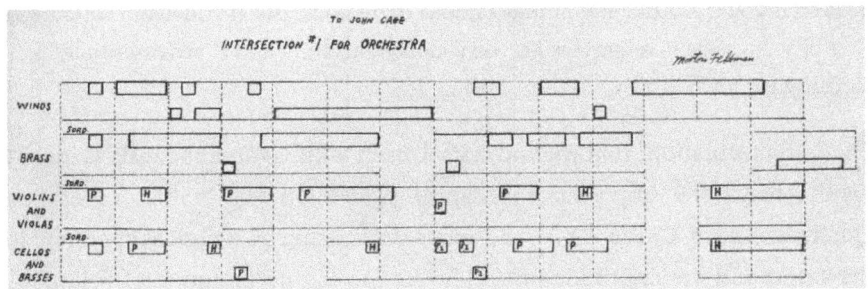

Figure 1.2 *Intersection* (page 1) by Morton Feldman © 1962 by C.F. Edition Peters Corporation. All rights reserved.

own sense of alienation produced by reification of his music and the blockage of its spontaneous dimensions. A vitalist phenomenology permeates the following passage of March 10, 1952, found in one of Feldman's composition sketchbooks (more on this quotation in Ch. 2):

> Yet one could think of each sound as a mov[emen]t of a sensibility and in a Proustian way investigate its countless juxtapositions for experience. But to see "things as they are" requires a vision of style which transcends detail and becomes the now moment, the experience rather than the fruits of experience. There is so much that conditions and shapes ourselves. My desire is to find what in myself can recreate myself as to alienation in my art as well as life. One thing certain. I must move, move. I must act regardless the action. Live regardless the living.[51]

This, along with his comments on "weight" quoted earlier, is among the earliest extant statements by Feldman that gives a sense of the metaphysics of his work. He desires direct experience, action, and attention to the present moment found also in the writings of Cage, Rosenberg, Rothko, and Arendt.

Cage, though, took this further, hearing in Feldman's *Intersection* the potential breakdown of art and life. In "Lecture on Something," Cage riffed on Feldman's instructions for the performance of his graphic scores to get at the point:

> High, middle, low; enter any time within the duration notated; this particular timbre. These are the somethings Feldman has chosen. They give him and his art character. It is quite useless in this situation for anyone to say Feldman's work is good or not good. Because we are in the direct situation: it is. If you don't like it you may choose to avoid it. But if you avoid it that's a pity, because it resembles life very closely, and life and it are essentially a cause for joy.[52]

The "direct situation" that we find ourselves in with Feldman's music is ideally joyful—recall the importance Schapiro placed on joy in his "Liberating Quality of Avant-Garde Art"—and *Intersection* achieves a radical openness to the world and the multitude of H.C.E. Yet Cage's interpretation of Feldman's *Intersection* is predicated on his own imagination of it. It had not been performed and had only just been finished. This strong reading of Feldman's music exemplifies what Guston called the "didactic" character of Cage: "one always felt that [Cage] was illustrating what he already believed—which is fine, but with Feldman the kinship he and I felt aesthetically had to do with the fact that we didn't know what we were going to do until we did it."[53] Guston's familial tie to Feldman came about from a shared attitude toward spontaneous action and its unknowability before the fact. That Cage was projecting onto Feldman is evident from his later writings on Robert Rauschenberg's *White Paintings* from 1961.

The substitution of Rauschenberg's *White Paintings* for Feldman's *Intersection* proved to be an easy one; Cage identified in both a rejection of the dialectic of art and life. In both, the former collapsed into the latter. Cage describes the paintings as "airports for the lights, shadows, and particles."[54] They are open canvases that accept intrusion—much like Cage's reading of Feldman's *Intersection*. The shadow motif was also first stated in "Lecture on Something": "I remember now that Feldman spoke of shadows. He said that the sounds were not sounds but shadows. They are obviously sounds; that's why they are shadows. Every something is an echo of nothing. Life goes on very much like a piece by Morty Feldman."[55] And later:

> The moment it becomes a special continuity of I am composing and nothing else should happen, then the rest of life is nothing but a series of interruptions, pleasant or catastrophic as the case may be. The truth, however, is that it is more like Feldman's music—anything may happen and it all does go together. This is no rest of life. Life is one.[56]

Following his appropriation of Feldman's music, Cage went on to say the same of Rauschenberg's *White Paintings* (1951), forging a genealogical link between them and his own *4'33"*.[57] Spontaneity is not, as with Feldman and Guston, the result of individual action or performer choice, but rather the acceptance of events beyond our control and beyond our ego's desire.

Cage delivered his "Lecture on Something" the week after Feldman's own lecture "The Unframed Frame" was given, on February 2, 1951. With Feldman's text lost, it is difficult to know the extent to which Cage referenced Feldman's ideas, though his quotation of Feldman suggests some possibility of recapitulation. The text of "Lecture on Something" went on to have a much more public life and moved the private debates of the Club into the public sphere. Beginning as a text for a specific semi-private world, it circulated publicly in Philip Pavia's journal *It is.* in 1959. There, in the house magazine of the Club, it was published to celebrate the release of Feldman's first LP on Columbia Records. It was more widely circulated in Cage's first book of collected writings, *Silence*, which appeared in 1961. There, removed from its earlier abstract expressionist contexts, it is read through the other texts of Cage and taken as evidence of a linear development toward indeterminacy. These shifting contexts track Feldman's movement from private to public though Cage's mediation, though Cage's revisionist anti-Club sentiments risked garbling Feldman's own desire to produce "a totally abstract sonic adventure," when in the 1960s, as Brett Boutwell notes, he took a more assertive hand in his reception.[58] Cage recognized the possibility of misinterpretation and included in both printed versions of "Lecture on Something" the disclaimer, "In the general moving around and talking that followed my Lecture on Something (ten years ago at the Club), somebody asked Morton Feldman whether he agreed with what I had said about him. He replied, 'That's not me; that's John.'"[59] At nearly a decade's remove and with knowledge of Cage's unreliable memory, it's uncertain as to whether Feldman actually said this. Regardless, it served to retrospectively distinguish Cage's non-subjective aesthetics from Feldman's faithfulness to abstract experience.

Marginal Intersection and the Failure of Cagean Acceptance

In the months following "Lecture on Something," Cage and Feldman entered into conflict over the meaning of the latter's graph music. The composition and first performance of one of the orchestral graphs, *Marginal Intersection* (see Figure 1.3), provides a foil for Cage's fantasies of radical acceptance. After completing *Intersection 1* in February, Feldman continued composing both graph and conventionally notated work—the soundtrack to Namuth's *Jackson Pollock 51* among them. Following the completion of the music for Pollock in May of 1951, Feldman began two *Intersections*: *Intersection 2* for piano solo (first performed by Tudor) and the aforementioned *Marginal Intersection*

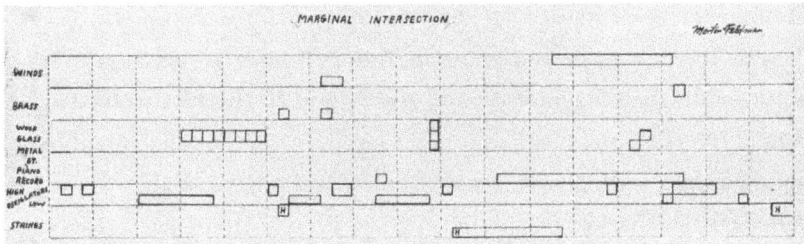

Figure 1.3 *Marginal Intersection* (page 1) by Morton Feldman © 1962 by C.F. Peters Corporation. All rights reserved.

for orchestra. In addition to conventional orchestral instruments, Feldman included amplified guitar, a battery of found percussion, a phonograph, and two oscillators. Cline notes that the inclusion of the oscillators and found percussion linked *Marginal Intersection* to Cage's earlier percussion pieces from the 1930s and 1940s and other works using solid state electronics, like *Imaginary Landscape No. 3* (1942).[60] Feldman remembered a number of influences on the sound world of *Marginal Intersection* in an interview with Jan Williams in 1983:

> I remember bringing in, for the first concert of *Marginal Intersection* at Cooper Union, plastic dishes and those old heavy aluminum pots and pans that I borrowed from my mother. My models for percussion at that time were from the Gamelan Orchestra, John Cage's early forties pieces, and Varèse's work, where the instruments were used en masse, not soloistically. I used that aspect as a model in *Marginal Intersection*, except I remember wanting the percussion to sound more like noise. I used "found objects" for sound sources.[61]

Of the oscillators, Feldman wrote in 1963 in the little magazine *Kulchur* that the oscillators "cannot be heard, but are 'felt'" as they are outside the range of human hearing.[62] This was an early iteration of what Feldman would later describe as his desire to push sound to the "periphery ... of human audibility."[63] Thus the titular emphasis on the "marginal" figured as the limits of perception.

Despite timbral similarities to Cage's work, *Marginal Intersection* revealed undergirding conflicts between Feldman and Cage over their respective conceptions of what the graph music was and how it had to remain distinct from other forms of modernist spontaneity, namely jazz. Initially, Cage was thrilled by the new piece and wrote to Tudor: "Morty + I get along very well (he's not yet finished the *Intersection* [*Intersection 2*]—he got involved in a new 'Marginal Intersection': that is, sounds heard between 2 limits: inaudible high + inaudible low!—which are notated but will not be heard)."[64] Some weeks later, he registers marked disappointment, writing to Tudor that "Morty is now in a period of not writing. He finished his marginal intersection, but rather as though he was dropping it; he gave it a real cadence (dim[inuendo] poco a poco) [decrease in loudness little by little]; I think his life has been taking his attention so that as he says he has lost contact with sound."[65] Cage refers to the fade-out effect Feldman required for the phonograph record at the end of *Marginal Intersection*. Because it is an obvious rhetorical gesture familiar from countless classical works, Cage rejects it. More troubling is Cage's concern with Feldman's loss of "contact with sound." Feldman emphasized his non-systematic, intuitive way of working, but this proved hard to sustain in the summer of 1951. "Life"—that is, his job at the family business—prevented him from accessing what he later described as the "'metaphysical place' which we all have but which so many of us are not sensitive to by previous conviction."[66]

Why should *Marginal Intersection* have proven to be such a challenge to Feldman compositionally and to Cage aesthetically? It is clear from Feldman's sketchbook containing work for *Marginal Intersection* and his soundtrack music for Namuth's Pollock film that his work falls off in the summer of 1951. After *Marginal Intersection* and *Intersection 2*, his next completed piece, *Extensions 1* for violin and piano, is not finished until November 12 of that year. With *Extensions 1*, his compositional fluency seems to return and a series of works in conventional notation follows: *Extensions 3 & 4* and the open-form piano solo, *Intermission 6*.[67] Feldman's working method for the graph pieces was to compose visually, directly on the grids. For large orchestral pieces, Feldman made individual parts for the players that were represented by notes placed on the top line, middle line, or bottom line of a five-line staff. The rhythms, with their regular pulse, were written out in conventional notation, though the freedom to enter at any point within an indicated beat was explicitly granted to the performers.[68] The sketches indicate a wider range of influences beyond those genres that Feldman selectively remembered. Next to the percussion part, he wrote, "For desired effect: each player should think of this part[,] percussion part I: concentrate on wood and solo xyl[ophone] but when possible play other parts as in a jazz ensemble."[69] Feldman's comments refer to a style of performance more than any specific citation of jazz, though his exclusion of this influence from his later commentary is evidence of an all-too-common erasure of jazz and its improvisatory spontaneity from the musical New York School.

Cage's increasing frustrations with Feldman in the summer of 1951 also hinged on the necessity of jazz's exclusion from chance music. In an undated letter to Tudor, but likely from August, Cage bluntly describes the difficulties facing his friendship with Feldman:

> Poor Morty's life is all mixed up + I'm afraid his present music too. At least I find I cannot "accept" his present work which is an Intersection over an Arty [sic] Shaw record. I feel we are somewhat estranged over this work which I find not "valable." It is psychological; however, he's breaking up with Val Lombard who inspired it and now he's again at sea, poor fellow, searching for something someone etc. I always thought we were close friends but in the last few days I realize something else; I too am at sea right now with regard to Morty. He looks always for an easy way out. Of course they're all around us and all "valable"; maybe you can put me straight about all this. I only feel helpless and silent for the words that reach him come from that ignoramus Danny Sterne [sic]. Then too, Morty's analyst has been away. An ugly paragraph (the above).[70]

With evidence of Feldman's diminished output between *Marginal Intersection* and *Extensions 1*, and no other surviving evidence for what this other *Intersection* might have been (certainly not *Intersection 2*, completed in July), just what Cage is referring to is unclear. The "present work" is likely *Marginal Intersection*. As noted earlier, the instrumentation included a phonograph, which the contemporaneous sketches and published score from 1962 indicate should play a sound-effects record of riveting. Cage's early fascination with *Marginal Intersection*, though, centers on the paraperceptual use of oscillators—he makes no mention of the sound-effects recording. Speculatively, I wonder if the recording of clarinetist and bandleader Artie Shaw might have stood in at some stage for the recording of riveting in Feldman's conception, given the indication for the percussionists to perform "like a jazz ensemble" (despite his stated distaste for the genre in his lecture at the Club the previous February).[71] Whether or not Cage's comments refer to *Marginal Intersection* or to some other aborted *Intersection*, the evidence indicates that Feldman briefly attempted a rapprochement between his graph music and jazz—each with their invitations to spontaneous, real-time music making.

Jazz, however, was what George Lewis has called an "epistemological other" for the composers of the New York School.[72] Its form of modernism was largely excluded from their work—though a notable exception is a piece by Cage for magnetic tape collaged from spliced jazz recordings, composed a year after Feldman's *Marginal Intersection*. Titled *Imaginary Landscape No. 5* (1952), Rebecca Kim argues that with this piece Cage came to "an acceptance of jazz on its own terms through a willing suspension of distaste."[73] The *Marginal Intersection* controversy documents a step on the path to that eventual (and rather anemic) acceptance of jazz, predicated on Cage's manipulation of it in recorded form. From the perspective of intersubjectivity and its relationship to aesthetics, Cage seems to recognize that a suspension of distaste might be required as inoculation against the infection of friendship by artistic preference. The rupture of Cage and Feldman's friendship over the issue of jazz (among others) indicates something else about the music's ambivalent place within midcentury modernism—it was ignored as a viable accompaniment to Pollock's filmic performance despite its actual role in accompanying the painter at work and shaping the sound world of the studio. It was subsequently blocked from intersecting with Feldman's graph music which Cage admired as long as it conformed to his idea of what it should be. Jazz was not, however, excluded from the Club, and there were a few jazz nights on the calendar in the early 1950s along with performances of Cage and Feldman's music. Other experimentalists—Edgard Varèse among them—pursued more lasting engagement with post-bop jazz in the late 1950s.[74]

Cage's ambivalence about his friendship with Feldman reveals the dark side of undoing the bifurcation of art and life. As he had in "Lecture on Something," Cage recognized the issue as one of acceptance. But whereas he there lauded Feldman's ability to accept any sound that emerged in a performance, in the letter he faults himself for being unable to accept the sounds in *Marginal*

Intersection. For as much as he criticizes Feldman, he critiques himself. We read him struggling to become the Cage we know today—to become as accepting as he found both Feldman and his music for *Intersection 1*. The archival record doesn't offer a full picture of the resolution of this conflict, but it is clear from later correspondence between Feldman and Cage that their relationship was particularly rocky over the next few years. Cage struggled to subordinate aesthetics to an ethics of acceptance that he celebrated in "Lecture on Something" and that could have salvaged his friendship with Feldman.

By erasing a distinction between "what one does and what was is" (as Feldman phrased it), Cage is not that different from his abstract expressionist colleagues and friends. Catherine Craft argues that "[i]n their dealings with one another, artwork and creator would be heavily identified, and critical judgments could be based on morality as much as aesthetics."[75] Similarly, Cage understood Feldman the composer and *Intersection 1* the piece as equivalent. The openness of the score's grid functions as evidence of Feldman's *personal* willingness to accept whatever sounds came along. But in the subsequent letter to Tudor we find an admission of failure and Cage's self-criticism in it. In a *parrēsiatic* gesture—borrowing Michel Foucault's formulation—he "implicates himself in what he says," so as to "strive to arrive at the [truth]": the renunciation of hierarchies of taste.[76] In so doing, however, he shows the risks such a collapse had for friendship, and the dangers of speaking for others about their work.

At its premiere on November 7, 1952, *Marginal Intersection* had as sour a reception publicly as it had had privately with Cage. It was featured on a concert series titled "Music in the Making," organized and conducted by David Broekman. Broekman framed the concert series as a critique of free market ideologies governing concert programs and argued that "The trouble is the market is rigged, and there is price control of the worst kind. . . . There is simply no money to play American music and repeat a piece often enough so that it has a chance to become a classic."[77] Building up a concert repertoire of new American music was only part of the goal. The concerts were collaborative events in which performers, composers, and critics were put into dialog with one another, with the composers and conductor commenting on the works. Broekman hoped "that paying jobs for professional musicians may come out of this new audience-composer-critic participation formula for concerts."[78] S. Stephenson Smith, managing editor of the union magazine *International Musician*, was similarly optimistic about the series, saying that it "has shown that a new audience, predominantly trade-unionists, can be one and held for American serious music."[79] Here the progressive values of labor and community exemplify a different kind of spontaneity—the organization of a multitude resistant to the exploitation of capitalism.[80] With its offering of spontaneous action and collective organization, Feldman's music could have been an ideal way to organize a creative collaboration between performers resistant to the alienation of labor so strongly critiqued by members of the Club.

Yet, even in this possibly ideal public presentation, Feldman's music was met with resistance from critics and performers. Performers and audience neither recognized, nor desired the spontaneity proffered by Feldman's graph music. Lester Trimble found it to be "a sado-masochistic enterprise which upset my viscera for days."[81] Peggy Glanville-Hicks, a composer-critic like Trimble, was similarly harsh in her judgment. She described Feldman as a representative of the "leave-it-to-chance school of esoteric sound-composers" and assessed the responses of those gathered for the performance: "The audience was not really fooled, and estimated the rather amusing experiment for what it was, the work of one of the philosophers of the negative who point up brilliantly the assets of a positive—any positive—way of working."[82] Glanville-Hicks, in the midst of her dismissal, also recorded Feldman's commentary from the stage:

> When asked by a curious member of the audience, "How do you indicate on such [graph] paper which note is to be played?" Feldman replied, "I don't, it doesn't matter. Any sound will do so long as the player does something at the point marked at his entry." He added by way of illumination that "it calls for rigorous self-discipline on the part of the members of the orchestra to perform this work."[83]

Feldman's acceptance, so lauded by Cage, is qualified by the need for discipline on the part of the performer. *Parrēsia* and *askēsis* were linked in the relational situation of *Marginal Intersection*. Feldman's hopes for this ascetic practice were that sound might be handled with "love or interest."[84] *Marginal Intersection*'s sounds, however, were not.

Frank O'Hara and the Limits of Spontaneity

In the domains of poesis, performance, and reception, *Marginal Intersection* is a musical object that materialized the tensions of Feldman's community. It was disparaged during its composition by Cage for its initial engagement with jazz and conventional musical rhetoric. It was realized in performance by musicians who mistook freedom for license, and rejected by critics for its negation of music itself. *Marginal Intersection* couldn't establish, even temporarily, an operative community on the private or public level. Nonetheless, the much-maligned piece shows up as a marker of community in an artwork by one of Feldman's closest friends—O'Hara's "Poem Read at Joan Mitchell's." Written in 1957, we find the echoes of *Marginal Intersection*'s performance four years after the fact:

> Tonight you probably walked over here from Bethune Street
> down Greenwich Avenue with its sneaky little bars and the Women's
>   Detention House,
> across 8th Street, by the acres of books and pillows and shoes and
>   illuminating lampshades,
> past Cooper Union where we heard the piece by Mortie Feldman with "The
>   Stars and Stripes Forever" in it
> and the Sagamore's terrific "coffee and, Andy," meaning "with a cheese
>   Danish"—
> did you spit on your index fingers and rub the CEDAR's neon circle for
>   luck?
> did you give a kind thought, hurrying, to Alger Hiss?[85]

O'Hara's verse confirms Feldman's recollection that musicians often mistook the graph score's openness as an invitation to do anything—undermining the piece by citing popular patriotic tunes, for example. Feldman recalled "Yankee Doodle" being interpolated in one performance. O'Hara documents in the foregoing stanza that he heard John Philip Sousa's "The Stars and Stripes Forever" march.[86] "Stars and Stripes" brings with it a world of associations attached to patriotic tunes. The nationalistic incursion into avant-garde performance exposes the risks of "giv[ing] a kind thought, hurrying," to Alger Hiss, an accused (and convicted) Soviet spy. O'Hara's recollection of *Marginal*

Intersection insists too that friendship is nurtured by memory and place. The translation of Feldman's music into "Poem Read at Joan Mitchell's" attests to the work O'Hara's coterie did to make a private claim on public space—as well as the tenuousness of that claim in the mid-1950s.

Shaw notes in a different way the "conflicted tonality" felt in O'Hara's poem as it circles around the theme of heterosexual marriage, and the tonal shift toward celebratory intimacy when it addresses "the shared aspects of the interwoven lives of both absent friends . . . and those present at Joan Mitchell's loft."[87] But even within that shift there remains in the stanza a thoroughgoing anxiety that haunts the shuttling between private friendship and the public sphere. The lesson Shaw draws out from O'Hara's "poetics of coterie" is frustrated by *Marginal Intersection*'s performance, which thematizes the risks to art and friendship that come with the movement—as Feldman defined it—between studio and world.

The anxiety over political blockage marks Feldman's appearance in "Poem Read at Joan Mitchell's" and recurs throughout documents of his friendship with O'Hara. Will Montgomery and I have each written on their friendship and the ways in which their relationship registers these feelings. Montgomery notes compellingly that "while both artists occasionally subscribed to a vocabulary of liberating immediacy and freeing personal 'expression' in their writings both held back from the implications of 'endlessness' and acknowledged a form of 'containment.'"[88] This containment is felt in the ambivalence of "Poem Read at Joan Mitchell's," which, like Cage's "Lecture on Something," began as a coterie text and was subsequently transformed into a published statement.[89] O'Hara's recognition of the limits on Feldman's experimentation is tonally distinct from his statements in their private correspondence. There the poet is unequivocally enthusiastic about the radical possibilities of composer's work. Following a concert in late 1953 or the first days of 1954, O'Hara wrote to Feldman, "it was so exciting and inspiring to find one's sensibility led into absolutely new experiences in such a subtle, authoritative way—without any posings or denial which only distract one when it's a matter of real music."[90] Though O'Hara's letters to Feldman are few they are filled with similar endearments couched within invitations to intimate artistic collaboration.[91] This optimism, however, is lost in O'Hara['s] subtle critique of the affective occlusion marking the performance of Feldman's music in the agonistic world mapped by "Poem Read at Joan Mitchell's."

O'Hara's first published writing on Feldman was part of a triple collaboration on Feldman's first LP, *New Directions in Music 2* (1959). O'Hara wrote the sleeve notes, and the cover art was a drawing by Feldman's close friend Guston titled *Head–Double View* (see Figure 1.4). That same year, O'Hara brought to fruition another major writing project, his monograph of Pollock, which followed on the heels of the Pollock retrospective at the Museum of Modern Art in 1957. The retrospective also prominently featured Namuth and Feldman's film as part of its programming.[92] O'Hara's interpretations of Feldman and Pollock are remarkably similar and the poet-critic feels this same stasis impacting Feldman's music.

In his writings on Pollock and Feldman, O'Hara celebrates the expressive capacities of both. Pollock attempted to produce a "drastic self-knowledge."[93] Feldman's music was similarly "a personal search for expression."[94] The painter

Figure 1.4 Philip Guston, *Head–Double View*, 1958. Brush and ink on paper, 20 × 24 7/8". Purchase. Digital Image © The Museum of Modern Art/Licensed by SCALA / Art Resource, NY. © The Estate of Philip Guston, courtesy Hauser & Wirth.

and composer were also allied in their approach to performance. Pollock struggled to achieve a vitalist state where "the spirit can act freely and with unpremeditated knowledge."⁹⁵ "Unpremeditated" evinces the value placed on direct non-conceptual action that the New York School inherited from Henri Bergson's philosophy. O'Hara reflected on the performance of Feldman's graph music in similar terms, which he connected explicitly to abstraction:

> To perform Feldman's graph pieces at all, the musician must reach the metaphysical place where each can occur, allying necessity with unpredictability. Where a virtuoso work places technical demands upon the performer, a Feldman piece seeks to engage his improvisatory collaboration, with its call on musical creativity as well as interpretative understanding. The performance on this record is proof of how beautifully this can all work out; yet, the performer could doubtless find other beauties in *Intersection III* on another occasion.⁹⁶

Perhaps thinking back to the performance of *Marginal Intersection* documented in "Poem Read at Joan Mitchell's," O'Hara leaves open the possibility that the performance of Feldman's graph music might also *not* work out so beautifully. Whereas Cage had focused on the *askēsis* modeled by Feldman's acceptance of any sounds, O'Hara recognizes the ascetic demand Feldman makes of performers who must cultivate their own "metaphysical place." It was a demand few performers—save Feldman's close collaborators such as Tudor or Daniel Stern—heeded in the 1950s.

O'Hara's metaphysical interpretations of Feldman and Pollock were not well received. Clement Greenberg dubbed the Pollock monograph "pseudo-poetry" while reviewers of Feldman's record found the liner notes to be "high flown."⁹⁷ Despite O'Hara's enthusiasm, it would be a mistake to read either document as unequivocally celebrating some sort of abstract expressionist ego. With his own experience of Feldman's music and knowledge of the reception of Pollock's painting, O'Hara was certainly aware of both the promise of the avant-garde and its risks of failure. In his monograph on Pollock, O'Hara provides the following reading of *Number 11, 1952* (known as *Blue Poles*):

> *Blue Poles* is our *Raft of the Medusa* and our *Embarkation for Cytherea* in one. I say *our*, because it is the drama of an American conscience, lavish,

bountiful, and rigid. It contains everything within itself, begging no quarter: a world of sentiment implied but denied; a map of sensual freedom, fenced; a careening licentiousness, guarded by eight totems native to its origins.[98]

O'Hara's interpretation of *Blue Poles* works along a spatial logic of outward expansion that is blocked by dominating forces. Fences and totems constrain the expression of sentiment and freedom. A logic of emotional occlusion is present here as it is in "Poem Read at Joan Mitchell's," where the vulgar nationalism of Sousa and red-baiting threaten the fragile cohesion of friendship. Shaw has argued that O'Hara's interpretation is that "Pollock's late works provide a drama of wild, affective energies undergoing a kind of neutralizing framing."[99] O'Hara identifies the same process as affecting Feldman's music.

O'Hara articulates the limits of Feldman's *askēsis* in his discussion of *Piece for Four Pianos* (1957), which exemplifies another notational development beyond the graph scores and which required spontaneous interaction in a different way. The performers were invited to choose the speed at which they move through the work, even though the pitches were fixed:

> Unpredictability is used in a different way still in the *Piece for Four Pianos* (1957). This work, scored in notation rather than graph, begins simultaneously for all four pianos, after which the following notes may be played to the end by each of the pianists at time intervals of their mutual or individual choice. Feldman has said, "The repeated notes are not musical pointillism, as in Webern, but they are where the mind rests on an image—the beginning of the piece is like a recognition, not a motif, and by virtue of the repetitions conditions one to listen." As we proceed to experience the individual time-responses of the four pianists we are moving inexorably toward the final image where the mind can rest, which is the end of the piece. In this particular performance it is as if one were traversing an enormous plain at the opposite ends of which were two huge monoliths, guarding its winds and grasses.[100]

O'Hara's metaphors qualify the spontaneity of Feldman's music that he had praised up to this point in his essay. O'Hara had used the metaphor of a restricted field as an image for his criticism of Pollock's *Blue Poles*, which was "guarded by eight totems native to its origins." In his critiques of both *Blue Poles* and *Piece for 4 Pianos*, O'Hara evokes primitivist objects (totems and monoliths) that curtail spontaneous action. Noting these limitations, O'Hara identifies a darker truth about cultural production at the end of the 1950s: that the affective experience of Abstract Expressionism and chance music remained a risky endeavor, despite the expressive autonomy that brought the works into being. In O'Hara's accounts of both Pollock and Feldman, aesthetic action offers the spontaneous overcoming of alienation. Still, these performances are stalked by ominous figures on the horizon.

Into the 1960s

The year 1959 saw a sharp increase in Feldman's public circulation with the release of his LP *New Directions in Music 2* on Columbia Records, accompanied by O'Hara's sleeve notes.[101] The occasion was also marked by the publication of Cage's "Lecture on Something" in *It is. A Magazine for Abstract Art*. Both documents found a newly developing anonymous audience for avant-garde art beyond the intimate sphere of studio and home that Feldman drew sustenance from. On the cusp of the counter-cultural revolution of the 1960s and the "incorporation of the avant-garde," Feldman circa 1959 was on the verge of garnering a much wider audience thanks to the availability of his recordings and writings.[102] While he had a stronger hand in his own narration in the 1960s, the 1950s was a decade of mediation by others. Feldman's relationships with Cage, Pollock, and O'Hara all register tensions felt by this community as artworks moved out of the studio and into the world. In contrast to Cage's non-relational acceptance, Feldman's music risked the affective stasis faced by artistic action once brought into the public sphere. Feldman's friends alternated between advocacy, truth-telling, and betrayal, and registered, even more than critical dismissal, the social dynamics of the New York School.

Feldman's failure to resolve the tensions of spontaneity and intimacy with the demands of publicness is perhaps the reason why we find him gradually reducing the frequency of performer choice and indeterminacy in his works throughout the 1960s, such that by 1970 he had returned to a fully prescriptive notation. Nonetheless, his music, regardless of its compositional style, continued to signify chance, spontaneity, and existential liberation. Yet,

Feldman's writings and lectures in the 1960s worked against this popular view. If spontaneity and intimacy could not both be had, Feldman cast his lot with intimacy and emphasized friendship's necessity for the proper performance of his music. In an interview with Robert Ashley in 1963, Feldman noted the importance of intimacy in a manner similar to Goodman, Schapiro, and Rosenberg:

> Well, I think it's important to know certain very personal things [about an artist]. I remember years ago the art critic Harold Rosenberg was criticized because he said that to really understand the painting that was being done at the time you should know the painter personally, and most people want to understand a work without knowing the painter. Last week David [Tudor] did my new piano piece, "Piano piece (to Philip Guston)," and he called me up and said, "Should I play it on the stage the way you wrote it, with the lid down?" Well, this was very important. He knows that when I give a concert I always keep the lid down; he knows I compose with the lid down. He also knows that I compose at a piano that's always perfectly in tune, so he's very concerned that the piano he is playing be perfectly in tune. So you see, with David's association from the beginning there was never an element of implication; everything was very explicit because of a close association.[103]

Piano Piece (to Philip Guston) (1963), as Feldman imagines it, is a relational object. The dedication is evidence of a continuing social life—one previously publicized through the mutual involvement of Guston, O'Hara, Tudor, and Feldman on *New Directions in Music 2*. Feldman reiterates the importance of personal knowledge—friendship—to artistic understanding and cites approvingly Tudor's conformation to the composer's habits—the atypical practice of keeping the lid down during performance. The public performance of Feldman's compositional comportment proceeded to make the spontaneous and private scene of composition available to the public through Tudor's mediation.

My account of questions about intimacy, spontaneity, and publicity dramatized by Feldman's friendships requires us to shift the foundation upon which we base our discussions of his community as well as how we conceptualize the relationship between the arts at midcentury. Feldman's laments for his community provide clear evidence that friendship in fact *produced* New York School modernism. Such friendships provided the "underlying network of awareness" that Robert Motherwell intuited among his peers.[104] Attention to Feldman's relationships allows us to know the affective and epistemological conditions of friendship. His compounding and conflicting ties reveal in sharp detail how friendship mediates aesthetic objects and leaves its traces on them. Poems, films, compositions, and recordings all register irresolvable conflicts between agapic friendship and agonistic authorship. Such tensions animated Feldman's idealization of musical performance as a form of intimate autonomy. This idealization is ultimately political and provides an alternative to both the vulgar expressionistic model of the free-but-lonely painter and Cage's non-relational idealism. It is, however, a melancholy heroism that has its limits—exemplified by Feldman's attempts to reproduce as much as possible the space of home, even as the wider world continually intruded upon it.

Notes

1 Morton Feldman, "The Anxiety of Art," in Morton Feldman, *Give My Regards to Eighth Street: Collected Writings of Morton Feldman*, ed. B. H. Friedman (Cambridge, MA: Exact Change, 2000), 24.
2 Amy Beal, "An Interview with Earle Brown," *Contemporary Music Review* 26, no. 3 (2007): 350.
3 Morton Feldman to John Cage, March 29, 1966, John Cage Correspondence, Northwestern University Music Library.
4 On Dominique de Menil's aesthetics, see Pamela Smart, "Possession: Intimate Artifice at the Menil Collection," *Modernism/modernity* 13, no. 1 (2006): 765–85.
5 Morton Feldman, "Four Lectures: N.Y. Style," Morton Feldman Collection, Paul Sacher Foundation.
6 Caroline A. Jones, *Machine in the Studio: Constructing the Postwar American Artist* (Chicago, IL: University of Chicago Press, 1996), 72–80.
7 "Four Artists in a 'Mansion,'" *Harper's Bazaar*, July 1952, 79.
8 Daniel Belgrad, *The Culture of Spontaneity: Improvisation and the Arts in Postwar America* (Chicago, IL: University of Chicago Press, 1998).

9 Philip Guston, "On Morton Feldman," in *Philip Guston: Collected Writings, Lectures, and Conversations,* ed. Clark Coolidge (Berkeley, CA: University of California Press, 2011), 76.
10 Ibid.
11 Dore Ashton, *Philip Guston* (New York: Grove Press, 1960), 53.
12 Meyer Schapiro, "The Liberating Quality of Avant-Garde Art," in *Reading Abstract Expressionism: Context and Critique,* ed. Ellen G. Landau (New Haven, CT: Yale University Press, 2005), 216.
13 Morton Feldman, "After Modernism," in Feldman, *Give My Regards to Eighth Street,* 79.
14 Paul Goodman, "Advance-Guard Writing: 1900–1950," *Kenyon Review* 13, no. 3 (1951): 375.
15 Ibid.
16 Frank O'Hara, "Personism: A Manifesto," in *The Collected Poems of Frank O'Hara,* ed. Donald Allen (Berkeley, CA: University of California Press, 1995), 499.
17 Goodman, "Advance-Guard Writing," 376.
18 On "New York Folk Art," see Francesco Pellizzi, "Morton Feldman and the Arts: A Recollection," in *Vertical Thoughts: Morton Feldman and the Visual Arts,* ed. Seán Kissane (Dublin: Irish Museum of Modern Art, 2010), 118. On "a new culture," see Richard Bernas and Adrian Jack, "The Brink of Silence," in *Morton Feldman Says,* ed. Chris Villars (London: Hyphen Press, 2006), 44.
19 Valerie Hellstein, "The Cage-iness of Abstract Expressionism," *American Art* 28, no. 1 (2014): 56–77.
20 Antoine Hennion, "The History of Art—Lessons in Mediation," *Réseaux* 3, no. 2 (1995): 238.
21 Or as Benjamin Piekut has put it, "every musical performance is a performance of relationship." Piekut, *Experimentalism Otherwise: The New York Avant-Garde and its Limits* (Berkeley, CA: University of California Press, 2011), 159.
22 Brenna Moore, "Friendship and the Cultivation of Religious Sensibilities," *Journal of the American Academy of Religion* 83, no. 2 (2015): 439.
23 Ibid.
24 Goodman, "Advance-Guard Writing," 377.
25 Morton Feldman, *Skizzenbuch* 3, Morton Feldman Collection.
26 Joel Nickels, *The Poetry of the Possible: Spontaneity, Modernism, and the Multitude* (Minneapolis, MN: University of Minnesota Press, 2012).

27 Hannah Arendt, *The Human Condition* (Chicago, IL: University of Chicago Press, 1998), 40.
28 On Wolpe, see Brigid Cohen, *Stefan Wolpe and the Avant-Garde Diaspora* (Cambridge: Cambridge University Press, 2012).
29 Morton Feldman and Thomas Moore, "Morton Feldman in Conversation with Thomas Moore, November 9, 1983," in *Morton Feldman Says: Selected Interviews and Lectures 1964–1987*, ed. Chris Villars (London: Hyphen Press, 2006), 181.
30 Morton Feldman, "I Met Heine on the Rue Fürstenburg," in Feldman, *Give My Regards to Eighth Street*, 114.
31 Morton Feldman, "Frank O'Hara: Lost Times and Future Hopes" in Feldman, *Give My Regards to Eighth Street*, 104.
32 Martine Cadieu, "Morton Feldman—Waiting," in *Morton Feldman Says*, 39.
33 John Cage, "Composition as Process," in *Silence: Lectures and Writings* (Middleton, CT: Wesleyan University Press, 1961), 35.
34 John Cage and Morton Feldman, "Radio Happening 1," in *Radio Happenings: Conversations/Gespräche, 1966–1967*, second edition, ed. Gisela Gronenmeyer and Reinhard Oehlschlägel (Cologne: MusikTexte, 2015), 20.
35 Program for Merce Cunningham performance, Hunter College, January 21, 1951, Merce Cunningham Dance Company Archives, New York Public Library.
36 John Holzaepfel, "Painting by Numbers," in *The New York Schools of Music and Visual Art*, ed. Stephen Johnson (New York: Routledge, 2002), 159–72.
37 Frank O'Hara, "New Directions in Music: Morton Feldman," in Feldman, *Give My Regards to Eighth Street*, 213.
38 John Cage, Morton Feldman, Christian Wolff, and Pierre Boulez, "Four Musicians at Work," *Transformation: Arts, Communication, Environment* 1, no. 3 (1952): 168; Henry Cowell, "Current Chronicle," *Musical Quarterly* 38, no. 1 (1952): 131.
39 Arthur Berger, "Music Notes: Jeritza Back, 'Dybbuk' Off; Chance Games," *New York Herald Tribune*, January 28, 1951. D8.
40 Sianne Ngai, "Theory of the Gimmick," *Critical Inquiry* 43, no. 2 (2017): 466–505, 467.
41 Berger, "Music Notes."
42 John Cage, "Lecture on Something," in *Silence*, 135. I have not kept Cage's typographical arrangement.
43 Ibid., 129.
44 Andrea Caffi, "On Mythology," *Possibilities* 1 (Winter 1947–48): 91.

45 Harold Rosenberg, "The American Action Painters," in *The Tradition of the New* (New York: McGraw Hill, 1959), 23–39.
46 Arendt, *The Human Condition*, 169.
47 Caroline A. Jones, "Finishing School: John Cage and the Abstract Expressionist Ego," *Critical Inquiry* 19, no. 4 (1993): 628–55.
48 Mark Rothko, "The Romantics Were Prompted," *Possibilities* 1 (1947–48): 84. Reprinted in Mark Rothko, *Writings on Art* (New Haven, CT: Yale University Press, 2006), 58–9.
49 Cage, "Lecture on Something," 129.
50 David Cline, *The Graph Music of Morton Feldman* (Cambridge: Cambridge University Press, 2016), 243.
51 Feldman, *Skizzenbuch* 3.
52 Cage, "Lecture on Something," 133.
53 Guston, "Interview with Jan Butterfield," in *Philip Guston*, 294.
54 John Cage, "On Robert Rauschenberg, Artist, and His Work," in *Silence*, 102.
55 Cage, "Lecture on Something," 131.
56 Ibid., 134.
57 Branden W. Joseph, *Random Order: Robert Rauschenberg and the Neo-Avant-Garde* (Cambridge, MA: The MIT Press, 2003), 49.
58 Brett Boutwell, "Morton Feldman's Graphic Notation: *Projections* and *Trajectories*," *Journal of the Society for American Music* 6, no. 4 (2012): 457–82.
59 Cage, "Lecture on Something," 128.
60 Cline, *Graph Music*, 31.
61 Jan Williams, "An Interview with Morton Feldman," *Percussive Notes* (1983): 4–14, reprinted in *Morton Feldman Says*, 151–2.
62 Morton Feldman, "Marginal Intersection, Intersection II, Intermission IV," *Kulchur* 3, no. 11 (1963): 33, reprinted in Feldman, *Give My Regards to Eighth Street*, 11.
63 Michael Auping and Morton Feldman, "Touch," in *30 Years: Interviews and Outtakes*, ed. Auping (Fort Worth, TX: Modern Art Museum of Fort Worth, 2007), 143.
64 John Cage to David Tudor, undated, David Tudor Papers, Getty Research Center, box 52, folder 3. Transcribed in *John Cage and David Tudor: Correspondence on Interpretation and Performance*, ed. Martin Iddon (Cambridge: Cambridge University Press, 2013), 13. Iddon estimates the date to be early June of 1951.
65 John Cage to David Tudor, undated, David Tudor Papers, Getty Research Center, box 52, folder 3. Transcribed in *John Cage and David Tudor*, 15–16.

66 Feldman, quoted in Frank O'Hara, liner notes to *New Directions in Music 2*, reprinted in Feldman, *Give My Regards to Eighth Street*, 212.
67 Feldman, *Skizzenbuch* 3.
68 See Cline, *The Graph Music of Morton Feldman*, 149–50 and 300–5.
69 Feldman, *Skizzenbuch* 3.
70 John Cage to David Tudor, undated, in Iddon, *Correspondences*, 27–28.
71 Philip Pavia recalls Feldman saying that jazz was too instrumental and "not human." Pavia, *Club without Walls: Selections from the Journals of Philip Pavia*, ed. Natalie Edgar (New York: Midmarch Arts Press, 2007), 61.
72 George E. Lewis, "Improvisation After 1950, Afrological and Eurological Perspectives," *Black Music Research Journal* 16, no. 1 (1996): 103.
73 Rebecca Y. Kim, "John Cage in Separate Togetherness with Jazz," *Contemporary Music Review* 31, no. 1 (2012): 63–89, 63. On Cage's work with jazz musicians in the genesis of his *Concert* in the late 1950s, see Martin Iddon and Philip Thomas, *John Cage's Concert for Piano and Orchestra* (New York: Oxford University Press, 2020).
74 Olivia Mattis, "From Bebop to Poo-Wip: Jazz Influences in Varèse's *Poème électronique*," in *Edgard Varèse: Composer, Sound Sculptor, Visionary*, ed. Felix Meyer and Heidy Zimmermann (Woodbridge: Boydell and Brewer, 2006), 309–17; Brigid Cohen, "Enigmas of the Third Space: Mingus and Varèse at Greenwich House, 1957," *Journal of the American Musicological Society* 70, no. 1 (2018): 155–211.
75 Catherine Craft, *An Audience of Artists: Dada, Neo-Dada, and the Emergence of Abstract Expressionism* (Chicago, IL: University of Chicago Press, 2012), 155.
76 Michel Foucault, "Parrēsia," trans. Graham Burchell, *Critical Inquiry* 41, no. 2 (2015): 247.
77 David Broekman, "Music in the Making May Make Jobs for Musicians," *International Musician* (Winter 1953): 10.
78 Ibid., 11.
79 S. Stephenson Smith, "Good Programs Mean Jobs," *International Musician* (March 1953): 13.
80 Nickels, *The Poetry of the Possible*, 9–13.
81 Lester Trimble, "Music," *The Nation*, February 20, 1960, 175.
82 Peggy Glanville-Hicks, "Music in the Making at Cooper Union," *International Musician* (March 1953): 13, 35.
83 Ibid., 35.

84 Robert Ashley and Morton Feldman, "Around Morton Feldman," 27, Morton Feldman Collection.

85 Frank O'Hara, "Poem Read at Joan Mitchell's," in *The Collected Poems of Frank O'Hara*, ed. Donald Allen (Berkeley, CA: University of California Press), 265.

86 Cf. Ashley and Feldman, "Around Morton Feldman," 14.

87 Lytle Shaw, *Frank O'Hara: The Poetics of Coterie* (Iowa City: University of Iowa Press, 2006), 53–54.

88 Will Montgomery, "'In Fatal Winds': Frank O'Hara and Morton Feldman," in *Frank O'Hara Now: New Essays on the New York Poet*, ed. Robert Hampson and Will Montgomery (Liverpool: Liverpool University Press, 2010), 195–210, 209.

89 Frank O'Hara, "Poem Read at Joan Mitchell's."

90 Frank O'Hara to Morton Feldman, January 2, 1954. Morton Feldman Collection.

91 On their friendship, see Chapter 3.

92 "Jackson Pollock Film to be Shown at Museum of Modern Art," January 11, 1957, Museum of Modern Art Archives, https://www.moma.org/docs/press_archives/2145/releases/MOMA_1957_0003.pdf?2010, accessed October 8, 2021.

93 Frank O'Hara, *Jackson Pollock* (New York: Braziller, 1959), 12.

94 O'Hara, "New Directions in Music," 212.

95 O'Hara, *Jackson Pollock*, 21.

96 O'Hara, "New Directions in Music," 213.

97 Clement Greenberg, "How Art Writing Earns Its Bad Name," in *The Collected Essays and Criticism, Volume 4: Modernism with a Vengeance, 1957–1969*, ed. John O'Brian (Chicago, IL: University of Chicago Press, 1995), 135–44; Albert Goldberg, "Record Reviews," *Los Angeles Times*, September 18, 1960, F7.

98 O'Hara, *Jackson Pollock*, 30–1.

99 Shaw, *Frank O'Hara*, 160.

100 O'Hara, "New Directions in Music," 214–15.

101 Feldman notes that by 1962 the record had sold 4,500 copies ("Brushed Off For Years, Avant Garde Music Finally Gaining Recognition," *Variety*, February 21, 1962, 53), 30–31.

102 Loren Glass, *Counterculture Colophon: Grove Press, the Evergreen Review, and the Incorporation of the Avant-Garde* (Stanford: Stanford University Press, 2013).

103 Ashley and Feldman, "Around Morton Feldman," 8.

104 Robert Motherwell quoted in Robert Goodnough, ed., "Artists Sessions at Studio 35," in Ellen G. Landau, ed., *Reading Abstract Expressionism*, 151.

2

"*Élan vital* . . . and how to fake it"

For Sabine Hänggi-Stampfli

In the years that I've been working with the Morton Feldman Collection at the Paul Sacher Stiftung, I've grown attached to particular objects. Those I'm most fond of provide portentous clues to Feldman's musical world but remain to some degree under-investigated. One such artifact is a notebook titled "Four Lectures: New York Style," which contains drafts and anecdotes for a series of talks given at the New York Studio School in the 1967–8 academic year.[1] The lectures are wide-ranging, referencing Claude Debussy, psychoanalysis, Zionism, Søren Kierkegaard, the Marquis de Sade, Pierre Boulez, Luciano Berio, John Cage, Norman O. Brown, and more. They develop themes of artistic anxiety and existentialist thinking explored in Feldman's published writing. Other traces evince concurrent—if somewhat mysterious—intellectual commitments. At the beginning of the notebook, for example, among a list of phrases that appear to be mnemonic devices for stories Feldman might tell during his talks, we find: "Henri Bergson's *élan vital* . . . and how to fake it."

Feldman leaves this statement largely undeveloped, though he evokes *élan vital* in a later discussion of feeling and fantasy couched in largely Freudian terms. There he writes, "the overall feeling of art was the belief in the immortality of its soul or the Jewish equivalent which is really Bergson's *élan vital*. The creative ghost that reappears in every age—not unlike the ancient Hebrew myth that as long as Jews survive—there will always be 10 just men . . . who carry on the Law."[2] From what little he gives us, it seems that Feldman interprets *élan vital* as a generative force. It is a "creative ghost" ensuring the continuity of art and the survival of the world. In a typical rhetorical gesture, he finds an analogy for artistic practice in a religious idea likened to a metaphysical concept. Bergson's vitalism is placed in dialog with a Jewish parable—the story of the ten just men whose righteousness sustains humanity.³ I've found no earlier named reference to the philosopher in any of Feldman's writings, published or unpublished, though we find circumstantial evidence of his awareness of Bergson in the titles of various composition series, including *Extensions* (from the early 1950s) and *Durations* (from 1959–61). "Extension" and "duration" are both fundamental concepts in Bergson's *Time and Free Will*.⁴

In his foundational work on Feldman, Sebastian Claren has cautioned against making too much of Bergson's role in Feldman's thinking, noting that "although a certain correspondence between Bergson's train of thought and Feldman's purpose is obvious, it would go too far to apply Bergson's theory to Feldman's understanding of the instrumental image, especially since Bergson's image plays only a subordinate role as mediator between reality and perception."⁵ My own goal is not to directly apply Bergson's vitalist philosophy to Feldman's musicality, but rather to identify vitalism as a metaphysical current running through the musician's community of friends and collaborators. Claren is certainly correct that attempting what he advises against would shoehorn Feldman's idiosyncratic metaphysics into something far too limiting, or expect him to maintain a philosophical consistency to which he did not aspire. Yet it was Bergson's presence in "Four Lectures: New York Style" and the evocation of *élan vital* that sparked my interest in exploring vitalism—the view of "life as a self-evident and comprehensive evolving force that could not be explained by a materialist mechanism"—in Feldman's work prior to 1967.⁶ Just how, I wondered, might Feldman "fake" *élan vital*?

In light of John Cage's reception of Bergson in the 1950s, it seems productive to consider how Feldman drew upon Bergson specifically as well as vitalist metaphysics more generally.⁷ Branden Joseph has made a strong claim about the importance of Bergson to Cage, arguing that "Cage's mature understanding of silence as formulated in [1951] can be related to (if it did not, in fact, derive from) Bergson's critique of non-being as expressed in *Creative Evolution*."⁸ No such claim can be made for Bergson's presence in Feldman's thought.

In the wake of Joseph's reading of Cage, there has been a broader reconsideration of vitalism's importance to the intellectual history of New

York School modernism.⁹ Art historians, including Ellen Landau, Jonathan Katz, and Valerie Hellstein have shown that an interest in vitalism cut across the interdisciplinary community of the Eighth Street Artists Club.¹⁰ Katz notes that "Vitalism . . . was one of many competing early-twentieth-century attempts to detect deep structuring first principles, the array of invisible forces that shape and determine all creation. . . . All living things possess a life force that can be sensed intuitively." He also notes that it was "less a systematic philosophy than grab bag metaphysics."¹¹ More pointedly, Hellstein argues that Zen, transcendentalism, Bergsonism, and so on comprised a sensibility—a vernacular metaphysics, really—held in common by figures as supposedly divergent as Harold Rosenberg and John Cage:

> Vitalism, although popular in the early part of the twentieth century, diminished as an influential discourse after 1930, but after World War II, with the disclosure of the horrors of the Holocaust, the building of atomic weaponry, and the mass destruction caused by two atomic bombs, many began to feel acutely that individuals were increasingly objectified. Vitalism's acknowledgment of a pervading, connecting rhythm, an *élan vital* in Henri Bergson's terms, throughout all of existence that cannot be reduced to mechanistic or chemical explanation made it particularly attractive at this moment, offering an alternative worldview in which relatedness and connectivity are as fundamental as individual autonomy.¹²

By calling this group's vitalism a vernacular metaphysics, I want to stress the avant-garde's interpenetration with some aspects of popular culture and explore how the Bergson craze of the early twentieth century had an afterlife in New York School modernism. It preceded the revival of the philosopher, precipitated by Gilles Deleuze's *Bergsonism*.¹³ This particular relationship between popular culture and avant-garde practices to some degree prefigures later formations of what Benjamin Piekut has called the "vernacular avant-garde" and Benjamin Lee—working on 1960s hipness—has termed "vernacular styles."¹⁴

Bergson's immense impact in the United States in the early years of the twentieth century was felt both in elite intellectual publics and popular culture.¹⁵ His concepts of becoming and creativity were profoundly influential on the British-born Harvard professor Alfred North Whitehead, who developed a metaphysics of creative novelty in his process philosophy.[16] Whitehead's importance to New York School modernism is hardly inconsequential;[17] Robert Motherwell studied with Whitehead at Harvard and credited his teacher—as well as Bergson—with a powerful impact on his painting and aesthetic theories.[18] Feldman was friends with Motherwell and it is plausible that Motherwell mediated these ideas in the 1950s. However, the case for any transmission of these ideas between them remains speculative. Feldman does reference Whitehead in the 1980s, but it is difficult to say when he first read him.[19] The tenor of Feldman's language suggests some familiarity with the spirit—if not the letter—of Whitehead's metaphysics, due in part to their shared interest in Bergson.

Hellstein, Katz, and Landau recognize a communal vitalism suffusing the New York avant-garde, which suggests that distinctions between Cagean indeterminacy and Abstract Expressionism may be less pronounced than scholars such as Joseph and Caroline Jones have argued.[20] I do not deny such distinctions were salient from the 1960s on—especially with the turn in Cage's work toward theater and anarchy. But such distinctions cannot be made on the grounds of the artist's supposed fealty to Bergson. Indeed, as Hellstein notes, if one turns toward the matter of artistic experience—particularly the de-centered, relational encounters proffered by Cage's indeterminacy, Feldman's notational experiments, and abstract expressionist painting—one finds a remarkably similar mode of reception. Recovering Feldman's vitalist interests and the broader circulation of such ideas among his friends may go a long way toward sharpening our understanding of the shared metaphysics of this community and the sociopolitical situation of the 1950s New York art world.

To begin, I home in on a particular rarity in Feldman's oeuvre—his use of open-form notation, in which musicians craft a performance from a cluster of small gestures or fragments. There are only two extant works of this kind: the much-discussed *Intermission 6* (1952) and the little-known *Figure of Memory* (1954), written for the dancer-choreographer Merle Marsicano (1903–83) and used as accompaniment for her solo dance of the same name. I'll consider the annotations from Feldman's first version of *Intermission 6* in his 1952–3 sketchbook, which attest to his absorption of vitalist ideas from the arts and philosophy. I'll then explore Feldman's collaboration with Marsicano on *Figure of Memory*. Marsicano herself developed through dance the vitalist concerns of the New York School and echoed many of Feldman's values. Their shared sentiments offer evidence of a vernacular metaphysics circulating among their friends. By vernacular metaphysics I mean the heterodox and pragmatic development of concepts through artistic practice—a kind of loose talk used for self-understanding. The resonances of Feldman and Marsicano's vitalism extended into the broader milieu of the Eighth Street Artists Club, especially in the genre of the artist film.[21] Following my discussion of Feldman and Marsicano, I'll offer an extended discussion of Herbert Matter's *Works of Calder*, Hans Namuth's *Jackson Pollock 51*, and Nathan Boxer's *Sculpture by Lipton*—films that thematize the connectedness of abstract gesture (sound, paint, movement) to natural energetic forces as representation of *élan vital*. It is no coincidence that these films were soundtracked by Feldman (*Pollock* and *Lipton*) and Cage (*Calder*). These collaborations suggest that by 1954 Feldman was well-versed in vitalist ideas and actively assimilating them to his musical aesthetics. Moreover, his music was by then already iconic of the sound of the communal vitalism shared by New York School modernism and embodied in dance and artist films.

". . . just the outlines of becoming": *Intermission 6*

Besides "Four Lectures: New York Style," another evocative object within the Feldman collection has long fascinated me: a sketchbook—designated *Skizzenbuch 3*—containing a number of works, drafts, and writings from mid-1951 through 1953. These include the soundtrack score for Hans Namuth's *Jackson Pollock 51*, notations for the graph score *Marginal Intersection*, bits of *Extensions 1, 3,* and *4*, incidental music for a production of Aristophanes's *The Frogs*, and the first version of *Intermission 6*.[22] *Skizzenbuch 3* is among the earliest sources of Feldman's writing about his own music. Another is the statement Henry Cowell published in his "Current Chronicle,"[23] which was republished in *trans/formation* that same year.[24] *Skizzenbuch 3* offers a number of insights into Feldman's early years of friendship with Cage as well as his participation in the

Eighth Street Artists Club. It also provides evidence for his early involvement with dance as we find references to collaborations with Katherine Litz and Jean Erdman.[25] As a document of his interdisciplinary community, it is invaluable, showing us the range of his involvement across the arts and the interpenetration of disciplines by means of aesthetics and friendship.

Feldman peppers his writings in *Skizzenbuch 3* with a vitalist vocabulary shared by Cage, Pollock, Seymour Lipton, Marsicano, Rosenberg, and many others. Feldman captures this in a note from March 10, 1953 (encountered previously in Chapter 1):

> Yet one could think of each sound as a [movement] of sensibility and in a Proustian way investigate its countless juxtapositions for experience. But to see "things as they are" requires a vision of style which transcends detail and becomes the now moment, the experience rather than the fruits of experience. This is so much that conditions and shapes ourselves. My desire is to find what in myself can recreate myself as to alienation in my art as well as life. One thing [is] certain. I must move, move. I must act regardless the action. Live regardless the living.[26]

He conveys an energetic urgency—"I must move, move"—and aspires to "live regardless the living." Two literary references tie Feldman's desire to vitalist matters. First, he imagines sound as "a movement of sensibility" via the excavation of memory performed in Proust's *In Search of Lost Time*. Feldman's desire to see "things as they are" points up anti-conceptualist and an anti-representational impulses that get to the truth of things by dissolving illusion. Feldman may well have borrowed the line "things as they are" from Gertrude Stein (whose novel of the same name was published in 1950); however, Wallace Steven's poem "The Man with the Blue Guitar" is a more likely candidate, given the relatively limited circulation of Stein's novel at the time. In Steven's poem, his refrain insists upon a renewed attention to the world and "the rhapsody of things as they are."[27] Each of these writers (Proust, Stein, and Stevens) was impacted by the vitalism emergent in the nineteenth century via Bergson, Whitehead, and Stein's teacher William James. Proust drew on Bergson's philosophy of memory[28] while Stein's anti-representational aesthetics were inflected by her studies in psychology and automatic writing with James.[29] Stevens was himself a devotee of Bergson.[30]

As Susanne K. Langer has noted, Bergson's "nearness to the problems of art has made him pre-eminently the artists' philosopher."[31] Bergson himself—in "The Perception of Change"—argued that artists had a special role in expanding our perceptions of reality:

> It will be said that this enlarging is impossible. How can one ask the eyes of the body, or those of the mind, to see more than they see? Our attention can increase precision, clarify and intensify; it cannot bring forth in the field of perception what was not there in the first place. That's the objection.—It is refuted in my opinion by experience. For hundreds of years, in fact, there have been men whose function has been precisely to see and to make us see what we do not naturally perceive. They are the artists.
>
> What is the aim of art if not to show us, in nature and in the mind, outside of us and within us, things which did not explicitly strike our senses and our consciousness?[32]

Bergson praises artists and glorifies their expansion of our capacity for feeling. This resonates with Feldman, who conceived of sound as emotionally energetic—a "movement of sensibility" akin to Proust's affective and involuntary memory. This takes on a more Bergsonian sheen when Feldman distinguishes between "experience" and the "fruits of experience" that remain in the wake of an authentic encounter with the absolute. Such encounters allow us to experience things—sounds, in this case—as they are. Feldman describes this as "the transcendence of detail," which "becomes the now moment." His valorization of immediacy shares more than a superficial relationship to Bergson's notion of experience that we find in *Creative Evolution*:

> Let us then concentrate attention on that which we have that is at the same time the most removed from externality and the least penetrated with intellectuality. Let us seek, in the depths of our experience, the point where we feel ourselves most intimately within our own life. It is into pure duration that we then plunge back, a duration in which the past, always moving on, is swelling unceasingly with a present that is absolutely new. But, at the same time, we feel the spring of our will strained to its utmost limit. We must, by a strong recoil of our personality on itself, gather up our past which is slipping away, in order to thrust it, compact and undivided, into a present

which it will create by entering. Rare indeed are the moments when we are self-possessed to this extent: it is then that our actions are truly free.[33]

The movement into the "now moment" (as Feldman calls it) echoes Bergson's plunge back "into pure duration," in which we overcome alienation and achieve freedom. The artist films on Pollock, Calder, and Lipton—for which Feldman and Cage composed music—each dramatize the act of creation and situate it within such a vitalist imaginary. Feldman's comments follow on his work on Namuth's Pollock film and show him developing a feeling for sound in terms of the vitalism coursing through his community.

Most relevant to my argument is the copresence in *Skizzenbuch 3* of *Intermission 6* (see Figure 2.1) with statements quoted earlier. We are most familiar with the 1963 version of the piano piece, published in the counterculture magazine *Kulchur* and as sheet music by Edition Peters. The most recent engraved edition by Edition Peters gives the date of composition as 1953, although I am in agreement with Alistair Noble that the correct year is 1952, based on its place between other dateable works in the sketchbook.[34] *Intermission 6* is one of two examples of Feldman's experimentation with "open form," or "mobile" notation—versions of which Cage, Earle Brown, Pierre Boulez, and Karlheinz Stockhausen also developed in the 1950s. In the 1963 version of *Intermission 6*, a pianist is confronted with a page sparsely covered with fragments of notation.[35] She is free to move between any of the fragments and improvise the continuity of the piece. There are no time constraints; a performance can continue as long as desired.

Feldman's spatialized conception of the piece is a far cry from its original notation in *Skizzenbuch 3* as well as the second iteration held in the Tudor archive at the Getty. Most interesting is the instruction that accompanies the notation: "THIS PIECE IS JUST THE OUTLINES OF BECOMING. IT CAN START ANYWHERE, GO ANYWHERE WITHIN THESE REFERENCES OF SOUNDS AND MAY BE ANY LENGTH."[36] A further direction instructs performers to "hold each measure until completely inaudible." Note the metaphysical charge of Feldman's language. To call this notation "just the outlines of becoming" suggests that the performance would be becoming itself. Thus, Feldman's attempt to fake *élan vital*. Furthermore, the anti-

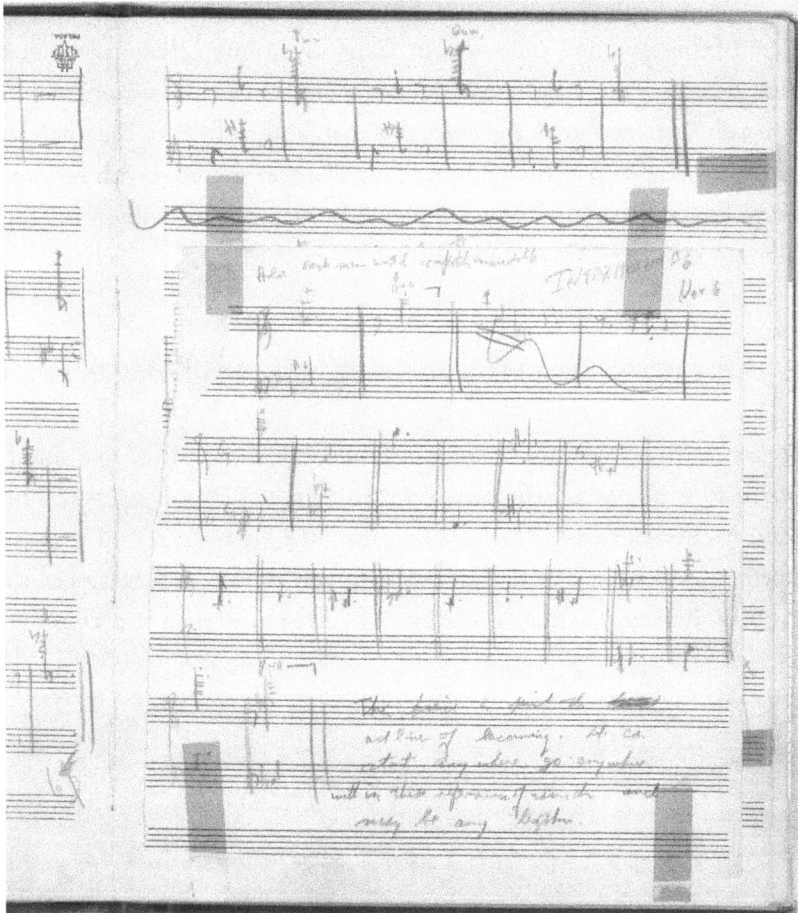

Figure 2.1 Morton Feldman, *Intermission 6*, first version. *Skizzenbuch 3*. Morton Feldman Collection. Paul Sacher Foundation.

conceptualism foundational to Bergson's philosophy—and, as Kevin Volans[37] insists, Feldman's musical practice—is evident only a few pages following *Intermission 6* in *Skizzenbuch 3*, where we find Feldman writing,

> Time as time; texture as time; texture as a plastic image creating itself only in execution. The happening in time is the reality. Space in music is Illusion. An image created by intuitive relationships defining itself in all degradation of this Illusion. Starve the Illusion and feed the energy that made it visible will then become an experience as yet unknown to me.[38]

Intuition is a method that allows him to "starve" the illusionary power of spatial representation in music in favor of an energetic surge that will produce new, as yet unknown experiences. What we can glean from Feldman's thinking documented in *Skizzenbuch 3* is that, at least in part, the open-form indeterminacy of *Intermission 6* was a way of experimenting with becoming. This novel notation might make audible his burgeoning metaphysics of sound itself.

"My person is a protean being": *Figure of Memory*

Little more than a year after its composition, Feldman returned to a variation of *Intermission 6*'s open-form notation with *Figure of Memory*. It was written for dancer-choreographer Merle Marsicano (see Figure 2.2) and premiered on April 3, 1954, with David Tudor at the piano.[39] The piece was performed extensively during Feldman's lifetime—likely more than *Intermission 6*.

Figure 2.2 Merle Marsicano. Photographer unknown. Edwin Hymovitz Collection. Paul Sacher Foundation.

Marsicano danced it regularly for twenty-five years, first with Tudor, and then with pianist Edwin Hymovitz. We have Hymovitz to thank for reconstructing the score, which Marsicano had lost by 1976. Hymovitz was able to reproduce it from memory and gave a photocopy of it to the Sacher Foundation along with a number of materials related to Marsicano's career.[40] Tragically, her husband, painter Nicholas Marsicano, threw out the vast majority of her archive after her death.

Marsicano—more than even Merce Cunningham—should be credited as Feldman's most important choreographic collaborator. Feldman's music was used for at least four of her dances and was included on many recitals she gave from the 1950s through the 1970s. She, too, was deeply enmeshed within the broader community of New York School modernists and present at the Eighth Street Artists Club. Her husband was a member of the Club and she encountered Feldman in this community of painters, dancers, and musicians.[41]

Marsicano was born in Philadelphia and began her dance training in ballet with Ethel Philips and Mikhail Mordkin. She trained in Spanish dance with Angel Cansino and received a two-year fellowship to study with Martha Graham and Louis Horst at the Neighborhood Playhouse. Her work with Graham put her in contact with Jean Erdman and Merce Cunningham, and these relationships led to her musical collaborations with Feldman as well as Cage. Feldman wrote three scores for Marsicano—*Three Dances* (1952), *Figure of Memory*, and *Dance Suite for Merle Marsicano* (1963). Marsicano also danced to other pieces by Feldman that were not written specifically for her, such as *Christian Wolff in Cambridge* (1963) and *Chorus and Instruments II* (1967). Recordings of both accompanied the dance *Fragment for a Greek Tragedy* in 1979. (It had previously been danced to music by Cage.)[42] Of these dance scores, *Figure of Memory* was the most frequently performed and critically acclaimed.[43]

Marsicano gave her debut New York recital on February 17, 1952, with a program that included Feldman's *Three Dances* for piano as well as dances with the music of Cage, Stefan Wolpe, and Jerry Petersen.[44] David Tudor played piano. She described her conception of dance a few years later:

> By the very nature of the dance, as differentiated from any of the plastic arts, each performance recapitulates the act of creation. The concept is alive and

working and confronts one as a living presence. The dance itself... confronts one as a living thing, with the mental concept and the vibrant actuality merged into one image. How could we say what living thing the dance symbolizes?[45]

Marsicano here adopts a vitalist vocabulary. Through dance, one activates living energy and recognizes the powerful agency of movement itself. She insists upon prolonging discovery through "the elasticity of a dance's duration."[46] This is also a form of anti-conceptualism. One could interpret her understanding of durational elasticity as a movement-based conception of the open-form approach Feldman took in *Intermission 6* and *Figure of Memory*. It certainly calls to mind the "elastic form" Cowell developed in his collaborations with Graham, and suggests that the elder composer's own notational invention may have played some part in Feldman's conception of *Figure of Memory* (see Figure 2.3).

Of *Figure of Memory*, dance critic Don McDonagh wrote:

[Marsicano's] feet are in constant motion, carrying her to all corners in her search. Her hands flicker momentarily, and then she will suddenly stretch

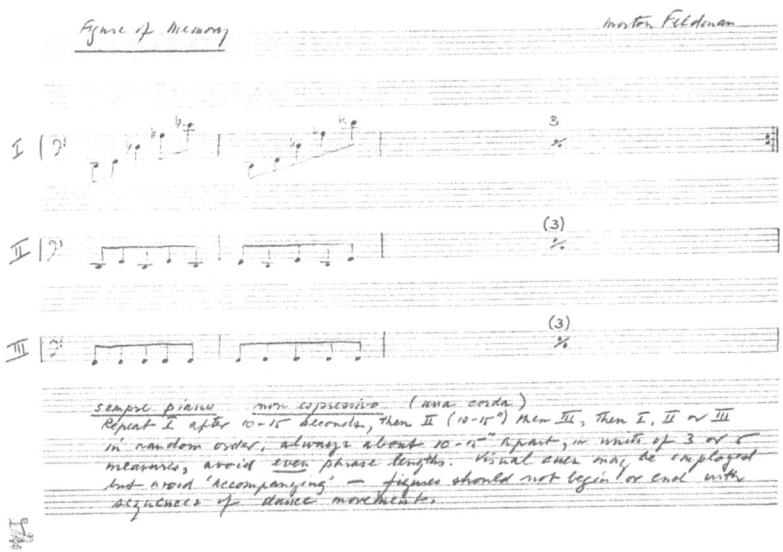

Figure 2.3 Morton Feldman, *Figure of Memory* (reconstruction by Edwin Hymovitz). Edwin Hymovitz Collection. Paul Sacher Foundation.

her arms straight out, but the object of her search remains beyond her grasp. The feeling evoked is that of perennial searching without violent anxiety.... One does not detect the familiar beginning, middle, and end development of the dance. It always seems to have been there and, when it ceases, it does not finish with a sense of resolve. It just trails away. One is not concerned with the individual moments of the dance but more with the over-all web that enmeshes the attention.[47]

McDonagh's language evokes Clement Greenberg's conception of "all-over" painting, in which a viewer's attention cannot settle on one area of the canvas but is continually activated by a non-hierarchical field of gestures.[48] The immediacy of the dance's image was reinforced by Feldman's music, which Hymovitz recalled: "When we used to do FIGURE OF MEMORY in concert to live music we spent a lot of time rehearsing Feldman's spare figurations so that they came in exactly the right places, not <u>in time</u> but at the right time. It sounded random but wasn't at all."[49]

Through her choice of collaborators for the recital on which *Figure of Memory* premiered, Marsicano emphasized the Eighth Street Artists Club's interdisciplinary ethos and foundation in friendship. In addition to her collaboration with Feldman, Marsicano choreographed *Jet Pears* to a recitation of Frank O'Hara's poem "Augustus." The sculptor Richard Lippold—another club member and friend of both Feldman and Cage—reviewed the performance. His review provides a sense of the reflexive nature of aesthetic discourse in which ideas were generated by the artists themselves. They set the terms of reception, which were confirmed by an audience of artists and friends and circulated in the public sphere. Lippold wrote, "Merle Marsicano is one of a small group of highly original dancers who, like the most experimental of today's painters, sculptors, composers, and poets, have put aside the rather tired concerns with narrative psychoanalysis, social awareness, or classically-inspired forms of the recent past."[50] Vitalism, though not named, is the guiding metaphysics of her work and it shares with Feldman's own thinking a stark anti-conceptualism and anti-representational bent.

Lippold went on to make the connections between Marsicano's dance and abstract painting explicit: "Some of Miss Marsicano's dances such as *Jet Pears* and *Green Song*, two group works, suggest more than a casual relationship to painting with their dependence on color and on choreography which uses individualized dancers to describe a complex space of independent, though overlapping shapes." Lippold describes a situation similar to Cage's compositional values of unimpededness and interpenetration, which mark most of the composer's works from the mid-1950s until the late 1970s. In Lippold's description, the tension between "independent" and "overlapping" forms Marsicano's conception of dance merging into "one image." Her taut, gestic movement operates on stage in a manner similar to the new abstract painting. Indeed, Lippold presaged McDonaugh's description of Marsicano's dance as an "over-all web." In his description of Feldman's *Three Dances*, Lippold elaborates: "These are a somewhat moody group, full of a continuous flow of movements, rich in invention, always surprising, yet seldom rising or falling to either side of a rather turgid line, making a complex and rich design, like the surface of a de Kooning or Pollock painting."[51] This pseudomorphic logic transposes the social basis of these collaborations to the level of form.

"Of the solo dances," Lippold writes, "Figure of Memory is undoubtedly the richest of Marsicano's efforts. It sustains a magical quality throughout, and succeeds best in accomplishing what seems to be her intent in all her works: a convincing emotion, compactly stated with such expert abstraction that the presence of the performer is forgotten and the audience is transported by the experience of pure movement."[52] As an "experience of pure movement," Marsicano's dance was capable of overcoming symbolization and returning to flux and flow—attempting, like Feldman, to "fake"—or evoke, really—*élan vital*.

Marsicano echoes the decentered, "all-over" experience favored by Feldman and Cage in draft writings that eventually became her essay "Thoughts on the Dance," which was published in the house magazine of the Eighth Street Artists Club, *It is*. She writes, "I think of music as an art of untouched white upon which I must breathe for my very existence, yet leave untouched, just as the music must pass through and around me without discoloring the white of my being. We must become one and yet retain the separateness of our souls."[53] Again we find hints of Cage's dialectic of unimpededness/interpenetration, but it also suggests the more generalized non-hierarchical relationship of music and dance in the post-Graham era of the New York avant-garde. Whiteness here figures as a kind of distinctness or independence from other aspects of the performance event. She is concerned with making (not faking) *élan vital*, producing an art that *is* becoming and resists being: "The dancing figure is the person and becomes in the next moment, the wind. Arrest the dancer anywhere on stage—her condition is flux. In stillness I change. And the composed shape of my figure suddenly explodes in a riot of configuration. My person is a protean being."[54]

Other passages from Marsicano's unpublished writings express stronger vitalist sentiments and emphasize notions of intuition and anti-conceptualism found in Bergson: "The innocence, the irrational, the inspiration and the improvisation of a living art such as the dance are lost when we attempt to rationalise [*sic*] the construction. The consciousness makes for self-conscious questioning, to which available answers can be supplied. The art suffers from rationalization."[55] She hoped to escape such rationalizing strictures of the known by means of her choreography:

> I find myself subjected to the most critical exposures of analytical sophistication in our sciences, histories, and physical probings and communications. How can we find again mysterious motivations and the innocence of no memory—reason to the point of being unreasonable? sense that makes no sense? How to blindfold my ability to construct a dance? How to render speechless the common instinct for taste? How to create a jungle, to find again the hopeless situation [in] which only a magnificent failure could be acceptable. To confuse the known! and then have to depend again upon inspiration or desperation.[56]

As with Feldman's desire to "step aside to be in control"[57] and to compose as a dead man[58]—or, similarly, with Cage's vast self-disciplinary apparatus of chance composition through the *I Ching*—Marsicano developed an ascetics to get beyond her training "in this school of contemporary taste."[59] Marsicano's anti-conceptualism gives free play to her emotions beyond intended meaning: "I should like to feel free to allow my feelings to construct whatever shape and form they take, give them whatever image would depict most intensely so that they should stand in themselves not for or against anything."[60] Her practice emerges as a kind of intuitive method that moves away from representation and toward the pure intensity of experience. She desired—as she said of *Figure of Memory*—"Powerful occurrence."[61]

Feldman's Filmic Vitalism

Feldman's music played an important role in producing the shared vitalist sensibility found in New York School modernism. His collaborative relationship with Marsicano is but one important example. The vitalist impulse in the New York avant-garde of the 1950s, with its quality of a vernacular metaphysics, subtended the practices of a number of artists. As such, it functioned as a kind of pseudomorphosis we don't usually attribute to midcentury modernism.[62] For too long, we've taken Greenberg's claims of medium-specificity as a rule when—as the work of Feldman and his coterie makes apparent—it was the exception. There was commerce between the arts. In the preceding sections I've show how attention to vitalist conceptions of becoming—powerfully shaped by Bergson—cut across Feldman's music as well as his and Mariscano's collaborative dance works. These emphasized mobile form, disorientation of memory (on both musical and physical planes), and anti-formalist structure. In what follows, I widen my scope to look at filmic collaborations between Feldman, Jackson Pollock, Hans Namuth, Seymour Lipton, and Nathan Boxer. My wager is that these films stage painting and sculpture as acts of nature, and Feldman's music has the privileged position of making this connection sensible. In vitalist terms, *elán vital* is a demiurgic natural process that artists can merge with in their creative work. No longer are artists assumed to paint *from* nature—"I am nature," Pollock once quipped in response to Hans Hoffman; creative abstraction from memory, from daily life, and from the natural world was represented on film and mended what Whitehead called "the bifurcation of nature."[63]

Despite Bergson's own antipathy for cinema—which he felt fixed becoming and staunched the flow of *élan vital*—members of the Club employed the medium as a means of materializing their vitalist metaphysics. *Works of Calder* (1950) was an important precursor to both Namuth's *Jackson Pollock 51* and Boxer's *Sculpture by Lipton*, establishing important representational precedents the later films would employ. *Work of Calder* brought together Herbert Matter as director, John Cage as composer, and Jackson Pollock as key grip to produce an artist film on Alexander Calder that unequivocally projected a vitalist interpretation of the kinetic sculptor's work. From the opening moments of the film, there is an energetic equivalence of organic and inorganic material. As Cage's prepared-piano score proffers metallic percussive sounds resonating with complex overtones, a close-up shot of a spinning Calder mobile is overlaid atop a mid-range shot of waves crashing on a beach. Lasting around twenty seconds, the scene does powerful semiotic work: the waves crash, the mobile turns, and the sounds whir along—all animated by some unseen force. It is a clear illustration of the Thomistic dictum often cited by Cage, that "art should imitate nature in its manner of operation."[64] Burgess Meredith—narrator and producer of the film—intones a ruminative text by John La Touche that details the adventure (leading to Calder's studio) of young Alexander "Pundy" Matter, the filmmaker's son.

Latouche's own vitalist commitments are unclear, but he made a powerful case for Calder's vitalist aesthetics in his description of the film's scenes. The narration draws out in particular the quality of *movement* central to the natural world. Over images of waves lapping upon a sandy shore intercut with shots of jellyfish in motion, Meredith recites, "Today this boy went to the beach. It was a sunny, windy day and he was alone. He wandered about and investigated. The wind made everything move. He found some jellyfish, and under the water they were moving too. So was the water and the milkweed and the sun." A powerful life force animates this world. The music preceding this section prepares us for such a description, as its prepared-piano tones gradually coalesce into a pregnant pulsion. The vital energy of pulse felt across domains was important to Herbert Matter; as Richard H. Brown notes, "he was deeply concerned with the rhythmic integration of sound and image, and Cage's work clearly followed Matter's vision."[65] Integration is certainly not a value we associate with Cage's mid-career aesthetic, yet we find him participating here in the communal elaboration of a vernacular vitalism.

These initial moments open up a whole world in which Calder's art finds its place: the energetic flow and rhythm of life. The next section of the film follows Pundy into Calder's studio, where we watch the artist work:

> There was a man in there, very busy. He was making the noise. Hammering and banging, scraping and bending things into shape. The boy asked the man why he was doing that; the man said he enjoyed doing so. He explained that

the things he made were called "mobiles," because they move by themselves. And mobiles were made out of everything, he said: tin, wood, steel, wire. He made them by himself. He worked hard as though in a factory, but the things came out different. Sometimes they moved all around him and he enjoyed that. It was like having his own private sky.

Latouche's script highlights the critique of post-Fordist capitalism we find in the New York avant-garde.[66] Calder works "as though in a factory," but where such work would usually produce identical commodities, the work of the artist produces *difference*. In fact, Calder's process is a radical criticism of capitalist waste as he takes up scrap metal and other detritus of the commercial process and reworks it into artifacts that achieve their own uniqueness. These objects in turn become activated by nature and move with a life of their own.

Matter took the animacy of Calder's sculptures seriously, and the final section of the film synthesizes the dialectical process between nature and culture (see Figure 2.4). We began in the rhythms of the natural world (wind, wave, bioenergetic motion) and turned to the rhythms of the artist's world (human labor, the movement of the mobiles). The discrete worlds are superimposed as Matter layers footage of Calder's mobiles over scenes from nature and stages sculptures in the landscape. This synthesis is presented as

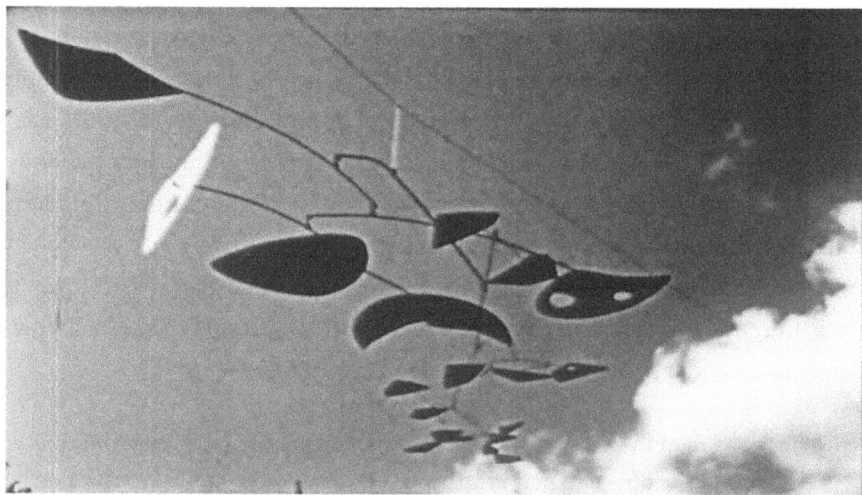

Figure 2.4 *Works of Calder*, directed by Herbert Matter, 1950.

the recovery of childlike powers of observation, with Pundy as the viewer's proxy. Again, Latouche's narration: "The boy watched them so long he got rather dreamy, and the things he saw in the house and the things he had seen outside got mixed up together in his head. The man said that was what they were *supposed* to do." Artistic labor, and especially the work of abstraction, reintegrates humankind with nature, thereby accessing its energies and perceptual possibilities.

Film, like Calder's sculpture, was a technology for revealing these latent connections. It was a medium Matter used to reveal the complexities of time and motion. He achieved this through stroboscopic photography of nature and Calder's mobiles. Matter's deployment of stroboscopic photography—a technique he had been using since as early as 1939—in the recuperation of nature is another instance of a techno-primitivism cutting across modernism, existing in agonistic tension with the Action Painters because of their resistance to commodification and suspicion of mechanical means.[67] It finds less dissonant resonances with Cage's embrace of technology as a tool for getting inside sounds and hearing the world without intention. In a way, Matter's stroboscopic photography, as well as his film of Calder, produces the illusion of vital movement through a concatenation of discrete instants, making perceptible the flow of Bergson's *durée*.

Works of Calder set up a template of focusing on vitalist metaphysics, which was followed by Namuth (in *Jackson Pollock 51*) and Boxer (in *Sculpture by Lipton*). *Sculpture by Lipton* hews closest to the structure of *Works of Calder*, recapitulating the superimposition of nature and artwork. *Jackson Pollock 51* dramatizes Pollock's personal identification with natural forces. Namuth places him outdoors, where his balletic dripping technique is likened to the wind itself. Lee Krasner's recollection of Pollock's invocation of natural forces (as well as her own) opens up an expansive claim of similitude between the work of abstraction and elemental forces. Their interpenetration reconciles humans to nature:

> LEE KRASNER: Well, I would say that up to the point of meeting Pollock—as I said, I'd worked with Hofmann who certainly brought an understanding of Cubism. I'd say my work at that point was still very

much under the so-called French influence and on meeting Pollock there was once more a violent transition and upheaval. And living with him and watching him work, well, certainly it had its effect and consequently the painting changed.

DOROTHY SECKLER: In your case, how did this express itself? Was it a matter of a more vehement approach to the actual handling of the paint or was there any kind of oh, type of mystique that emerged?

LEE KRASNER: Well, in my own experience after it occurred it not only was more vehement, it became infinitely, well, one might say from a loud sound to a grain of sand. In other words, I went through a kind of black-out period or a painting of nothing but gray building up, because the big transition there is that up to that point, and including Hofmann, I had worked from nature. Now let me try to explain that in a more simple way. When I brought Hofmann up to meet Pollock and see his work which was before we moved here, Hofmann's reaction was—one of the questions he asked Jackson was, do you work from nature? There were no still lifes around or models around and Jackson's answer was, "I am nature." And Hofmann's reply was, "Ah, but if you work by heart, you will repeat yourself." To which Jackson did not reply at all. Now then, this is what was happening to me: as I had worked so-called, from nature, that is, I am here and Nature is out there, whether it be in the form of a woman or an apple or anything else, the concept was broken and you faced a black canvas. Well, with the knowledge that I am nature and try to make something happen on that canvas, now this is the real transition that took place.[68]

While usually reduced to Krasner's recollection of Pollock's response to Hoffman—"I am nature"—the fuller context of the discussion with Seckler reveals Krasner's own powerful conception of non-bifurcated practice in which the illusion of the nature/culture binary is collapsed. What is striking about Krasner's description of Pollock is its similarity to John Cage's own position and alignment with Bergson's philosophy. Like Cage, Krasner rejected the notion that "I am here and Nature is out there." She and Pollock identified with an outside, but unlike Cage, this outside was accessible through subjectivity and artistic agency. It did not require the "state of mind of wanting to become a weed"—as Yoko Ono described Cage and his adoption of chance methods.[69]

Pollock and Krasner understood consciousness as an extension of nature. Their reconfiguring the practice of painting—not as the mimesis of nature, but as a natural process itself—offers another variation on vitalists themes, one related to but distinct from the sensibility we find in *Works of Calder*. There, La Touche and Matter replaced the artist within nature and likened artistic action to the energetic flows of wind and water. Calder himself remains, in their estimation, *homo faber*—a laboring artisan manipulating the refuse of post-Fordist production.

Pollock found a vocabulary for his own views of painting through his long friendship with Matter and their collaboration on *Works of Calder*. Ellen G. Landau notes the resonance between Matter's thought and statements of Pollock's—for example, his claim to be nature and his statement that "my concern is with the rhythms of nature... The way the ocean moves... I work inside out like nature."[70] Herbert Matter's pantheistic interpretation of artistic practice proliferated into Namuth's and Boxer's artist films. The vitalist bona fides of both *Jackson Pollock 51* and *Sculpture by Lipton* were enhanced by Morton Feldman, whose music shaped—and indeed was *shaped by*—the vitalist visions of those films.

Namuth's *Jackson Pollock 51* and the Space of Freedom

Photographer Hans Namuth approached Pollock with the idea of making a film in 1950 in the midst of his long photographic documentation of the painter's practice. Initially, it was Cage who was approached to score the film. As is well known, Cage demurred (out of distaste for Pollock) and suggested Feldman in his place. *Jackson Pollock 51* and *Works of Calder* share many tropes that structure their vitalist sensibilities. Both highlight nature as a setting for artistic creation. In *Works of Calder*, the relationship is figured through analogy, given that the studio space is closed off from the elements. As the film eventually shows, however, the products of that studio are then moved into nature in order to become part of it—to become "mixed up" with the sea and the trees in order to reveal the undergirding rhythm uniting all things. *Jackson Pollock 51* figures this relationship somewhat differently, but in a no less vitalist fashion.

Because of the exigencies of filming and lighting difficulties, Namuth asked Pollock to paint outside, *in nature*, instead of in the barn studio that was his usual workplace. Thus, Pollock's stated connection with nature is staged explicitly. Pollock's statement (in the voiceover) that "my paintings have a life of their own, so I try to let them live" seems all the more plausible with those paintings liberated from the confines of the studio and the gallery—free to interact with the natural world. I argue later that this sense of freedom—its expansion and curtailing—is something both the film and Feldman's music for it dramatizes. Unlike Calder's mobiles—whose movement from the studio into nature is tracked in Matter's film—Pollock's paintings are presented to us as works that *come into existence* in nature and are only subsequently brought into the gallery, a space of observation and consumption.

Feldman understood the potential for reconciling the human and the natural, undoing the supposed bifurcation of nature (á la Whitehead): "If I want my music to demonstrate anything, it is that 'nature and human nature are one.'"[71] Feldman's equation of nature and human nature, uttered in the 1960s, was of immense importance to his avant-garde community. Though Cage articulates it differently—and he devalued human agency and aimed to disable it—his insistence upon art's imitation of natural processes is rooted in this concern. With Matter's and Namuth's films as evidence, the abstract expressionist ego seems less involved with the expression of repressed psychic energies that it figured as the becoming-nature of artistic action and the recognition of one's creativity pulsing with the rhythms of *élan vital*.

Namuth's film is organized into four discrete scenes: a brief title sequence of Pollock painting his signature on glass; an extended sequence of Pollock working on his property in the Hamptons; a scene of shadow painting intercut with close-up shots of paintings that segues into a shot of Pollock and Krasner in a gallery; and a final scene that takes us inside one of Pollock's paintings as he works on glass. We move with Pollock from the natural scene of artistic production to the public presentation of the work back into nature and finally into the painting itself. Feldman's soundtrack is scored for two cellos, both played (and overdubbed) by Daniel Stern. The soundtrack articulates Pollock's movement through nature and sociocultural space. Feldman deploys two types of sonic cues, both present in the opening title sequence: gestural music that emphasizes the physicality of the performer, and longer, dissonant drones. The physical structure of the cello allows for a wide variety of timbres and textures, and Feldman explores these capacities for sonic variety from the outset.

Feldman's manuscript indicates that, in the title sequence, the "music starts on writing of last name."[72] The first cello plays harmonic glissandi, producing an eerie whistle sliding between the interval of major third (Ab and C). The glissandi are produced by Stern's left hand gently touching the string, without pressing fully against the fingerboard, and sliding up and down the neck of the cello. These glissandi are iconic musical gestures that emphasize corporality in such a way that suggests physical motion of a body in sound. This carnal action is further set off when it is juxtaposed with the second cello's dissonant double-stop drone, a major seventh between D and C#—(wherein Stern's bow makes contact with two strings simultaneously, producing two pitches at once). The pitch content of these opening moments is limited to only four notes (D and C-sharp in cello 2; Ab and C in cello 1), but the affect feels fraught due to the clashes between them. This is alleviated only slightly when the second cello's drone shifts, in measure 11, to an open-fifth interval (E and B). This provides some relief from the earlier, dissonant D-C#, but the continued presence of the Ab-C glissando slithering above it denies a full resolution. Long, sustained tones such as those in the second cello provide an affective contrast with the gestural sounds above them.

As the film continues, these drones become a representation of Pollock's emotional and energetic stasis, in contrast to the plucked sounds that punctuate the soundscape and mime Pollock's dripping actions. This relationship is set up in the title scene with the initial sliding tone juxtaposed against a double-stop drone. Though not mapped precisely onto Pollock's signature, the glissandi suggest the brush strokes of the artist signing his name. The signature scene sets up the dialectic of Feldman's soundtrack in which active, gestural music evocative of Pollock's physicality is one term and sustained droning retarding that physicality is the other. Feldman pins these sustained sonorities to moments in which we observe Pollock's paintings. The sounds have the effect of attenuating Pollock's action and inhibiting our ability to fully entrain both with the plucked sounds of Pollock's movement. This dialectic of direct action and distant observation is also linked to the distinct spaces represented in the film. The natural world of the outdoor painting sequence is dominated by the plucked tones of the action-music. The sustained tones dominate the next scene set in the public space of the gallery. The final scene submerges us in Pollock's painting, with the frenetic action-music returning to prominence, and the sustained tones vanishing entirely.

The second scene opens with shots of Pollock preparing to paint, accompanied by a voiceover narrative extracted from his statement in the sole issue of *Possibilities*.[73] Feldman's music begins as Pollock takes up his brushes and begins to paint. The gestic music transforms from the glissandi of the title sequence into a flurry of plucked strings in both cellos that is occasionally interrupted with sustained, bowed double stops, which slow the music's pointillistic propulsion. These drones frustrate our ability to correlate the gestic music with Pollock's body and entrain our own bodies to their energies. Despite this resistance, the scene is suffused with plucked string sounds and sharp bowed strokes—one such stroke even coordinating exactly with Pollock's violent cigarette toss (see Figure 2.5). The vibrant scene translates Pollock's desire to "express my feelings and not illustrate them" into

Figure 2.5 *Jackson Pollock 51*, directed by Hans Namuth, 1951.

a flurry of sound. On the gestural aspects of Feldman's music, Olivia Mattis suggests that the soundtrack "reflects the abstract artistic gestures depicted on screen without precisely imitating them."[74] Jonathan Bernard, too, notes that "it is hard to miss the overtly *gestural* character of Feldman's writing [in the film], suggestive of Pollock's gestures even though no attempt was made to coordinate music and visual image precisely."[75] Regardless of the lack of exact coordination, the music in this scene makes felt—in its saturation of our visual and aural senses—the excessive, "all-over" aspect of Pollock's work.[76] Physical and musical gestures fill up our experience of Pollock in (and *as*) nature, the space where—in Feldman's idealization of vitalism more broadly—artistic action brings about a synthesis between action and subjectivity.

While the meaning of the active musical sounds is produced through their relationship with Pollock's movements, the meaning of the drones is clarified only in the next section of the film. As the location shifts to a scene of shadow painting and gallery display, the gestic music ceases, replaced by a preponderance of sustained, rasping dyads. Pollock's physical body, too, is rendered invisible and inaudible in this scene: we see only his shadow. The dyads are synchronized with shots of individual paintings or slow pans over canvases. Namuth seems to dramatize our sudden awareness of the paintings' surfaces. There are two instances in which an out-of-focus shot of a canvas is keyed with the onset of a sustained, crescendoing tone in the soundtrack. The emotional effect is that of a momentary vertigo produced by the camera's sharpening focus and the increased volume of the dissonant simultaneities. There is only visual resolution with the camera's coming-into-focus; Feldman's dissonant dyad remains, proffering an intensification of anxiety yoked to the clarification of the image. Gestic plucks occur in isolation and recall Pollock's painting in the first scene. When juxtaposed with images of the canvases they offer the memory of action but no longer action itself. The sonic transformation of the filmic world in this scene suggests something larger: that the movement of the artist and his work into a space of public display has the detrimental effect of attenuating action. It produces anxiety that energizes our perception of the paintings. This is further established by Namuth's pan across the gallery space—we glimpse both Pollock and Krasner from behind—which is accompanied by a major seventh dyad, linking public display with affective immobility. The film to this point has reversed the movement traced in *Works of Calder*. Pollock's painting is extracted from the natural world (where it gets its strength) and placed in the gallery, where its powers are restrained (see Figure 2.6).

The association between nature and enabled action is made all the more poignant in the film's final scene. We are returned to nature, with Pollock's glass canvas becoming window onto the sky—and onto Pollock himself. Musically, the sustained tones are now wholly absent, indicating no synthesis between the terms of the sonic dialectic. The soundtrack has become saturated solely with the gestic music of Pollock's painterly practice. The excited plucks we have experienced prior lock into what we might fairly call "a groove" for the first time in the film. The music of action triumphs over the immobilizing music of public display.

In summary, Feldman's music heightens the emotional sensation of this transition, with sounds that move from crackling *pizzicatti* to off-kilter grooves in the scene of Pollock painting on the grounds of his East Hampton

Figure 2.6 *Jackson Pollock 51*, directed by Hans Namuth, 1951.

property. This *energy made audible* is curtailed in the previous scene, in which Pollock's paintings are offered up for display and the rhythmic propulsion felt in the outdoor painting scene grinds down into static droning chords. Once we return to nature as the space of Pollock's creative action, Feldman's music resumes its flow with even greater rhythmic drive and propels Pollock's painting on glass in the final scene. The film, and the glass-painting sequence in particular, resonates not only with Matter's direction of *Works on Calder*—in which we observe Calder in his studio—but also with Matter's work with stroboscopic effects and montage with which he captured still photography. Landau argues that Pollock's comments on nature and vitalism—some of which were heard as voiceover in Namuth's film—"could just as easily be used to delineate the successive effects of individual frames in *Works of Calder*" and indeed shared much with Matter's own commentary on artistic energy.[77] But Calder's studio practice is not romanticized by Matter to the degree that Pollock's is by Namuth. *Jackson Pollock 51* thus resonates less with the image of Calder and more with Matter's stroboscopic photography. The final scene of Namuth's film vivifies Matter's process via Pollock's body, producing an affective atmosphere that Feldman's music is essential in generating.[78] The metaphysical ideals developed in the 1940s by Matter and Pollock—and the sonic signifiers developed by Feldman and Cage—coalesced into semiotics legible across both films. Indeed audiences had had the opportunity to compare the two films and note their similarities and divergences as both were shown at an art film festival in Woodstock, NY, in 1951.[79]

Sculpture by Lipton and the Germinal Force of Life

Seymour Lipton, though less well known today than Matter or Pollock, was just as invested in vitalist thought. The film documenting and dramatizing his work, *Sculpture by Lipton*, marked the third (along with Matter's and Namuth's) in a series of films involving artists and musicians associated with the Eighth Street Artists Club. Lipton's involvement with the Club in the early 1950s is less documented than that of Feldman, Cage, Pollock, or Matter. In Philip Pavia's 1952 membership list, Lipton is noted only as being on the mailing list, but his inclusion in the 1956 exhibition of *12 Americans* at the Museum of Modern Art along with Club regulars Philip Guston, Franz Kline, Grace Hartigan, and Larry Rivers suggests that he was moving in the same circles by mid-decade and was recognized by curators as a fellow traveler with the group.[80] The fact that Feldman served as soundtrack composer for *Sculpture by Lipton* is additional evidence that Lipton was part of the community.

Lipton expressed his creative practice in unequivocally vitalist terms that were inflected with evolutionary and organicist metaphors along with the natural energetics found in the words of Matter and Pollock. Lipton's statements in catalogs and the film share with Pollock the energetic autonomy of each artwork. As Pollock wrote in *Possibilities* (a text subsequently adapted for Namuth's film), "I have no fears about making changes, destroying the image, etc., because each painting has a life of its own. I try to let it come through."[81] Lipton described himself as being held by "Forms that have a catalytic force growing from an ambiguous but strongly felt fountainhead in nature."[82] He continues in language that echoes Bergson's conception of creative evolution and *élan vital*:

> To catch a glimpse of the bird on the wing of chance, the dissonant, the unrhythmic, is the stuff of onrushing experience. However, a sense of unwinding of such things in myself and in the world is always bounded by laws. In sculpture it is the law of organization. But to maintain and shape in three dimensions the mood of these reverberating excitements, both pleasurable and painful, is a provocative need.[83]

Compare with Pollock on artistic practice as an energetic compulsion: "A method of painting is a natural growth out of a need. I want to express my feelings rather than illustrate them."[84] The act of expression is less about pouring one's guts onto a canvas—a vulgar Abstract Expressionism that few ascribed to—and more about accessing natural forces and creating communicative forms that attest to the power of what Lipton calls "onrushing experience." Elsewhere, Lipton described this imperative in his concept of the seed motif:

> The germinal force of life is a reality rich in sculptural possibilities. To open up and unfold these dark beginnings, to peer into their interiors that they

disclose, themselves as feeling and symbols pointing to the entire process of life, struggle, change, death, and rebirth. To activate the quiet seed, to bring out the energy lying dormant within the shell of the seed, my present concern is to bring all these into the realm of active, vital sculpture.[85]

Both Pollock and Lipton distinguish between representation and the authentic expression of life. Their filmic portraits each narrate this distinction explicitly. Feldman, both with his music and in his own sparse writings from the 1950s, espoused a similar desire to eschew representation in favor of direct experience.[86] Juxtaposed with the creative processes of Pollock and Lipton, Feldman's music in the 1950s was tied to a non-representational artistic theory that short-circuited historical symbolism for an energetic, relational encounter with an *other*—be it painting, sculpture, or sound.

Sculpture by Lipton (1954) was produced in the wake of both *Works of Calder* and *Jackson Pollock 51*, and shares with them a vitalist narrative that draws its audience into a metaphysical place where nature, artist, and art objects interpenetrate. In each film, the copresence of music, art, and nature encourages us to "get rather dreamy" as we find them "mixed up together in [our] heads."[87] *Sculpture of Lipton* literalizes this mix-up just as *Works of Calder* had: by overlaying shots of natural landscapes/vegetation and the sculptor's works. These indexical editing techniques produced complex signs that equate the natural and the man-made, undoing a strong nature/culture binary that has otherwise governed Western modernity. Lipton's statement in the first scene is a case in point:

> The sounds in the sculptor's studio are no longer familiar. There are new materials and new techniques. I'm concerned with forms that suggest the inner core of things. I look for the mysterious activity that goes on inside of flowers, seeds, and embryos: forms that speak of the germinal force of life, not as a quiet dream but active, struggling, and evolving.[88]

Feldman's soundtrack begins in the second scene—an extended interlude in which viewers are taken along on a nature walk and shown close-up shots of trees, flowers, and seed pods. We watch Lipton walk through the landscape—perhaps gathering sources of inspiration, or imagining ways to shape his materials as nature shapes its own. Feldman's music in this scene is sparse and very much of a piece with his piano music around this time (particularly *Extensions 3* and *Intermission 6*). In contrast to *Works of Calder*, Lipton himself moves out of the studio and into the natural world. In the Calder film, this role is filled by the director's son, who acts as our surrogate in the filmic world while Meredith's narration offers us a vitalist interpretation of Calder's mobiles. In his filmic portrait, Lipton does the mediating work (in both voice and physical presence) directly. He moves from studio into nature in order to adapt its "germinal force" to his "new materials and new techniques." The Lipton and Calder films are similar in their demarcation of nature and studio space even as they insist upon their interpenetration. Like *Works of Calder*, *Sculpture by Lipton* charges the work of industrial manufacturing with vitality and creativity. Lipton repurposes metalworking techniques familiar to post-Fordist factory work and reconciles them to a vitalist creative practice.

In the fourth scene, Boxer alternates between shots of Lipton's sculptures outdoors (where they become part of nature [see Figure 2.7]) and shots of the works in gallery spaces. The presentation of each sculpture is loosely

Figure 2.7 *Sculpture by Lipton*, directed by Nathan Boxer, 1954.

coordinated with a single chord that is struck suddenly and then allowed to decay. Feldman's soundtrack in this final section of the film is remarkable for its sheer verticality. The occasional glint of linear polyphony or potential segmentation of musical events heard in the music of the second scene is replaced by static music charged with potential. Each chord is presented as an object for reflection, like a sculpture. In contrast to the furtive germination of the nature walk in the second scene, we are here presented with sound block after sound block, each numinously shining and only occasionally linking up to subsequent sounds in a way that might suggest linear continuity. At the end of the scene, Lipton is shown again walking in the woods and stooping down to pick up a pinecone. The camera zooms in and cuts to the interior of his sculpture *Sanctuary*, establishing the equivalence of nature and art. Along with *Works of Calder, Jackson Pollock 51,* and Marsicano's dances, we're given another means of "faking" *élan vital.* All of these works, animated by the music of Feldman and Cage, dramatize artistic practices as a process of becoming—one that returns to the undifferentiated vital impulse of life itself. The artists provide a necessary act of mediation for *élan vital.* As Bergson writes,

> The impetus of life . . . consists in a need of creation. It cannot create absolutely, because it is confronted with matter, that is to say with the movement that is the inverse of its own. But it seizes upon this matter, which is necessity itself, and strives to introduce into it the largest possible amount of indetermination and liberty.[89]

New York School Vitalism

What Branden Joseph recognized in Cage is just as true for Feldman, Marsicano, Pollock, and Lipton:

> For his part, Cage never explicitly echoed Bergson's interest in intuition, nor the typically Bergsonian emphasis on evolution and biology. Combined as they were with his interest in Zen, Cage's borrowings were generally more abstract and less strident than Bergson's *Lebensphilosophie.* Yet Cage did adopt Bergson's ideas of nature as flux in duration, of the role of temporality in the perpetual creation of the new, and of the interrelated functioning of

intellect and memory. Like Bergson, Cage saw that to dissociate oneself from the intellect's instrumental predispositions, one had to turn away from the anthropocentric point of view and identify with nature—or, as Cage termed it, the "outside."[90]

We've seen how these artists discussed earlier developed ascetic procedures—such as Marsicano's intention to "blindfold her ability to construct a dance"—in order to escape personal taste and leap into the immediacy of intuition. This community of artists developed vitalist spiritual exercises that operated as a "secular metaphysics."[91]

Jonathan Katz gets at the vernacular quality of this shared sensibility, though he does not call it that: "Indeed, the very casualness of Pollock's vitalism suggests that it was probably picked up third hand, less the product of direct study than of ordinary conversations among friends."[92] The casual circulation of these ideas does not diminish their pervasiveness or seriousness, realized as they were through open-form compositions and imagistic dance abstractions, glimpsed in filmic experiments documenting artistic practice, and argued over at the Cedar Tavern. More than through direct philosophical engagement, the vitalist sensibility of New York School modernism emerged through gossip, close listening, and extended attention to artworks. Feldman's attempts at faking *élan vital* with *Intermission 6* and his work with Marsicano on *Figure of Memory* are marginal but telling documents of the wider importance of intuitive method and its metaphysical implications—a metaphysics developed further in artist films on Calder, Pollock, and Lipton.

Lastly, I want to make a point on method and return briefly to my interest in those seemingly recalcitrant, mysterious objects within Feldman's archive. What I've tried to do in this chapter is to make sense of some curious statements by Feldman and account for the resonances of latent vitalist metaphysics within his practice. These are usually drowned out by Feldman's Kierkegaardianism, Cagean indeterminacy, or reductive conceptions of Abstract Expressionism as gut-spilling masculinist hysteria. By turning to a little-known collaboration with Marsicano and his soundtracks for artist films, I've attempted to recover something that might account for these eccentric metaphysical references, namely, Feldman's participation within a broader vitalist field of relations, of which Abstract Expressionism was an important part (as was Cage). Also, my attention to obscured figures like Marsicano and Lipton is meant to extend Joseph's method of "minor history," which offers tools to rethink the post-Cage avant-garde.[93] By extending his minoritizing historiography backward, we can see that the social situation pertaining to Cage, Feldman, and Abstract Expressionism—especially in the 1950s—may be more in flux than we had previously thought.

Notes

1 Morton Feldman, "Four Lectures: New York Style," Morton Feldman Collection, Paul Sacher Foundation, 1965, n.p.
2 Ibid.
3 On Judaic references in Feldman's work, see Benjamin Levy, "Vertical Thoughts: Feldman, Judaism, and the Open Aesthetic," *Contemporary Music Review* 32, no. 6 (2013): 571–88.
4 Henri Bergson, *Time and Free Will: An Essay on the Immediate Data of Consciousness*, trans. Arthur Mitchell (1910; Mineola, NY: Dover, 1998). There is a later reference to Bergson's idea of cognition in the Darmstadt Lecture of 1984. See Morton Feldman, "Darmstadt Lecture," in *Morton Feldman Says: Collected Interviews and Lectures 1964–1987*, ed. Chris Villars (London: Hyphen, 2006), 193.
5 Sebastian Claren, *Neither: Die Musik Morton Feldman* (Hofheim am Tanus: Wolke Verlag, 2000), 119. "*Obwohl eine gewisse Übereinstimmung zwischen Bergsons Gedankengang und Feldmans Zielrichtung offensichtlich ist, würde es zu weit führen, Bergsons Theorie auf Feldmans Verständnis des instrumentalen Bildes zu übertragen, zumal das Bild selbst bei Bergson nur die untergeordnete Rolle eines Vermittlers zwischen Realität und Wahrnehmung spielt.*"
6 Tom Quirk, *Bergson in American Culture: The Worlds of Willa Cather and Wallace Stevens* (Chapel Hill: University of North Caroline Press, 1990), 42.
7 Branden W. Joseph, *Random Order: Robert Rauschenberg and the Neo-Avant-Garde* (Cambridge, MA: MIT Press, 2003) and "Chance, Indeterminacy, Multiplicity," in *Experimentations: John Cage on Music, Art, and Architecture* (New York and London: Bloomsbury, 2016), 133–72.

8 Joseph, "Chance, Indeterminacy, Multiplicity," 146.
9 My use of "New York School modernism" refers to the interdisciplinary community to which Feldman belonged and references a collective sensibility across the arts—one undergirded not only by friendship but also by the vernacular metaphysics of vitalism I elaborate upon herein.
10 Ellen G. Landau, "Action/Re-Action: The Artistic Friendship of Herbert Matter and Jackson Pollock," in *Pollock/Matters*, ed. Ellen G. Landau (Boston, MA: McMullen Museum of Art, 2007), 9–58; Jonathan Katz, "Jackson Pollock's Vitalism: Herbert Matter and the Vitalist Tradition," in *Pollock/Matters*, ed. Ellen G. Landau (Boston, MA: McMullen Museum of Art, 2007), 59–72; Valerie Hellstein, "The Cage-iness of Abstract Expressionism," *American Art* 28, no. 1 (Spring 2014): 56–77.
11 Katz, "Jackson Pollock's Vitalism," 61.
12 Hellstein, "The Cage-iness of Abstract Expressionism," 60.
13 Gilles Deleuze, *Bergsonism*, trans. Hugh Tomlinson and Barbara Habberjam (New York: Zone Books, 1988 [1966]).
14 Benjamin Piekut, *Henry Cow: The World Is a Problem* (Durham, NC: Duke University Press, 2019); Benjamin Lee, "Avant-Garde Poetry as Subcultural Practice: Mailer and Di Prima's Hipsters," *New Literary History* 41, no. 4 (Autumn 2010): 775.
15 Quirk, *Bergson and American Culture*.
16 Alfred North Whitehead, *Process and Reality. An Essay in Cosmology. Gifford Lectures Delivered in the University of Edinburgh During the Session 1927–1928* (New York: The Free Press, 1978 [1929]).
17 Daniel Belgrad, *The Culture of Spontaneity: Improvisations and the Arts in Postwar America* (Chicago, IL: University of Chicago Press, 1998), 120–41.
18 Manfred Milz, "Essay in Honor of Robert Motherwell's Centenary: 'Temporalized Form': Mediating Romanticism and American Expressionism—Robert Motherwell, Henri Bergson, and the ontological origins of abstraction around 1800," *Journal of Aesthetics and Culture* 8 (2016): 1–22.
19 Morton Feldman, "Toronto Lecture," in *Morton Feldman Says: Selected Interviews and Lectures 1964–1987*, ed. Chris Villars (London: Hyphen, 2005), 137, 144.
20 Joseph, *Random Order*; "Chance, Indeterminacy, Multiplicity"; and Caroline Jones, "Finishing School: John Cage and the Abstract Expressionist Ego," *Critical Inquiry* 19, no. 4 (Summer 1993): 628–65.
21 Caroline Jones, *Machine in the Studio: Constructing the Postwar American Artist* (Chicago, IL: University of Chicago Press, 1996).

22 On the various versions of *Intermission 6*, see Alastair Nobel, *Composing Ambiguity: The Early Music of Morton Feldman* (Burlington, VT: Ashgate, 2013): 111–13.

23 Henry Cowell, "Current Chronicle," *The Musical Quarterly* 38, no. 1 (1952): 123–36.

24 Morton Feldman, John Cage, Pierre Boulez, and Christian Wolff, "4 Musicians at Work," *Trans/Formation: Arts, Communication, Environment* 1, no. 3 (1952): 168–72.

25 Morton Feldman, *Skizzenbuch* 3, Morton Feldman Collection, Paul Sacher Foundation, 1953, n.p. *Skizzenbuch 3* contains references to Litz's dance *Thoughts out of Season*, for which Feldman wrote "4 1/2 minutes of music which can be inserted anywhere within the structure of the dance." *Skizzenbuch 3* also contains a draft letter to Jean Erdman that indicates some trouble over their collaboration on the dance *Changing Woman*. Feldman's music, though used in the original 1952 performance, seems to have been subsequently replaced with music by Henry Cowell. Feldman's draft reads,

> I'm writing this letter with greater sorrow not for the money involved in the transaction but neither for our relationship. It is things like this which subtly come between people and before you know it they are not speaking to each other [and] resent working together.
>
> I don't want this to happen to us since I enjoyed working with you so much. I'm afraid that the remainder of the money will have to stand and be sent to me as soon as you can manage it.

26 Feldman, *Skizzenbuch 3*.

27 Wallace Stevens, "The Man with the Blue Guitar," *Poetry* 50, no. 2 (1937): 69. I am exceedingly grateful to William Brooks on this point.

28 Peter A. Y. Gunter, "Bergson and Proust: A Question of Influence," in *Understanding Bergson, Understanding Modernism*, ed. P. Ardoin, S. E. Gontarski, and L. Mattison (New York: Bloomsburg, 2013): 157–76.

29 Stephen Meyer, *Irresistible Dictation: Gertrude Stein and the Correlations of Writings and Science* (Palo Alto, CA: Stanford University Press, 2001).

30 Quirk, *Bergson and American Culture*, 189–91.

31 Susanne K. Langer, *Feelings and Form: A Theory of Art* (New York: Scribner, 1953), 114.

32 Henri Bergson, "The Perception of Change," in *The Creative Mind: An Introduction to Metaphysics*, trans. M. L. Andison [1946] (Mineola, NY: Dover, 2007), 133–4.
33 Henri Bergson, *Creative Evolution*, trans. Arthur Mitchell [1911] (Mineola, NY: Dover 1998), 212.
34 Nobel, *Composing Ambiguity*, 111–13.
35 Feldman, "Marginal Intersection, Intersection II, Intermission VI," *Kulchur* 3, no. 11 (Autumn 1963): 33.
36 Feldman, *Skizzenbuch 3*.
37 Kevin Volans, "What Is Feldman?" *Tempo* 68, no. 270 (2014): 7–14.
38 Feldman, *Skizzenbuch 3*.
39 Other scholars have consistently misdated it. John Holzapfel is off by a year and places it in 1955; see John Holzapfel, "David Tudor and the Performance of American Experimental Music, 1950–1959," (PhD diss., City University of New York, 1994), 340. David Cline recently hypothesized that *Figure of Memory* "is undated but probably contemporary with *Ixion*," which would date it as 1958; see David Cline, *The Graph Music of Morton Feldman* (Cambridge: Cambridge University Press, 2016), 214.
40 These materials are held in the Edwin Hymovitz Collection at the Paul Sacher Stiftung.
41 Philip Pavia, *Club without Walls: Selections from the Journals of Philip Pavia*, ed. Natalie Edgar (New York: Midmarch Arts Press, 2007).
42 See video of the performance: *Fragments for a Greek Tragedy*, 1979. Jerome Robbins Dance Collection, New York Public Library, NYPL *MGZIDF 6468.
43 Biographical material gathered from an unnamed and undated grant application in the Merle Marsicano Papers in the New York Public Library Jerome Robins Dance Division. See folder *MGZMD 308.
44 See Merle Marsicano, "Program of a Dance Recital at the YM-YWHA Dance Center, 17 February 1952," Edwin Hymovitz Collection, Paul Sacher Foundation.
45 Merle Marsicano, "Speech—Henry Street Playhouse," 1. Merle Marsicano Papers, New York Public Library Jerome Robbins Dance Division, (S)*MGZMD 308, Box 1, folder 20.
46 Merle Marsicano, "The Dance-Further Thoughts," 1. Merle Marsicano Papers, New York Public Library Jerome Robbins Dance Division, (S)*MGZMD 308, Box 1, folder 21.

47 Donald McDonagh, *The Complete Guide to Modern Dance* (New York: Doubleday, 1976), 218.
48 Clement Greenberg, "The Crisis of the Easel Picture," in *Clement Greenberg: The Collected Essays and Criticism, Vol 2: Arrogant Purpose, 1945-1949*, ed. John O'Brian (Chicago, IL: University of Chicago Press, 1986 [1948]), 222.
49 Edwin Hymovitz, "Letter to Arlene Croce, 25 June 1976," Edwin Hymovitz Collection, Paul Sacher Stiftung.
50 Richard Lippold, "Merle Marsicano," *Dance Observer* 21, no. 5 (May 1954): 71.
51 Ibid., 72.
52 Ibid.
53 Marsicano, "Speech—Henry Street Playhouse," 3.
54 Marsicano, "The Dance—Further Thoughts," 3.
55 Merle Marsicano, "Meditations of a Dancer," 4. Merle Marsicano Papers, New York Public Library Jerome Robbins Dance Division, (S)*MGZMD 308, Box 1, folder 21.
56 Marsicano, "Meditations of a Dance," 4–5. I have retained Marsicano's capitalization. "[in]" is in the original typescript.
57 Morton Feldman, "The Anxiety of Art," in *Give My Regards to Eighth Street: Collected Writings of Morton Feldman*, ed. B. H. Friedman (Cambridge, MA: Exact Change, 2000 [1966]), 26.
58 John Cage, "Composition as Process II. Indeterminacy," in *Silence: Lectures and Writings* (Middleton, CT: Wesleyan University Press, 1961), 37.
59 Marsicano, "Meditations of a Dancer," 4.
60 Ibid., 2.
61 Ibid., 1. On affective formalism, see Todd Cronan, *Against Affective Formalism: Matisse, Bergson, Modernism* (Minneapolis, MN: University of Minnesota Press, 2013).
62 On pseudomorphosis and modernism, see Theodor Adorno, "On Some Relationships between Music and Painting," *The Musical Quarterly* 79, no. 1 (Spring 1995): 66–79; as well as Theodor Adorno, *Philosophy of New Music*, Trans. Robert Hullot-Kentor (Minneapolis, MN: University of Minnesota Press, 2006).
63 Alfred North Whitehead, *The Concept of Nature: The Tarner Lectures Delivered in Trinity College, November, 1919* (1920; Mineola, NY: Dover, 2004), 26–48.
64 See, for example, John Cage, "On Robert Rauschenberg, the Artist and his Work," in *Silence: Lectures and Writings* (Middleton, CT: Wesleyan University Press: 1961), 96–108, 100.

65 Richard H. Brown, *Through the Looking Glass: John Cage and Avant-Garde Film* (New York: Oxford University Press, 2019), 99.
66 See Chapter 1. See also David Craven, *Abstract Expressionism as Cultural Critique: Dissent during the McCarthy Period* (Cambridge: Cambridge University Press, 1998), 133–50.
67 Ibid., 151–70.
68 Dorothy Streckler, "Oral history interview with Lee Krasner, 1964 Nov. 2–1968 Apr. 11." *Smithsonian Archives of American Art*. https://www.aaa.si.edu/download_pdf_transcript/ajax?record_id=edanmdm-AAADCD_oh_214115, accessed October 8, 2021.
69 Yoko Ono, "Word of a Fabricator," in *From Postwar to Postmodern: Art in Japan 1945–1989: Primary Documents*, ed. Doryun Chong, Michio Hayashi, Fumihiko Sumitomo, and Kenji Kajiya (New York: Museum of Modern Art, 2012), 136.
70 Landau, "Action/Re-Action," 36.
71 Morton Feldman, "A Life without Bach and Beethoven," in *Give My Regards to Eighth Street: Collected Writings of Morton Feldman*, ed. B. H. Friedman (Cambridge, MA: Exact Change, 2000 [1964]), 18.
72 Morton Feldman, *Skizzenbuch 3*.
73 Jackson Pollock, "My Painting," *Possibilities* 1 (Winter 1947–48): 79.
74 Olivia Mattis, "Morton Feldman: Music for the Film *Jackson Pollock* (1951)," in *Settling New Scores: Music Manuscripts from the Paul Sacher Foundation*, ed. Felix Meyer (Mainz: Schott, 1998), 166.
75 Jonathan Bernard, "Feldman's Painters," in *The New York Schools of Music and the Visual Arts*, ed. Steven Johnson (New York: Routledge, 2002), 193.
76 See Greenberg, "Crisis of the Easel Picture."
77 Landau, "Action/Re-Action," 36.
78 On Affective Atmospheres, see Ben Anderson, "Affective Atmospheres," *Emotion, Space and Society* 2, no. 2 (December 2009): 77–81.
79 Aline B. Louchheim, "An Art Film Festival," *The New York Times*, September 9, 1951, X8.
80 Pavia, *Club Without Walls*, 154.
81 Pollock, "My Painting," 79. Significantly, this quotation was radically different in the film. Pollock's reading of it changes implied punctuation as well as increases the vitality of the painting by altering the last line to "I try to let it live" (from "I try to let it come through").
82 Seymour Lipton, "Statement," in *12 Americans*, ed. Dorothy C. Miller (New York: The Museum of Modern Art, 1956), 72.

83 Ibid., 72.
84 Jackson Pollock, in *Jackson Pollock 51*, directed by Hans Namuth (Museum at Large, New York, 1950), 16 mm slides.
85 Seymour Lipton, quoted in Lori Verderame, *An American Sculptor: Seymour Lipton* (State College, PA: Palmer Museum of Art, 1999), 26.
86 On this point, see Chapter 1 of Ryan Dohoney, *Saving Abstraction: Morton Feldman, the de Menils, and the Rothko Chapel* (New York: Oxford University Press, 2019).
87 Narration for *Works of Calder*, directed by Herbert Matter (New World Film Productions for the New York Museum of Modern Art, 1950), 16 mm slides.
88 Nathan Boxer, *Sculpture by Lipton*, Scene 1 (Film Images, New York, 1954), 16 mm slides.
89 Bergson, *Creative Evolution*, 262.
90 Joseph, *Random Order*, 53–54.
91 Katz, "Jackson Pollock's Vitalism," 62.
92 Ibid., 63.
93 Branden W. Joseph, *Beyond the Dream Syndicate: Tony Conrad and the Arts after Cage* (New York: Zone, 2008).

Intermission

The Necessary Other

For Scott Krafft

All revolutions are misunderstood. Donatello misunderstood Greek sculpture. And if it wasn't for the misunderstanding maybe we wouldn't have anything new.

Morton Feldman[1]

In an interview conducted in the spring prior to Charlotte Moorman's first Avant Garde Festival in 1963, Robert Ashley asked fellow composer Morton Feldman to assess the contemporary landscape of experimental performance:

> Robert Ashley: You will agree that a certain "revolution" happened in music in the early 50's in America. You were a main part of it. If we may skip over for the moment all of the precedents for that revolution, I would like to talk about its consequences. For instance, you might say, "We wanted to emancipate the sound—which is an end in itself." But in fact you may have emancipated something else.
>
> Morton Feldman: Of course, more than sound. For example we emancipated the musician, the performer. That certainly wasn't part of the deal; I mean the sounds were to be free, but not the performer. But it happened; it happened with David Tudor, and it happened with other very good people; so it more or less "came to pass," I would say.[2]

Feldman's comments point to the early 1960s as a moment of crisis within the avant-garde. What was the meaning of the "revolution" begun in the 1950s? What were the ends of liberation? Feldman is unequivocal here as he is elsewhere: "I was not only allowing the sounds to be free—I was also liberating the performer. I had never thought of the graph [score] as an art of improvisation, but more as a totally abstract sonic adventure."³ Feldman's concern here is with the shift in the idea of "freedom" from the "originators"—the New York School musicians of Feldman, John Cage, Christian Wolff, Earle Brown, Edgard Varèse, Stefan Wolpe, and David Tudor—and those who extended their work into the 1960s. Moorman (see Figure I.1) is certainly to be counted as essential to the New York School's second generation along with Robert Ashley, Gordon Mumma, Yoko Ono, Jackson Mac Low, Alan Kaprow, and the numerous other artists who moved the avant-garde toward performance, theatricality, and the further exploration of new technologies. Yet Moorman's work as an *impresaria* and performer of this music affords us a unique vantage point on this controversy— on what Benjamin Piekut has called the "actually existing experimentalism" as it was practiced and proliferated beyond any single intention.⁴

Figure I.1 William Lovelace. L to R: Nicholas Zumbro, Morton Feldman, Edgard Varèse, Frederic Rzweski, Charlotte Moorman, 1963, Charlotte Moorman Collection. Northwestern University. © Daily Express, Reach Publishing Service.

The previous generation of avant-gardists described their work in ascetic, almost religious terms. As Christian Wolff wrote in 1958, "Roughly, since 1950, . . . One finds a concern for a kind of objectivity, almost anonymity—sound comes into its own."[5] Objectivity was not aspirational for Moorman and her generation, nor was fidelity to the intentions of Feldman, Cage, or Wolff. Respect was, though, and one can hear in Moorman's programming for the early Festivals of the Avant-garde an honoring of those who came before as well as an extension of their so-called revolution. The generational tension enacted through the Festival's programs had been noted by Feldman in the moths prior to their inauguration. His interview with Ashley continued:

> Ashley: Last time we talked you did, offhandedly, somewhat reject the composers of this kind of music as being the inheritors of your revolution, you know, you said that they weren't part of your revolution.
> Feldman: I'm ambivalent about the whole question myself. I know that in performance I have occasions within my works where I would designate a certain amount of notes to play in the graph things, and I would hear "Yankee Doodle" coming out of the horn section. The players decide together, before the concert, actually to sabotage it—and they decided in this particular section they were going to play "Yankee Doodle," with the amount of notes called for and in the register in the score—there was nothing I could say about it that wasn't inherent in the instructions of the piece. But of course I said, "Manslaughter is one thing, but not homicide; I have not given you license to murder the piece." So for the younger generation the implication is a moral question that has to be decided ultimately. For example, that Korean fellow in Germany, [Nam June] Paik, does he have that? Whether or not he brings it to an element of violence that was never wholly inherited from John [Cage], but you could say the implication was there?[6]

It is doubtful that Moorman also understood the stakes of the new music in such moralizing terms and Feldman himself seems ambivalent about how he has framed the issue (though he does not seem hopeful that Paik, with his implicit violence, will answer the question in an ethical manner).

By raising the question of tensions within the 1960s avant-garde, I do not mean to side with Feldman, who seems to have valued musicians in as much as their performances recreated the scene of composition, handling sound with "love or interest."[7] Moorman certainly approached her music-making with love and interest and took full advantage of the new freedoms that had "come to pass." By the early 1960s, Euro-American modernists and avant-gardists recognized that since Feldman and Cage, composers and performers had transformed the hierarchy of musical roles.[8] Practices usually associated with composition—the fixing of sonic parameters of pitch, duration, instrumentation, articulation— were transferred to performers. Creativity, already distributed and relational as is the case with all musical performance, became more so as performers including Moorman and Tudor began "realizing" the open works of Cage, Feldman, Earle Brown, Sylvano Bussotti, and others.

"Realization" is a strange description of this practice. Co-composition might be a better word that more honestly recognizes the myriad mediations at play in the performance of indeterminate, graphic, event, or instruction-based scores.[9] Feldman describes the practice of realization in uncertain terms:

> I think, for example, that while David [Tudor] now will "realize" a [Sylvano] Bussotti score, or a John Cage score (say the imperfections on the paper), in the early days I never really felt that there was any realization involved. I'm not clear myself what is meant by "realization" now. Does it mean that the situation is ambiguous and has to be "realized?" I think that as the music of the scores became, in a sense, much more ambiguous, the sophistication of the performers and the realization also increased certainly in tightening the gradual gradations of ambiguity that make a part in these graphic scores.[10]

Within Western musical performance, the word "realization" was first used in 1911 to describe a performer's role in harmonizing a bass line in seventeenth- and eighteenth-century compositions. This work was originally done through improvisation on the part of a keyboardist but was gradually abandoned as composers did the work of realization themselves and improvisation fell out of much Euro-American musical practice. During the early music revival in the early twentieth century, "realization" became the composing-out of a bass line by editors, musicologists, and musicians no longer skilled in the improvisatory practices that would have been expected of the musicians of Claudio Monteverdi's or J. S. Bach's day.[11] Composer Benjamin Britten

(1917–76) used the term "realizations" in the 1940s when he developed new accompaniments to songs by Henry Purcell (1659–95) based on the extant bass lines. Britten's connection to the US avant-garde is tenuous at best, but his adoption of the term for his practice of finishing the composition of another gives a sense of its currency. Yet, the exact moment that it leapt from early music performance practice to experimental music is unclear. By 1963, Feldman places realization in scare quotes. This indicates perhaps its newness and its fraught adoption as a term that is at best an approximation for what is really going on in the performance practice of Moorman, Tudor, Ashley, Mumma, and others.

Though it may seem perverse to invite such a comparison, Moorman's realization of Feldman's *Projection 1* is conceptually similar to working out a figured-bass notation. Instead of harmonizing a given bass line, however, Feldman asks his performers to choose a specific pitch within a given set of parameters, and Moorman follows suit (see Figure I.2). Moorman described the piece in the WBAI broadcast of her performance:

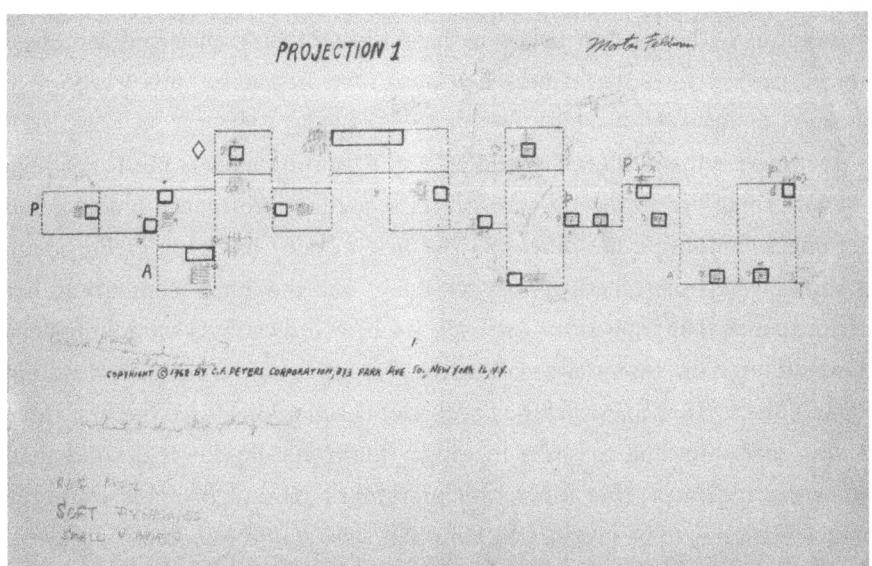

Figure I.2 *Projection 1* (page 1) by Morton Feldman with Charlotte Moorman's realization. Charlotte Moorman Collection. McCormick Library. Northwestern University. © 1962 by C.F. Peters Corporation. All rights reserved.

> *Projection 1* that you are about to hear is an unaccompanied cello piece written in graphic notation. It is the first graphic piece ever written. It is simply soft, pure sounds projected into space. The composer projects rhythm, register, quality, and duration, allowing the performer freedom of specific choice of notes.[12]

Moorman here understands Feldman as offering freedom of choice within an otherwise determined situation (indicating that Moorman "misunderstood" Feldman's goal of freeing sound). With her detailed realization of the score for *Projection 1*, Moorman offers us an important document of experimental performance practice as it had developed in the twelve years since *Projection 1*'s composition. In their earliest performances, Feldman did envision his *Projections* as a form of real-time music-making arising from interaction with the graphic notation, even though he later eschewed improvisation as a descriptive term. In a program note for the 1952 premier of *Projection 2*, Feldman states that "What particular sounds these are is left to the choice of the musicians at the moment of playing. . . . Since each performance of this composition is different, yet essentially the same, it will be played twice in succession."[13] The tension between these ideas of difference and sameness hinged on the ways performers like Moorman negotiated this freedom of choice.

In 1951 Feldman offers the grid as a spur to spontaneous music making, but Moorman's realization demonstrates that the performance practice had become something quite different. The first page of her copy of *Projection 1* shows Moorman meticulously working out the pitch content of her performances. She transforms each specific box (indicating a sounding pitch) into staff notation, essentially making the grid into a conventional performing score.[14] She further fixes each box with clef designations (save the first three boxes) corresponding to shifts in range (high, middle, low). Beyond that, Moorman indicates other mnemonic markings—reminders about what type of articulation is to be produced—natural bowed sound (marked A for *arco*), plucked string sound (marked P for *pizzicato*), or a harmonic effect (marked by a lozenge).[15] Moorman's choices of notes indicate her willingness to use the graph to extend her technical abilities by producing very high sounds or difficult-to-produce harmonics. Feldman's specifications regarding every aspect of sound (save pitch) marks a similar aesthetic found in works by Cage (*26'1.1499" for a string player*) and Brown (*Music for Cello and Piano*) that break down and reconfigure every sonic parameter. However, Feldman's affection for slow, quiet sounds distinguishes his work from the more violent and technically deconstructive compositions of Cage and Brown.[16]

With its fixed pitches, Moorman's realization of *Projection 1* (see Figure I.2) trades in the freedom of spontaneity (which would yield a different version in each performance) for the freedom to compose out her own repeatable version. While this might be construed as yet another willful refusal of the "true" revolution initiated by the New York School, it bears noting that Moorman's realization strategy was itself congruent with the performance practice of Feldman's graphically notated works that had, in fact, been initiated by the authority of pianist-composer David Tudor. After performing Feldman's graphically notated piano solos *Intersection 2* (1951) and *Intersection 3* (1953) with the grids scores alone, Tudor made a fully realized version of the latter and left a partial realization of the former which resulted in repeatable versions from performance to performance.[17] Though as Feldman increasingly distanced himself from improvisatory music-making and overwhelmingly preferred Tudor's performances, it is likely that Moorman's mode of working out the grid was at least tacitly approved by Feldman. The recorded documentation, however, indicates that she deviated from her realization, altering numerous pitches and making some mistakes in articulation. Unlike Tudor's fixed *Intersections*, Moorman's *Projection* likely maintained a degree of openness and spontaneity from performance to performance.[18]

With the evidence not only of *Projection 1*, but also her realization of scores by Earle Brown, it is clear that Moorman depended upon the tenuous but extant performance practice tradition that ran alongside and occasionally intersected the pianistic performance practice developed by Tudor. Moorman extended the "tradition of the new" developed in the 1950s by cellists Seymour Barab and David Soyer, whose recording of Brown's *Music for Cello and Piano* Moorman studied in preparation for her own performance of the piece with Tudor.[19] Even as Moorman drew upon these precursors, she transformed experimental musical agency into the perfection of "an imagery of personality" that emphasized "the way music spread out into other things," and which Robert Ashley argued was the "inheritance of [Feldman and Cage's] revolution."[20]

The new composer-performer relationship presented new questions about creative agency within experimental performance. The image of personality recognized by Ashley and discounted by Feldman extended beyond the composer, to encompass a new conception of theatricality that, while born from the spirit of music, did not aspire to the identity of "composer." Rather, it required a form of distributed creativity and co-authorship. Though not fully developed until the emergence of Fluxus in the late 1950s, strands of this newly expanded performer role were apparent in the early work of the New York School and were drawn out in Moorman's performance of Earle Brown's *Synergy* (1952). Moorman performed *Synergy* on a solo concert during the second Avant Garde Festival in 1964 along with Giuseppe Chiari's *Per Archo* (which would become a signature work of hers) and others. Brown's performance instructions read:

> To be performed in any direction from any point in the defined space.
> Tempo—as fast as possible to as slow as possible—inclusion.
> Lines and spaces may be thought of as tracks moving in either direction and at any speeds—clef signs thought of as floating in the field. This indicates the theoretical possibility of all the attacks occurring at the same instant, or any other expression of simultaneity.[21]

In developing her performance of *Synergy*, Moorman did much more than add exact pitches (as she had with Feldman's graph). Brown's instructions afford multiple options for the production of a performable piece. The work of realization involves a high degree of composition to determine what exactly the piece will become. Moorman's decisions seem to have explored the concept of the "floating field" as a compositional ideal. Her performance joined a live reading of the score with two prerecorded tape versions played on loudspeakers that distributed sound across the space of the concert hall and immersed the audience in her imaginative rendering of Brown's score. Most striking is the effectiveness of the spatialization in emphasizing the multiple temporalities sounding out from the one actual and two virtual Moormans. Moorman expanded the sonic possibilities beyond Brown's notation by saturating her *Synergy* with *glissandi*—bent notes and slid pitches—that are not indicated on Brown's score.[22] Brown was unable to attend Moorman's performance, as he was working in Europe at the time, but he wrote to her on October 2, 1964, with compliments saying, "So what else is new now that you are the Cecil B. DeMoorman of the music world? I heard good reports from your perf[ormance] of "Synergy"—thanks piles."[23] Moorman's version of *Synergy* gained currency beyond her performance on the Festival and Brown wrote to her again on February 10, 1965, to inquire after the tapes of her realization:

> [Giuseppe] Chiari did concert here with *Dec. '52* and wants you to send him y[ou]r background tape of cello "Synergy" over which, I assume, with proper credit he will impose some piano renditions. A guy from San Fran[cisco] may write and ask you the same. How do you feel about that?? I feel o.k.—at least as far as Chiari is concerned—don't knock yourself out for S.F. Play me well, you clown! (that's, CLOWN—in the appreciative sense).[24]

Apparent in Brown's exchanges with Moorman is a more complicated version of artistic agency, one exemplary of the shift within the New York City avant-garde identified by Feldman and Ashley. Brown recognizes her role as *impresaria*, lovingly christening her "Cecil B. DeMoorman" after that director of ostentatious spectacles, Cecil B. DeMille. He also feels she deserves authorial credit for her work in producing the tapes for *Synergy* which are taken up into circulation in the trans-Atlantic avant-garde. The version of *Synergy* later performed by Chiari became the product of multiple compositional and performance agents: Brown's production of the score, Moorman's taped realization, and Chiari's real-time piano interpretation. This desire to give credit and recognition to his collaborators was typical of Brown who, unlike Feldman, valued the chain of mediators his music had to go through for a performance to occur. Musicians were, in the words of philosopher Adriana Cavarero, "necessary others" coming together to collaboratively produce the work.[25]

Moorman's realizations of Feldman's *Projection 1* and Brown's *Synergy* demonstrate the conflicted lineage of the New York avant-garde, even within its coterie of originators. Sound itself was in tension with the image of personality, and we see Moorman negotiating those poles of aesthetic commitment in these two realizations—a faithful working out of Feldman's aesthetics of sound itself along with the assertion of a creative agency beyond mere executant to one who transformed Brown's notation into vibrating, fleshy, metallic sound. Lukas Foss was correct writing in 1963 that the composer/performer relationship had indeed changed, though what had changed was perhaps the recognition and intensification of the mediations at play in any musical performance.[26] Experimentalism had brought the play of forces and relationships to the fore, out from an aged ideology that idealized the role of the composer at the expense of the performer. The newly configured relationship calls to my mind the working relationship between Gertrude Stein and Alice B. Toklas as described by Adriana Cavarero:

> As the fruit of a curious fiction that clearly refutes itself, the text [of *The Autobiography of Alice B. Toklas*] is therefore interesting not only as the transgression of the autobiographical genre, but also for the desire that sustains its ingenious mechanism. That this desire is tightly bound to a lesbian relationship has been made clear by feminist literary criticism. What is remarkable, however, is the capacity of the book to stage a relationship between Alice and Gertrude that refigures itself in terms of both a visual and narrative reciprocity. Indeed, the game is found out. The two are accomplices. Alice types—or, rather, first reads, and then rewrites, the pages that Gertrude has written by hand. Alice was not a typist by trade. She had to learn how to use the typewriter in order to support Gertrude's work.[27]

Moorman resembles Toklas in this account. Like Toklas, Moorman's collaborative ethos came from a place of love and commitment. She also transformed and made presentable the texts (scores) given to her. Like Toklas, Moorman found a need to extend her abilities, to learn to do what she did not know how in order to realize a vision to which she was essential. Her collaborations with composers and musicians were based on a similar foundation of reciprocal trust, devotion, and commitment. But unlike Toklas, Moorman's role was not simply to transcribe, but to co-compose, to bring forth her personality as the medium of her collaborative endeavors—be they with Brown, Paik, Cage, or Feldman.

Yet, perhaps she thought herself more like Toklas. Until now, Moorman's agency and creative contribution to the works she herself performed remains suspended between mere interpreter and full collaborator. Despite performing the most radically open and indeterminate works of the time she often downplayed her creative agency, most famously (and strategically) in her trial on charges of indecent exposure and obscenity resulting from a performance of Nam June Paik's *Opera Sextronique*. She described herself as doing what the composer told her, and as such she seems beholden to a classical music ideology. Yet Moorman's occasional rejection of her creative agency masks a radical practice of freedom that was latent in the first generation of the New York School and became a fully developed performance practice through Moorman's committed labor. She, along with her community of fellow travelers in the avant-garde, practiced a reciprocal self-donation in which they saw each other as necessary, but not sufficient, to the task at hand.

Notes

1. Robert Ashley and Morton Feldman, "Around Morton Feldman," Unpublished typescript. Morton Feldman Collection, Paul Sacher Foundation. 6.
2. Ibid., 1.
3. Morton Feldman, "Liner Notes," in *Give My Regards to Eighth Street*, ed. B. H. Friedman (Cambridge, MA: Exact Change, 2000), 6. Feldman's comments were initially published as album notes to *Feldman/Brown*, Time Records 58007/S8007. They also appeared in *Kulchur* 2/6 (Summer 1963), 57–60. *Kulchur* was one of the "little magazines" of the New York avant-garde that published writing by Feldman's friend Frank O'Hara, Amiri Baraka (then LeRoi Jones), La Monte Young, and Feldman himself.
4. See Benjamin Piekut, *Experimentalism Otherwise: The Avant-Garde and Its Limits* (Berkeley, CA: University of California Press, 2011), *passim*.
5. Christian Wolff, "New and Electronic Music," in *Writings about John Cage*, ed. Richard Kostelanetz (Ann Arbor: University of Michigan Press, 1996), 85–92, 85. For an exploration of this idea in terms of John Cage's "politics of nature," see Benjamin Piekut, "Chance and Certainty: John Cage's Politics of Nature," *Cultural Critique* 84 (Spring 2013): 134–63.

6   Ashley and Feldman, "Around Morton Feldman," 14.
7   Feldman recalled how David Tudor asked for explicit instructions on how to perform his *Piano Piece (to Philip Guston)* that matched both how Feldman composed and how the composer performed in public. Ashley and Feldman, "Around Morton Feldman," 8. Feldman expresses his ethics of "love and interest" on 16.
8   See, for example, Lukas Foss, "The Changing Composer-Relationship: A Monologue and a Dialogue," *Perspectives of New Music* 1/2 (1963): 45–53.
9   On the genealogy of this performance mode and its development in Fluxus, see Liz Kotz, *Words to Be Looked At: Language in 1960s Art* (Cambridge, MA: Massachusetts Institute of Technology Press, 2007).
10   Ashley and Feldman, "Around Morton Feldman," 2.
11   The *Oxford English Dictionary* notes the earliest use of the word realization for this practice is 1911. I am grateful to Kyle Kaplan for reminding me of realization's connection to early music performance.
12   Charlotte Moorman, WBAI Broadcast recording. November 2 and 9, 1963. 10.5" reel recording in the Charlotte Moorman Collection, Northwestern University Library Special Collections. Moorman performed *Projection 1* first on April 15, 1963, and then again on the first Avant Garde Festival. See Joan Rothfuss, *Topless Cellist* (Cambridge, MA: MIT Press, 2014), 60. Feldman, though he later abandoned such indeterminate notation, took every opportunity to position himself as the *fons et origo* of "chance" notation. See Bret Boutwell, "Morton Feldman's Graphic Notation: *Projections* and Trajectories," *Journal of the Society for American Music* 6, no. 4 (2012): 457–82.
13   Morton Feldman, program note for Merce Cunningham Dance Company at Hunter College. January 21, 1951. Merce Cunningham Dance Company Archive.
14   Moorman's manner of realization resembles a style of notation that John Cage turned to in the 1979 for his vocal ensemble composition *Hymns and Variations*.
15   My study of the score indicates two primary layers of annotations—the realization done in graphite pencil indicating specific pitch content along with additional markings and marginalia. A later set of markings in blue pencil indicates notes toward editing a recording of the piece that seems to have never materialized. The live performance broadcast on WBAI is the only extant recording. See Morton Feldman, *Projection 1*. Annotated Copy by Charlotte Moorman. Charlotte Moorman Collection. Northwestern University Special Collections.

16 On Moorman's performance of Cage's *26'1.1499" for a string player*, see Jason Rosenholtz-Witt in this volume and Piekut, *Experimentalism Otherwise*, 140–75.
17 Both realizations are held in the David Tudor Collection at the Getty Research Institute, Los Angeles. Tudor also left a partial realization of the grid notation of Feldman's *Ixion* (1958) which accompanied the touring version of Merce Cunningham's *Summerspace*. Tudor performed *Ixion* for many decades and pianist Joseph Kubera notes that Tudor would play from the graph notation itself. Joseph Kubera, personal communication with the author, June 2007. On Tudor's realizations, see John Holzaepfel, "Painting by Numbers: The Intersections of Morton Feldman and David Tudor," in *The New York Schools of Music and Visual Arts*, ed. Steven Johnson (New York: Routledge, 2002), 159–72.
18 I say "likely" because there is only one extant recording with which Moorman's realization can be compared.
19 "Tradition of the new" is Harold Rosenberg's phrase. See Rosenberg, *The Tradition of the New* (New York: Horizon Press, 1959). For Moorman's references to Soyer, see her extensive annotation and comparisons with Soyer's recording on her copy of Earl Brown, *Music for Cello and Piano*. Annotations by Charlotte Moorman. Charlotte Moorman Collection.
20 Ashley and Feldman, "Around Morton Feldman," 9–10.
21 Earle Brown, performance directions to *Synergy* in *An Anthology of Chance Operations*, ed. La Monte Young and Jackson Mac Low, 1963 n.p. Moorman had two copies of the score to *Synergy* in her possession: one in the printed score of *Folio and 4 Systems* as well as the copy in *An Anthology of Chance Operations*.
22 A recording of Moorman's performance of *Synergy* is available on Charlotte Moorman, *Cello Anthology* (Alga Marghen, 2006).
23 Earle Brown. Letter to Charlotte Moorman. October 2, 1964. Charlotte Moorman Collection.
24 Earle Brown. Letter to Charlotte Moorman. February 10, 1965. Charlotte Moorman Collection.
25 Adriana Cavarero, *Relating Narratives: Storytelling and Selfhood*, trans. and with an introduction by Paul A. Kottman (New York: Routledge, 2000), 81–94.
26 Foss, "The Changing Composer-Performer Relationship."
27 Cavarero, *Relating Narratives*, 83.

3

The Elegiac Science

For Sianne Ngai

What then exactly constitutes the basis of our community?[1]

Robert Motherwell

And must I express the science of legendary elegies.[2]

Frank O'Hara, "Second Avenue"

In the previous chapters, I have explored Feldman's social world—its antagonisms and intimacies, inspirations and failures—through a hermeneutics of friendship. I've argued that Feldman's friendships and collaborations through the 1950s and 1960s provide fruitful ground upon which to conduct our analyses of inter-art collaborations that emerge in those years. Mutual affection and agonism were generative forces that gave rise to a specific form of midcentury modernism cutting across the arts. What I've shown in the previous chapters is how the arts were entangled with one another well before the advent of postmodernism. Such entanglement attests to an ontological character belying the purity of medium-specificity that Clement Greenberg insisted upon. Music, painting, poetry, dance, film, and festival were co-constitutive by virtue of their grounding in friendship. They were expressive results of a community sharing *some* aesthetic concerns while being held together by eros, agon, and agape.

Death—that inevitable part of life—intervened in Feldman's friendships with disturbing regularity: Jackson Pollock died in 1956, and Franz Kline in 1962. The tragic death of Frank O'Hara, in 1966, was probably the most damaging to Feldman's community. Beginning with Kline's death—and particularly after the death of O'Hara—Feldman would mark these losses musically, conceiving of his art as a memento mori.³ In dialog with John Cage, he stated that "I know that when I write a piece, sometimes I'm telling people, 'We're not going to be here very long.'"⁴ We might say—to borrow a phrase from O'Hara—that Feldman began to practice "a science of legendary elegies." This elegiac tone, established in the 1960s and 1970s, is especially pronounced in the 1980s, with a proliferation of dedicatory piece titles (*For Philip Guston, For Stefan Wolpe*, etc.). This chapter explores Feldman's grief work, looking in particular at the ways in which his interpretation of O'Hara's art (as being "like death") had a thoroughgoing impact on his music from the 1970s until his own death. I raise the important matter of mourning and explore its place in friendship—especially the maintenance of friendship after death. Collaboration continues to figure prominently, as it has in the previous chapters. In the final section of this chapter, I explore Joan La Barbara's mediumship—referring both to her as a mediator through which music passes into being, and one who is capable of channeling the voices of the dead—in realizing *Three Voices*, Feldman's last elegy for O'Hara and first (failed) attempt at musically mourning Philip Guston. Mourning, especially musical mourning, is a collective endeavor, and Feldman depended on necessary others in his late elegies no less than he had in the realization of his indeterminate music. Feldman's communal mourning is also aberrated—that is, it is divergent and unfinished. In much the same way that Gillian Rose has described Walter Benjamin as "the taxonomist of sadness," I propose that we think of Feldman as "the elegiac scientist" whose resistant mourning kept alive—and continues to keep alive—the specters of his friends.⁵

"Happy to be 'set' by you": Feldman and O'Hara's Friendship

By thinking through community elegiacally, we begin to discover how affective modes of sociability offer ways of interpreting the collaborations between the New York School poets and their musician and artist compatriots.⁶ The friendship of composer Morton Feldman and writer Frank O'Hara—one of the most important relationships of the New York School—exemplifies this mournful mode of sociability.

In my research in the Morton Feldman Collection at the Paul Sacher Stiftung, I discovered artifacts of the pair's extensive engagement with each other's work that enhance our understanding of their friendship and collaborations. In particular, several "posthumous collaborations"—compositions and writings by Feldman completed after 1966 and related in varied ways to O'Hara—will serve as the foundation for this chapter. While others have explored Feldman and O'Hara's friendship in relation to ideologies of freedom and aesthetic unpredictability during their lives,[7] I track how Feldman's mourning for O'Hara works as a strategy for perpetuating what Lytle Shaw has described as "coterie."[8] In the years after O'Hara's death, the New York School no longer existed as a physically proximate reality, but rather as a dispersed network of actors, objects, and performances. Feldman's music encourages us to hear and feel this loss of coterie as an afterimage—something vanished yet affectively present.

As Feldman noted in his obituary for O'Hara, "to die early—before one's time—was to make the biggest coup of all, for in such a case the work perpetuated not only itself, but also the pain of everybody's loss."[9] The pain of loss among the New York avant-garde of the 1950s and 1960s was as essential to a sense of group identity as the collaborations between members. Feldman's production of mournful affects in artworks and compositions became a way to sustain loss while also indicating the composer's place among a group of artists with increasing cultural capital. I want to consider Feldman's collaboration as a type of association that can be understood as affective investment; thus I'm interested in collaborative artworks as traces of a larger project of group formation in the New York School.[10] As Bruno Latour has argued, groups are never stable; instead, we can track processes of group assembly that provide momentary stability through repetition, reiteration, and the establishment of ever more durable networks of associations. Musical performance is one such mode of group formation.

With Latour's central insight in mind, we can reconceptualize collaborations as simultaneously aesthetic products and attempts at group formation. Feldman and O'Hara's relationship provides evidence for a sociability performed through the production of aesthetic feeling notable for its unpredictability and emotional impact. Because the New York School defined its collectivity largely on the basis of a shared interest in specific affective experience, the examples that follow move between documentation of community and the intensities afforded by the music, poetry, and art produced by this social network. Feldman, from the time of O'Hara's death until his own, makes a veritable cottage industry of memorializing his friend (as well as other members of the New York School), and inscribes this mourning into his music through compositional strategies modeled on his reading of O'Hara's poetry itself.

Morton Feldman and Frank O'Hara met at the Eighth Street Artists Club in late 1951 or early 1952. Feldman was a fixture at the Club by 1951, after having been brought there by his composition teacher Stefan Wolpe and friend John Cage. Feldman's earliest reference to O'Hara is found in one of his sketchbooks from 1952, soon after the poet arrived in the city. On the back cover, Feldman drew up plans for an opera based on André Gide's novel *Straight Is the Gate* with a libretto by O'Hara. Their stellar (yet, imagined) cast and crew included the singers Patricia Neway and Leslie Chabay in starring roles, Stella Adler as director, and lyricist John La Touche as producer (who, as we saw in the last chapter, provided the script for *Works of Calder*).[11] Such daydreaming evinces an already close friendship that brought Feldman into O'Hara's circle of young poets and painters. This group would serve as the composer's first—and perhaps most enthusiastic—audience. O'Hara's early opinion of Feldman is documented in a post-concert note from poet to composer in 1954:

> Just a note to thank you for such a beautiful concert. The performance was wonderful and it was so exciting and inspiring to find one's sensibility led into absolutely new experiences in such a subtle, authoritative way—without any posings or denial which only distract one when it's a matter of real music.[12]

O'Hara highlights elements of Feldman's music that he elaborated on in later writings, particularly his "subtle authority" unencumbered by "posings"—which the poet understood to be technical systems, such as twelve-tone composition.[13]

In 1959, O'Hara began a more public promotion of his friend when he provided the sleeve notes for Feldman's first recording for Columbia Records'

New Directions in Music series.¹⁴ In those notes, O'Hara helped shape Feldman's reception in terms that strengthened the composer's identification with abstract expressionist aesthetics.¹⁵ O'Hara's critical appraisal of Feldman shared a great deal with the poet's description of Jackson Pollock's work in his 1959 monograph.¹⁶ Both, in O'Hara's estimation, created works of unpremeditated expression working through an aesthetics and poetics of individualistic action. Feldman's album further documents the collective sociability of the New York School with its reproduction of Philip Guston's ink drawing *Head–Double View* (1958) on the cover (See Chapter 1 for more on this). This multidisciplinary collaboration indexed a social network invested in the mutual interpretation and promotion of its members and their work. Collaboration was for these artists as much about defining and sustaining a group identity as it was about the production of poems, paintings, or compositions.

It was only in 1962, however, with *The O'Hara Songs*, that Feldman and O'Hara realized the musical collaboration hinted at earlier. Setting to music O'Hara's poem "Wind" (for an ensemble of bass-baritone voice, chimes, piano, violin, viola, and cello), Feldman continued the compositional practice he had developed in 1958.¹⁷ Performers are given specific pitches to sound at minimal volume, but decisions regarding the duration of those pitches and the alignment between the parts are left largely to the musicians. As such, each performance is unique and unrepeatable. The two outer movements use the complete text of O'Hara's poem, while the middle movement uses repetitions of the line "Who'd have thought / that snow falls." Following the completion of *The O'Hara Songs*, O'Hara invited further collaboration with Feldman, evoking film noir in a letter saying, "I am very happy to be 'set' by you (and not in a bridge)."¹⁸ Included in the letter was a version of the poem "It seems far away and gentle now."¹⁹ There, O'Hara titles the poem, "To Philip Guston," noting, "This thing was inspired specifically by Philip's *Painting 1954* in the Modern Museum's collection, that mostly orange one that's somewhat like *Attar* [the Guston painting owned by Feldman], so it's nice that the three of us are somehow involved in this like with your record."²⁰ Feldman did not end up setting that poem, though he later returned to the text of "Wind" in his *Three Voices* (1982).

After O'Hara's death, Feldman eulogized his friend in an essay, "Frank O'Hara: Lost Times and Future Hopes," delivered at the New York Studio School on October 30, 1968, and later published in *Art in America*.[21] The piece is both a personal remembrance and an insightful interpretation of the writer's work. Feldman begins the essay by noting the inevitability and intensity of death with regard to the New York School's sociability: "It was big stakes we were after in those times. Through the years we have watched each other's deaths like the final stock quotations of the day."[22] He goes on to use death as a means of understanding O'Hara's poetry. Feldman was particularly drawn to the unpredictability of the poems and the sense of risk that he felt when encountering them:

> As a literary artist he was a sort of latter-day Chekhov on the New York scene. When we read O'Hara we are going along and everything seems very casual, but as we come to the end of the poem we hear the gunshot of *The Sea Gull*. There is no time to analyze, to evaluate. We are faced with something as definite and real and finite as a sudden death.[23]

Unpredictable affective events proliferate throughout the poems with an intensity that Feldman associates with unspeakable loss. Consider the final lines of "The Day Lady Died," particularly the musicality with which sudden death is figured:

> and I am sweating a lot by now and thinking of
> leaning on the john door in the 5 SPOT
> while she whispered a song along the keyboard
> to Mal Waldron and everyone and I stopped breathing.[24]

The poem, as Feldman might describe it, goes along, seeming "very casual," yet the closing lines draw us into a sensuous remembrance of the voice of Billie Holiday when she "whispered a song" that stopped the breath of everyone in earshot. Musical experience in this poem is figured as a loss—of breath, of life—and its impact sears the memory, forging a relay from seemingly workaday tasks of getting lunch and buying gifts to a sonic experience rendered as a visceral near-death response. O'Hara's poems, as much as they work though a poetics of process and coterie, also map dynamic affective landscapes in which hearts suddenly harden or the pleasures of sound stifle our bodily processes. This sense of affects and intensities undergirds the notion of a collective sensibility that O'Hara and Feldman are at pains to emphasize in their writing about one another.

Mourning Coterie

O'Hara and Feldman noted in each other's works a common affective atmosphere—an intensity of sensation emerging from an unpredictable sonic or linguistic construction. With this in mind, let us consider the ways in which their aesthetic disposition was continued in Feldman's music from the early 1970s, a few years after O'Hara's death. The pieces I focus on—*Three Clarinets, Cello, and Piano* and *For Frank O'Hara*—were written in a period in which Feldman had become particularly invested in subtle gradations of emotional expression. Both works also bear a connection to O'Hara's poetry.

In his music from 1970 to 1972, Feldman was concerned with what he called "the illusion of feeling," a name he gave to a phase of his compositional output marked by pervasive nostalgia, fragmentary melody, and strong emotional evocation. He described it in an unpublished lecture given in 1972 at the State University of New York at Buffalo (where he was made a professor of music in 1973):

> It appears that this new period of mine was short lived—from 1970 until 1972—beginning with *Madame Press* [*Died Last Week at Ninety*] and then *The Viola in My Life* right into *The Rothko Chapel* immediately followed by *I Met Heine on the Rue Fürstenberg* and then ending with a composition called *Three Clarinets, Cello and Piano*.
>
> After the three clarinet piece I was what the romantics call "lost"— uprooted and living in Europe added to the ambivalence of what to do next. While living in Berlin throughout all of last year—I abandoned what I called the "Illusion of Feeling" for again the "Illusion of Art" that is—I went back to a more abstract music—less detailed—still precisely notated but with another big change—longer, large works.[25]

Feldman sets up an evocative dialectic of feeling versus art and defines which pieces fall under the rubric of the former, but he's less willing to describe just what in those pieces—beyond their generalized musical characteristics—"the illusion of feeling" might refer to. A clearer sense of Feldman's meaning emerges when noting that *Madame Press* and *Rothko Chapel* are elegies in memory of deceased friends, and that *The Viola in My Life* was a cycle written out of deep feeling as well—in this case, newfound affection for the violist Karen Phillips, for whom Feldman had also composed the solo viola part of *Rothko Chapel*.[26]

The emotional tone Feldman projects in his music from this period is one of quiet mourning punctured by sudden violent intensities that rupture the musical fabric. As a listener, I hear a tension between a decaying sonorous landscape and a contrary impulse to "get on with something"—an attempt to coalesce or get moving. These impulses are crosscut by jarring gestural interventions that fracture the otherwise delicate sound worlds of the pieces. To understand the novelty of the latter development, it's important to note that Feldman's music had been marked by a singular quietude since the 1950s. "As soft as possible" is the instruction given to performers of his music in *The O'Hara Songs* and elsewhere, and Feldman's ideal performances hover on the edge of audibility. He cultivated what he called "flat" sonic surfaces with a minimum of timbral, gestural, or dynamic contrast. This flatness engenders varying affective responses in listeners. One valid response is frustration with a music that seems directionless, floating, and (if quiet enough) literally unlistenable. Another response, and one that I like to encourage in light of Feldman and O'Hara's shared aesthetic, is the sense that the music's quiet intensity can, and often does, draw one into a field of difference figured as sonic uniqueness. This notion of aural singularity may seem far from the relational sociability of Feldman's lectures and O'Hara's poems—and it very well would be, if the uniqueness of sonorous objects implied their autonomy. Clearly, that is not Feldman's intention, any more than it was O'Hara's to create assemblages of unrelated words. The aesthetic and affective force of Feldman's music comes precisely from the relationships that emerge and dissolve among the sounds.

Further indications of Feldman's understanding of "the illusion of feeling," and its resonance with the composer's reading of O'Hara, can be gleaned from studying the compositional sketches for *Three Clarinets, Cello, and Piano* (see Figure 3.1). Though published with a flatly descriptive title listing its instrumentation, Feldman's manuscript copy of *Three Clarinets* bears the title "In Memory of My Feelings"—a play on the title of an early O'Hara poem,

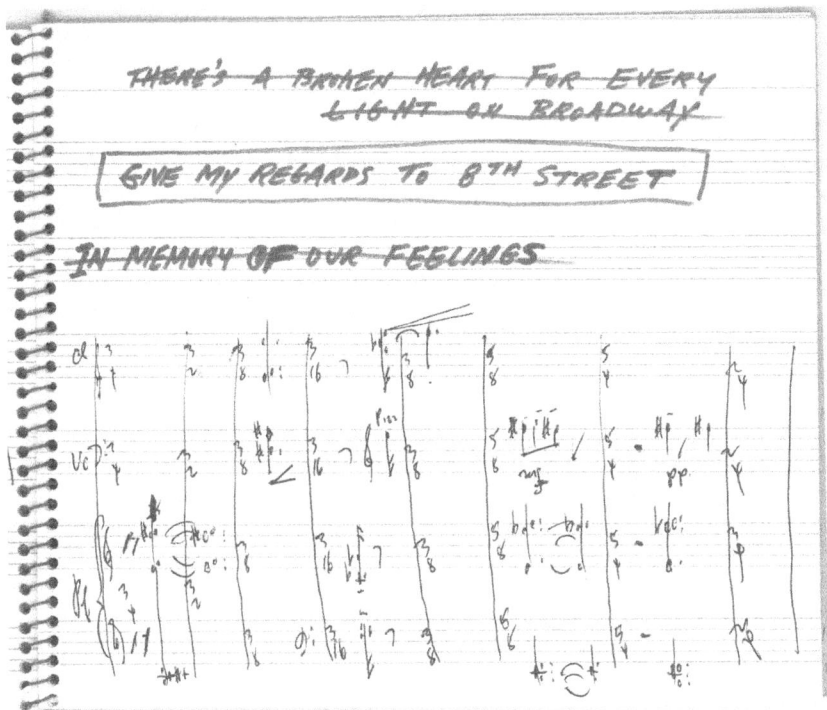

Figure 3.1 Morton Feldman, "Give My Regards to Eighth Street," working copy of *Three Clarinets, Cello, and Piano*, 1971. Morton Feldman Collection. Paul Sacher Foundation.

"In Memory of My Feelings."[27] He subsequently crossed this out and added another title, "There's a Broken Heart for Every Light on Broadway," taken from a Tin Pan Alley tune by Howard Johnson and Fred Fischer. He also crossed out this title. The sketches indicate that he settled on the title "Give My Regards to Eighth Street," only to finally change it once more to the austere *Three Clarinets, Cello, and Piano*.

"Give My Regards to Eighth Street" is also the title Feldman gave to an autobiographical essay published in *Art in America* in 1971. The theme of "Give My Regards" is nostalgia and, more explicitly, mourning for a lost coterie, such that the essay reads as a sequel to his obituary for O'Hara. In the early 1970s, Feldman had moved first to Berlin and then to Buffalo and was no doubt "at sea" socially, having lost the vital network that the New York artists and poets had provided. As we saw in Chapter 1, he gives a sense of this in "Give My Regards" when he writes,

> When you begin to work—until that unlucky day when you are no longer involved with just a handful of friends, admirers, complainers—there is no separation between what you do and who you are . . . . In some cases the work leads to a concept of music or of art that draws attention, and you find yourself in the world . . . . Yet there was another "world." Of conversation, of anonymity, of seeing paintings in the intimacy of a studio instead of a museum, of playing a new piece on the piano in your home instead of in a concert hall.[28]

Giving up the illusion of feeling could have meant giving up on a music that projected affects of loss and love into sound, and the music of the early 1970s certainly mourns for lost intimacy.

"In Memory of My Feelings" resurfaced as a possible title in 1973 when it was given to an ensemble piece for flute, clarinet, violin, percussion, cello, and piano—the piece known today as *For Frank O'Hara* (1973). Feldman's manuscript retains "In Memory of My Feelings" as the title, indicating that it was replaced at a very late stage, perhaps just as Feldman's manuscript was drafted in fair copy and sent to his publisher, Universal Edition (see Figure 3.2). With the replacement title, Feldman recalls two things: his 1962 piece titled *For Franz Kline*, and the elegiac music of the immediately preceding years.[29] But the question naturally arises of the ways this elegiac tone is produced and its debt to O'Hara's poetry.

As discussed earlier, Feldman described O'Hara's poems as capable of delivering sudden, devastating turns of phrase that are "as definite and real and finite as a sudden death." "In Memory of My Feelings" is just such a poem. In addition, as numerous commentators have noted, it deals with an unpredictable and fluid conception of subjectivity.[30] No doubt the poem's opening lines appealed to Feldman, perhaps through a shock of recognition: "My quietness has a man in it, he is transparent / and he carries me quietly, like a gondola, through the streets."[31] Quietness is, after all, at the heart of Feldman's aesthetic, with its emphasis on the barely or semi-audible. "In Memory of My Feelings" also takes up the theme of death, particularly in its second section beginning with the lines "The dead hunting / and the alive, ahunted."[32] Small wonder, then, that it would come to mind as a title for Feldman's musical elegy for the poet. As Nick Selby notes, the final sections

Figure 3.2 Morton Feldman, "In Memory of My Feelings," working copy of *For Frank O'Hara*, 1973. Morton Feldman Collection. Paul Sacher Foundation.

of the poem are marked by an attempt to reconfigure a sense of self out of the collage of images and experiences.[33] This corresponds to Feldman's own creation of music, which attempts to get itself together, to build up a coherent sense of progression or movement from fragmentary gestures that can seem aimless or inchoate.

Feldman had marked an end to emotional projection in his music with *Three Clarinets, Cello, and Piano*, yet *For Frank O'Hara* inhabits a markedly similar sound world. That the composer considered "In Memory of My Feelings" as a title for both pieces suggests that we could hear in each a translation of O'Hara's (sudden) death into the realm of Feldman's sounds. In these pieces Feldman seems to craft a musical analog to the intensities of O'Hara's verse, not just in the quick gestural turn, but also in generating musical experiences of focused attention like those the poet valorized in "The Day Lady Died." To get at this type of experience, I'll describe two moments in *Three Clarinets* and *For Frank O'Hara*, bolstered with references to Feldman's later exploration of melancholy and what he calls "atmosphere."

Listening to Feldman's *Three Clarinets, Cello, and Piano*, I'm often struck by its varied sonic textures and how the feeling of the piece can be construed as both a physical sensation and an atmosphere of anxiety.[34] As with much of his "illusion of feeling" music, gradations of dynamics in *Three Clarinets* range from extremely quiet to shatteringly loud, whereas before 1970, an all-pervasive near-silence was the norm. In *Three Clarinets*, long tones in the cello and clarinets begin on the edge of intelligibility and gradually fill up our senses, only to quickly vanish. These waxing and waning tones contrast with static fields of sound (produced by multiple instruments) that are more felt than heard, that register their presence in our bodies before we understand them as sonorities. The clarinets play sharply dissonant intervals—often minor seconds—which produce rapid oscillations and fluctuations in the sonorities that give them a buzzing, slightly irritating quality—an acoustic phenomenon called "beating." Yet Feldman takes the edge off the sound by keeping the clarinets quiet, rendering them focused fields of energy that draw the listener in. In contrast to these more textural sonic events, Feldman occasionally gives us short, two-note melodies: first in the cello and later in one clarinet. These melodies inject a more rhetorical music, in that they seem to get something going both lyrically and rhythmically in a way that the other musical events do not. They give an otherwise amorphous composition a bit of a tune—even if it is a tune marked by brevity, repetition, and unexpected disappearance.

With these types of sounds—long tones gradually increasing in volume, vibrating tone clusters, and fragmentary, repetitive melodies—Feldman spins out a ten-minute piece that retreats into silence, ending as it began. Yet one moment interrupts the otherwise flat musical scene. Approximately two minutes into the performance, the three clarinets interrupt the musical fabric with a loud, dissonant erruption of four quivering chords, then suddenly return to disconnected, quiet sounds. The curious thing about this moment is that it feels like a progression—that is to say, the sounds go somewhere amid music that otherwise doesn't feel like it's going anywhere. The four chords sound connected, and provide a brief narrative arc of a consequential phrase. It is a kind of music that gets it together long enough to say something instead of hanging on to its tremulous reticence. To call the four chords *narrative* may seem to overstate the case, but to notice that such a progression could even appear in Feldman's compositional practice is also to recognize the singularity of his sounds and the way he crafts hermetic atmospheres that lack drama. Drama in this moment comes from a sudden, singular interruption in the midst of an otherwise static sonic situation.

The music following the clamorous outburst of the clarinets is unchanged from that which comes before it. The sounds seem willfully ignorant of the event that has just transpired, and go along unperturbed. But the event causes my own hearing to be shot through with intense anxiety about what *else* might happen. I now hear the quiet tensions, the little anxious textures, and the fragmentary melodies with new suspicion. I thought I knew what the music was capable of doing, but my expectations have been radically revised. Feldman plays on this newly created anxiousness at the end of the piece. There he sets up a situation similar to the one in which the loud clarinet chords intervened: the clarinets begin an unexpected crescendo, as they had before the disruptive progression earlier in the piece. Instead of repeating the dissonant four chord progression, however, the music pulls back and dies away—a receding landscape that drags our attachment to the sounds with it into silence. At the risk of being too literal, we can recall Feldman's initial, though later redacted, connection of *Three Clarinets* with O'Hara's "In Memory of My Feelings"; indeed, Feldman seems primarily interested in playing on the memory of our feelings as listeners with his evocation of the memory of the violent event.

An analogous rupturing event occurs in *For Frank O'Hara* from 1973. As Catherine Hirata has noted about the piece, Feldman seems more interested than before in using his gestures to set up musical progressions (sounds that get on with something, go somewhere)—only to undercut those progressions. This is distinct from the way in which the violent event of *Three Clarinets* was disruptive (because that felt like a progression). In *For Frank O'Hara*, a violent event interrupts a play of sounds passing back and forth between coalescence and dissolution. Hirata describes *For Frank O'Hara* in her characteristically trenchant way:

> Heard in the context of the more fragmentary passages of *For Frank O'Hara*, a passage [in which sounds seem to come together and accompany one another] seems vigorous. It is as though suddenly the music gets off the ground, as it were. Each sound rather than seeming isolated from the next, combines with the next so as to create that effect so uncharacteristic for Feldman, namely of a musical progression. . . . At the same time that Feldman enables these sounds to be heard as a progression, he also undercuts this progression. This assures that the passage still seems to fit with those which are more fragmented (and that it still sounds like Feldman).[35]

A feeling of coming together and falling apart pervades *For Frank O'Hara*, yet a singular moment of rupture threatens to tear the music asunder. Near the two-thirds mark of the performance (mm. 177–8), the two percussionists execute a snare drum roll that is sudden, brief, incredibly loud, and devastating in its visceral, terrifying impact. Again, a sudden increase in volume intrudes upon the quiet of the sound; as in *Three Clarinets*, however, the violent event seems to go unnoticed (or is deliberately ignored) by the other music. It simply goes on with the winding up and unraveling that Hirata describes. We sense that we're again in a musical landscape in which anything might happen, occasionally does, and we should be ready for it—even if that readiness becomes dread.

In the preceding paragraphs I've explored affective events in two of Feldman's compositions and suggested that they might have something to do with Feldman's reading of O'Hara's poetry. Each piece was titled, up to a very late point in its compositional genesis, with a version of O'Hara's "In Memory of My Feelings," and while I don't mean to suggest that these pieces are programmatic or that they refer specifically to the poem, I do want to consider how Feldman's reading of O'Hara may be related to the violent sonic interventions in each composition.

Feldman preferred not to think of the snare drum event in *For Frank O'Hara* as necessarily dramatic:

> [Emphatic events] become something else in music. Recently, for example, in my Frank O'Hara piece when I got the two drum guys, now it seems dramatic in context of the musical composition. I didn't think of it as dramatic at the time. If there was an airplane coming over here we would talk a little louder and we are not even conscious how we are affected. But in music we demand other kinds of priorities.[36]

At the time of this interview—in the mid-1970s—Feldman was invested in an "illusion of art" produced in longer, repetitive, abstract works. Regarding the earlier O'Hara-connected pieces from 1972 to 1973, it bears recalling how Feldman in 1968 described the poet's verse. He defined affective events in O'Hara's poems through a discussion of the poem "Mayakovsky":

> In an extraordinary poem Frank O'Hara describes his love for the poet Mayakovsky. After an outburst of feeling, he writes "but I'm turning to my verses / and my heart is closing / like a fist." What he is telling us is something unbelievably painful. Secreted in O'Hara's thought is the possibility that we create only as dead men. . . . Only the artist who is close to his own life gives us an art that is like death.[37]

The drastic turn of the line "closing like a fist" illustrates what Feldman means when he describes O'Hara's verse as presenting a "gunshot" or "sudden death." These are drastic moments that explode the atmosphere of the poem and, at times, render a violent or disruptive effect—for example, the quoted lines of "Mayakovsky," with their "outburst of feeling." Yet the poem simply moves on, apostrophizing to "Words!" in the subsequent stanza, indifferent to what has happened.[38] Resembling O'Hara's interruptions and sudden shifts of register, tone, and address, Feldman's sonic interruptions work as musical translations of the poet's technique, in which O'Hara "dispenses with everything in his work but his feelings."[39] Feldman's reading of O'Hara—in which gunshots go off, characters die or go missing, or registers suddenly shift from the comic to the placid to the tragic—helps us understand the bewildering disjunctions within the composer's music from the early 1970s: its propensity to fall apart just as it seems to be getting together, the intrusion of sounds that are ill-fitted to their situations, and the tendency of the music after interruptions to simply go on doing what it was doing before, without attending to the effects of sudden violence. In these compositions—*Three Clarinets, Cello, and Piano* and *For Frank O'Hara*—a posthumous collaboration between poet and composer found Feldman learning from O'Hara's poetry and letting it influence, at least for a time, his compositional method and the musical atmospheres he created.

Late-style Mourning

After *For Frank O'Hara*, Feldman focused his compositional practice on the creation of monumental works, such as the six-hour *String Quartet No. 2* (1983), the four-hour *For Philip Guston* (1984), and the ninety-minute *Three Voices* (1982), based on fragments of O'Hara's poem "Wind," which he had set previously in his *O'Hara Songs* (1962).[40] His interest in musical memory and mourning expanded, such that the sense of loss he described in "Lost Times and Future Hopes" and explored in his "illusion of feeling" period became a more generalized "affective atmosphere."[41] He described his understanding of feeling and atmosphere in a 1985 lecture in Middelburg:

> I think the most important thing in my music is the gradations of feeling in the music. You can't discuss that. The music has a certain atmosphere that changes. The atmosphere itself is not monolithic. . . If we could come to some kind of consensus on what I mean by atmosphere, the way D. H. Lawrence would write about the atmosphere of Hawthorne.[42]

Feldman's conception of "atmosphere" resonates with that of Ben Anderson, in which atmospheres convey a sense of collective, diffused feeling. Building on the work of phenomenologist Mikel Dufrenne,[43] Anderson describes affective atmospheres as "autonomous from the bodies that they emerge from, enable and perish with. As such, to attend to affective atmospheres is to learn to be affected by the ambiguities of affect/emotion, by that which is determinate and indeterminate, present and absent, singular and vague."[44] While Anderson, following Dufrenne, imagines affective atmospheres as expressing singularity, Feldman's interest in the production of "gradations of feeling" motivates his music's propensity to shape and suddenly transform an atmosphere. This also suggests that music is an ideal medium through which to document the effects of affective atmospheres that Anderson has in mind. Far from being floating or ineffable, the specific set of actors (musicians), technologies (instruments, recording and reproduction machinery), and listeners in musical performance provides concrete channels through which to think of atmospheres as material networks engendered through specific sets of mediators and events. As such, performance-dependent atmospheres are mutable and subject to sudden changes of mood or tone. This is what impresses me about the moments of rupture in *Three Clarinets, Cello, and Piano* and *For Frank O'Hara*: the feeling of the piece changes suddenly, and that change affects one's future listening, yet the music seems to go on as though nothing dramatic has happened.

Beyond the production of a generalized affect, Feldman's idea of atmosphere is integrated with the work of mourning begun in his obituary for O'Hara and continued in his music of the early 1970s—those elegies of sudden death. Moreover, this morbid sensibility is felt even in his earliest memorial piece, *For Franz Kline*, as well as in *Vertical Thoughts 3* and *5*, in which Feldman ruminates musically on a line from the Talmud: "life is a passing shadow." We can gain further insight into Feldman's concept of atmosphere by following his reference in the Middelburg lecture to D. H. Lawrence's *Studies in Classic American Literature*.[45]

In a chapter on Nathaniel Hawthorne's *The Blithedale Romance*—a book concerned with the fracturing of relationships amid debates about the veracity of spiritualism—Lawrence reflects on the supernatural forces at play in the novel: "Is it all bunkum, this spiritualism? . . . Not quite. Apart even from telepathy, the apparatus of human consciousness is the most wonderful message-receiver in existence. Beats a wireless station to nothing."[46] He goes on to offer an account of how the mediumship of Hawthorne's character Priscilla ("the little psychic prostitute") could work authentically via trance. Lawrence develops this idea via the metaphor of wireless transmission:

> A trance means that all her *individual*, personal intelligence goes to sleep, like a hen with a head under her wing. But the *apparatus* of consciousness remains working. Without a soul in it.
>
> And what can this apparatus of consciousness do, when it works? Why surely something. A wireless apparatus goes tick-tick-tick, taking down messages. So does your human apparatus. All kinds of messages. Only the

soul, or the under-consciousness deals with these messages in the dark, in the under-conscious. Which is the natural course of events.[47]

Lawrence's discussion of "atmosphere" arises in this broader context of mediumship, in which Priscilla submerges her personality and gives her will over to others, to the various dead wills that surround her. These ghosts use her "human apparatus" as one would use a wireless telegraph. As Jonathan Sterne and others have noted, sound technologies—in this instance telephony—have always been figured as potential lines of communication with the dead.[48] The mediumship associated with spiritualism was itself linked with sound reproduction technologies beyond the metaphorical and enrolled the emergent technologies of not only telephony but also sound recording in the practice of séance.[49] Lawrence continues and finally arrives at the metaphor of atmosphere that Feldman found so descriptive for his music:

> But what sorts of messages [come through]? All sorts. . . . The human apparatus receives them all, and they are all dealt with in the under-conscious. . . . There may even be vibrations of ghosts in the air. Ghosts being dead *wills*, mind you, not dead souls. The soul has nothing to do with these dodges.
>
> But some unit of force may persist for a time, after the death of an individual—some associations of vibrations may linger like little clouds in the etheric atmosphere after the death of a human being, or an animal. And these little clots of vibration may transfer themselves to the conscious-apparatus of the medium. . . .
>
> There is never much worth in these "messages." Because they are never more than fragmentary items of the dead, disintegrated consciousnesses. And the medium has and always will have a hopeless job, trying to disentangle the muddle of messages.[50]

Elucidating Feldman's invocation of Lawrence gives us a clearer sense of how the musician thinks of atmosphere: as a field of ghostly fragments struggling for intelligibility and spectral vibrations that provide a tantalizing concept with which to describe the effect of the taut dissonances in *Three Clarinets, Cello, and Piano* and *For Frank O'Hara*. Atmospheres are always already haunted, and Feldman's music conveys this idea from the early 1960s until his own death in 1987.

Though Feldman doesn't draw out the point in his Middelburg lecture, the fact that Lawrence's evocation of atmosphere is situated in a discussion of mediumship is salient to his mourning of O'Hara for a number of reasons—not least that it gets to a fact about musical performance: the shifting agencies and myriad relationships that obtain to it are transpersonal and transhistorical. Performers constantly submerge their personalities to transmit the messages of others—the "fragmentary items of the dead." Benjamin Piekut and Jason Stanyek write about such morbidity effects, labeling them "deadness" as a performative effect: "Deadness speaks to the distended temporalities and spatialities of all performance, much the way all ontologies are really hauntologies, spurred into being through the portended traces of too many histories to name and too many futures to subsume in a stable, locatable present."[51] As performances of such *deadness*, Feldman's musical elegies for O'Hara are acts of mourning that demonstrate the afterlife of his friendships—the residual traces of group formation structured on his attachment to and interpretation of O'Hara's poetry.

Even after *For Frank O'Hara*, Feldman continued to work with O'Hara's poetry and memory in *Three Voices*. In this late work, Feldman prolonged his posthumous collaboration with O'Hara while also making a first attempt at mourning Philip Guston. It is a work deeply concerned with the production of deadness and dramatizes musical mediumship through the performance of Joan La Barbara. *Three Voices*, as Scott Klein has noted, is partially "an aesthetic response to O'Hara's aesthetics, a formal homage to the varied aesthetic flattenings of the Abstract Expressionists, and to the different kinds of emptying-out of language represented by [Jenny] Holzer or by the late works of Beckett."[52] While the work certainly is that, it is also effectively a séance over which Joan La Barbara (in the first performance and in decades of performances since) presides as medium (see Figure 3.3). Feldman's description of the work to John Rockwell in 1985 gets at these qualities:

> One of my closest friends, the painter Philip Guston had died; Frank O'Hara had died several years before. I saw the piece with Joan in front and the two loudspeakers, behind her. There is something kind of tombstoney about the look of the loudspeaker. I thought of the piece as an exchange of the live voice with the dead ones—a mixture of the living and the dead.[53]

Figure 3.3 Paula Court. Joan La Barbara. © 1983.

Feldman's annotations to his working manuscript of the score strengthen his interpretation and give us a sharper sense of the work's *intermundane* character—that is, its staging of a sentimental colloquy between living and dead friends.[54]

Feldman's description of the piece three years after its completion wasn't a retrospective interpretation. We can see in Feldman's working manuscript of *Three Voices* that its seánce-like character and graveyard setting were part of the piece's conception:

1) Three voices in dialogue between the dead and the living.
2) Two deceased friends: Philip Guston and Frank O'Hara are the voices from the speakers which ~~Joan La Barbara~~ in themselves are for me the "grave stones" of live acoustical music. Though entombed in the electronic medium they speak with the same thoughts and with the same voice as the performer.[55]

La Barbara's voice is both the literal and figurative medium through which O'Hara and Guston return. The "electronic medium" refers to the preparation of the work by La Barbara. She performed one of the voices live; the other two were prerecorded and synchronized to accompany her live voice. Tape music, about which Feldman was ambivalent at best, is here used to hermeneutic ends as the voices of his dead friends. O'Hara and Guston are "entombed in the electronic medium," projected out of speakers marking the graves of living dead. Feldman presents a rich archive of fantasies about death, embalming, mediumship, and voice in *Three Voices*. We find him valorizing *liveness* by foregrounding the *deadness* of the prerecorded music. We also find him insisting upon the mediumship of La Barbara and her voice—the voices speak "with the same thoughts and with the same voice as the performer." These are ideas found in the long history of sound's relationship to death. Jonathan Sterne, getting at the matter of death and recorded sound, describes a view that echoes Feldman's: "the voices of the dead no longer emanate from bodies that serve as containers for self-awareness. The recording is, therefore, a resonant tomb, offering the exteriority of the voice with none of its interior self-awareness."[56] This lack of self-awareness, I would argue, is also a lack of authentic presence. Thus the voice of La Barbara is needed as the material medium through which the voices of O'Hara and Guston return. Before advancing this claim and questioning if Feldman's friends successfully came through, we need to attend to the voice who first made *Three Voices*, recognizing La Barbara's role not only in commissioning the piece but in contributing to the form it took and the haunted sensibility it proffers.

The Mediumship of Joan La Barbara

Three Voices was the product of a large-scale commissioning project La Barbara undertook in the early 1980s. In addition to Feldman, John Cage, James Tenney, Roger Reynolds, Charles Dodge, Rhys Chatham, and Morton Subotnick wrote works tailored for her particular abilities.[57] By the time of the commission, Feldman and La Barbara had known each other for nearly a decade. They had met at the Metamusik Festival in Berlin in 1974, and Feldman soon became a staunch supporter of her work. He served on the committee of CAPS (Creative Artists Public Service program, a division of the New York State Council for the Arts), which provided a composition grant allowing La Barbara to realize her composition *Thunder* (1975–6), a work for voice, electronics and two timpani. It was recorded for La Barbara's second LP, *Tapesongs*, and released on her own label in 1977 (along with *Cathing* and Cage's *Solo for Voice 45*). Feldman also invited La Barbara to be an artist in residence with the Creative Associates at the University of Buffalo, where he took up the Edgard Varèse Chair in composition following his return from Berlin. Her brief time with Creative Associates allowed her to present *Circular Song* and *Vocal Extensions* at the Carnegie Recital Hall in 1977. She also continued to develop *Thunder* along with *Ides of March*, which she presented at the Kitchen that same year. La Barbara's star rose dramatically in the late 1970s as she made a name for herself as both composer and vocalist while becoming a specialist in the performance of Feldman's music.

On May 23, 1981, she sent a note from Berlin, reminding Feldman of the commission while also giving the specifics of her abilities. She listed performance opportunities she had on the horizon, hoping to include his new work:

> Just a short note to remind you to think seriously about writing a piece for me. I've already contacted Frans de Ruiter at the Holland Festival about possibilities for next year, though that may be too soon. If you have any thoughts about the ensemble instrumentation, or whether it will be for orchestra, do let me know.
>
> For your general information, my (normal singing—not "extended" techniques) vocal range is: 3 octaves d–d lowest tones are rather quiet unless amplified (that is, low d–e-flat–e will be relatively quiet no matter what dynamic you write, some power comes in at f).
>
> We'll be in Berlin, generally, until about mid-October ... back to the East Coast U.S. early November. Perhaps we could arrange to meet in New York in early November to do some preliminary work?
>
> Hope all is well with you. Best to Bunny [Bunita Marcus].[58]

Almost a year later, on April 23, 1982, Feldman sent the completed score to La Barbara with this letter:

> Dear Joan,
>
> Well, here it is.
> I'm somewhat shocked with the more sensuous if not "gorgeous" sound of most of it—never expecting it would go that way. The words are from the

two opening lines of *WIND*, a poem by Frank O'Hara dedicated to me. I think Frank had a lot to do with some of the "gorgeous" aspect of the piece.

The bottom system is what you sing "live," the other two are layered in—where the 2 loud speakers should be placed I have no idea—it is also one of the very few pieces where I didn't indicate a metronome marking—feeling that your tone and how you breathe should pace it—it sounds good both "slow" as well as a "fast" slowness (whatever that means).

I know that putting this work together is a horrendous undertaking! I feel that the work is you like "Joan that's your color—what a beautiful neck line—and the length though somewhat long (whoever heard of an afternoon dress with a long trail?)—still—buy it!"

> Of course you can always return it for whatever reason.
> All love to you and Mort
> from the other
> Morty[59]

What has until now gone unnoticed about *Three Voices* is that Feldman adapted La Barbara's tape music practice to his own music. Starting in the late 1970s, La Barbara has made numerous tape works that she calls "sound paintings." In works such as *Twelvesong, October Music, Erin*, and others, La Barbara layers multiple recorded tracks of her vocal performances. In many of these works, she produced a version for performance in which the tape part accompanies her live vocalizations. *Erin* (1980) and *Twelvesong (Zwölfgesang)* (1977) layered sixteen and twelve vocal tracks (respectively); Feldman's request that La Barbara produce two prerecorded tracks was tame by comparison, making the preparation of *Three Voices* likely somewhat less of a "horrendous undertaking" than Feldman imagined.

In terms of reference and inspiration, La Barbara's 1979 tape pieces *ShadowSong* and *Klee Alee* provide compelling points of thematic comparison with *Three Voices*. Recordings of both would have been available to Feldman on La Barbara's third LP, *Reluctant Gypsy* (1980). *ShadowSong* is a five-minute investigation into the limits of perception, consciousness, audibility, and form. The piece begins with whispered sounds, unintelligible on the edges of the stereo field. Tremulous melodies suddenly and erratically float into awareness—providing momentary anchors—only to vanish again. The work gradually coalesces into thick, pulsating all-La Barbara chords that assert themselves through the final minute of the piece. An aspirated "HUH" cuts the work off suddenly, as if waking us up from an uncanny dream that had threatened to become a nightmare. *ShadowSong*, La Barbara writes,

> explored . . . a psychological state—in this case, the idea that as one moves through the day, or through life, one encounters distractions, images on the periphery of sight or thought. One constantly has to choose to continue with one's chosen path, or to diverge and move into the realm controlled by the "distractions," a kind of "road not taken" exploration, with language playing a subtle part. Words for ghosts, specters, shadows in several languages, drift into audibility and melt away again.[60]

ShadowSong continued La Barbara's investigation into the relations between mental states and the phenomenology of sound. While her description begins in the seemingly objective realm of psychology, the form that these encountered "distractions" take is revealed as "ghosts, specters, shadows." Their polyglot evocation is likely an artifact of La Barbara's time living and working in Berlin, where she was a DAAD fellow in 1979 and where she would return in 1981. The tape medium retains its mystical ability to capture—"entomb"—the voices of the dead and evoke spectral presences. La Barbara, like Feldman, insists upon the relationship between recorded voice and haunting. In *ShadowSong* La Barbara dramatizes our perception of intermundane phenomena, while leaving in abeyance the question of their objective reality. *ShadowSong*, unlike *Three Voices*, is less séance than it is an Electronic Voice Phenomena (EVP) recording session, in which our perceptual capacities and abilities to hear voices of the dead is tested and the veracity of these experiences remains questionable.[61] We are on our own to make sense of these ghostly sounds—and wonder whether they are ghosts at all.

While *Three Voices* shares its content with La Barbara's *ShadowSong*, it shares its form and texture with another of her 1979 Berlin works, *Klee Alee*. The "sound painting" is a masterpiece of pseudomorphosis, in which the abstract chromatic grid of Paul Klee's *Hauptweg und Nebenweg* (1929)—which La Barbara saw in Köln—is translated into a dense vocal weave. In a manner similar to yet distinct from Feldman's musical translation of action painting,

La Barbara worked with the surface of Klee's painting to make her own sound world:

> I made extensive notes about the colors and structure and thickness of the paint and the figures scratched into it by the artist. . . . I constructed sound blocks of particular timbres which reflected for me the greens and blues of the painting. I then "scratched" into the thickness of the vocal sound blocks as Klee had scratched into the thickness of the paint, creating tiny figures using inhaled sounds, some thin, some click-like, some pensive, some wailing and distressed.[62]

La Barbara's conception of sonic abstraction comes to the fore in "the thickness of vocal sound blocks." Much like the frontality of Mark Rothko or the flattened picture plane of Guston's dark paintings from the 1960s, La Barbara pushes her sound blocks to the front of the stereo field—almost to the point of distortion—while other sounds remain hidden behind this wall of sound.

La Barbara succeeds in flattening out her sound world through the illusory medium of tape. In doing so, she translates Rothko and Adolf Gottlieb's maxim into sound: "We wish to reassert the picture plane. We are for flat forms because they destroy illusion and reveal truth."[63] Taking up Klee's flatness, she actualizes at the same time Feldman's own sense of surface—a musical picture plane in which there is a minimum of contrast.[64] Stereo recording, ideally used to recreate a full sense of worldly listening, can be used (as La Barbara does) to create a flat aural plane, one that comes to signify abstraction in *Klee Alee*.

The haunted flatness of *Three Voices* resonates with the oeuvre of its commissioning artist. Its "gorgeousness" had other sources though, and Feldman attributed the beauty of the work to the spirit of Frank O'Hara. In a lecture from 1982 he took up the question of sensuality in *Three Voices* and its relationship to his broader investment in abstraction. To capture his prolix logic, I quote Feldman at length:

> Usually what happens in a piece, I just wrote a piece now, for three voices, in which it was very disconcerting because I don't want to write pretty music, I don't even want to write beautiful music. . . . It's a dangerous word to use. . . . I really want everything, *alles*, in one piece.

> But never an obvious type of sensual beauty, and certainly not something that is communicable in terms of its motivic imagery or its harmonic language, even if that language is non-functional, whatever that means, it still in a sense can be very very beautiful, and you can handle it beautifully. And what was happening in this piece that I'm writing now, which I just finished the other day, is that I really wanted to write an abstract thing, called *Three Voices*, with just three singers, and I really, my dream always when I write, is that I want to do it abstractly. Because I feel that if you finally do it abstractly nothing could equal it. . . . No representational painting can equal maybe one or two paintings where Rothko made it. That's my feeling, it's almost political. . . . So I have a total political conviction in that abstract sensation, without the help of an iconic, iconography, no matter how startling, or no matter how fantastic it is.[65]

Feldman's public commentary on *Three Voices* obscures the more personal references that he inscribes in the working copy of the score but in no way diminishes the work's haunted affect. Indeed, the gorgeousness of O'Hara—his sensuous presence—has intruded upon the work, coming into conflict with Feldman's desire for abstract experience. He wanted to "do it abstractly" but "it doesn't happen that it works out sometimes, like in this vocal piece." He continued, "It went the other way. It is luscious, it's sexy, it's gorgeous, you swoon with it, and there's nothing I could have done with it short of throwing it out."[66]

As any medium knows, you can't control exactly what or who comes through in a séance. The same appears true in the creative act of composition. To create art like a dead man—as Feldman insisted O'Hara did—means that you don't exert *your* will. You give yourself over to the atmosphere that surrounds you and tune into what wants to come through. Feldman recalled his struggle in composing *Three Voices* regarding whether beauty or abstraction would dominate the work: "You can make a virtue of all these things, and you could say, 'oh, I was fighting it, and I fight it and I really surrendered to it,' and it's as if I came through some kind of spiritual and emotional cleansing. I didn't . . . I was weak, I couldn't say no [to beauty]."[67] When we realize that beauty was intimately bound up with Feldman's affection for O'Hara's gorgeousness, *Three Voices* seems even more like a work that mourns coterie. And though it's set in a technological graveyard, the sounds that emerged ended up being ravishing—a gift from O'Hara, from the other side.

The sheer loveliness of *Three Voices* did not go unnoticed by Feldman's friends. John Cage, in particular, was troubled by its beauty as well as the technological mediation. He discussed it in conversation with Michael Bach and Joan Retallack in 1992:

> Michael Bach: There is one problem with this [Feldman's] piece I think, apart from the acoustics—it's different if something comes out of the loudspeaker or if it's played—but the voices had to be together.
> John Cage: Yes, the fact that it is the score is difficult, hmm? Is it a fixed score?
> MB: I think so.
> JC: O.K., well that's an error, yes, that's a mistake, And the other error—well, go ahead, what do you think?
> MB: The singer [La Barbara] is always trying to—
> JC: —Be with herself.
> MB: —To follow the loudspeakers
> JC: Yes. Well, we won't have that problem
> MB: Yes, that's the problem with the Feldman piece, I think.
> JC: Yes, and the other problem is it's too beautiful.
> MB: So it's very obvious if the beauty is disturbed by a bad performance?
> JC: A good performance is even worse! Because it's *more* beautiful. *(laughter)* It's in meter too. It's in threes, isn't it?—one two three, one two three, one two three . . . Isn't it something like that?
> MB: Oh, I don't remember that.
> JC: I think so. It's like a triplet.
> MB: Like a waltz . . .
> JC: Triplets. Ta ta ta, ta ta ta. It's enough to drive you crazy. Finally, if you pay attention to it, it's irritating, triplets.
> Joan Retallack: Yes, triplets *can* drive you crazy. Oom-pah-pah cultures are frightening.[68]

Along with begrudgingly accepting beauty, Feldman also accepts certain conventions of musical semiosis. The triple-time "waltz" becomes a significant musical topic in *Three Voices*. It gives the work a tipsy dance-like feel that comes frighteningly close to undisguised text painting. The lines of O'Hara's poetry that Feldman sets are only a fragment of the full poem:

Who'd have thought
        that snow falls
. . .
snow whirled
        nothing ever fell[69]

"Whirling" becomes the operative verb and we spin around again and again. Grounded in this swirling dance, *Three Voices* goes on to play with our perception of consonance and dissonance as well as our ability to interpret language. Though Feldman gives in to beauty, tensions remain between abstract vocal sound and signification. While the music is remarkably concrete in its beauty, Feldman uses that beauty to explore the formation and degradation of language. He lets the material be as lovely as it wants to be, while O'Hara's poetry comes in and out of focus for the duration of the work. Such textual ambiguity challenges our ability to make meaning from sounds and project sense into what we hear.

For a musician so resistant to musical conceptualization and references, Feldman's tug-of-war between beauty and abstraction seems an odd lapse of, well, *taste*. As a late piece of the composer, we might expect what Feldman referred to as "the degradation of beautiful material." That is, the translation of his sudden-death sonic effects into long-duration exercises in decomposition. What is so radical and astonishing about *Three Voices* when viewed in his series of late works is how little the material changes when compared to other works of the period. Feldman wallows in the sheer pleasure of the sounds La Barbara brings into the world through her voice. Much of the work's material is recycled without alteration or transposition. Music from page 1 returns as page 15. Page 2 returns as page 16. Portions of page 6 come back as part of page 17. Page 10 returns as page 18, though the final utterance of "Who'd have thought that snow falls" is transposed up a whole step, making it shine even brighter in La Barbara's middle register. This is quite different from how Feldman worked in the 1980s. Material is rarely repeated literally; it is instead refracted through the prism of memory. This work with memory produces subtle variations that give the music what Joseph Dubiel would call a handmade, or bespoke quality.⁷⁰ Beauty is something that Feldman has a hard time accepting. In the 1980s he lets it be there, but it can't remain in its original form for long. He noted this procedure to John Cage, using his *String Quartet 2* (composed immediately after *Three Voices*) as his main example:

> Now, what my *String Quartet* [2] is, is a complete disintegration of very beautiful material . . . where things would follow things which before I found unacceptable and now sounded gorgeous. So it's very much like the *I-Ching*, in that I would put one sound against another sound that initially I would not find acceptable. And it winds up toward the end where I'm beginning to accept everything. But I can't go through stages. I can't start at the end like [Francesco] Clemente, you see; I have to start from the beginning, and I then have to kind of plow through every idea to which I decide to give that X-ray scrutiny, and I then disintegrate all the material. So what the material really is, is that it starts out like Proust and winds up like *Finnegans Wake*. And it's very painful and it adds to the beauty of the piece actually. . . . I never really wrote a piece like that, but it seems that the way it was is the complete destroying, so to speak, of all that which say, two or three years ago I would have been so lucky to have had as material.⁷¹

Given his refusal to allow beauty to disintegrate in *Three Voices*, Feldman performs an act of resistant mourning, refusing to allow his friendship with O'Hara to be degraded by memory. Instead, he preserves not only the text of his friend but the sheer beauty of his personage. Resistant mourning, following both Tamara Levitz and Jacques Derrida, is an expressive practice in which the mourner refuses to give up the lost object. Levitz puts it this way: "[the mourner] responsibly and ethically acknowledges the lost object in all perpetuity by allowing it to remain 'other' as memory, distinct from the self, undigested as an encrypted memory."⁷²

Glossing Derrida, Levitz elaborates, noting that this encryption is realized artistically through borrowing: "A writer interiorizes a friend in interminable mourning by using, incorporating, and citing texts by that friend, thereby 'enact[ing] or reenact[ing] an inimitable gesture, a singular way of thinking, a unique manner of speaking' of the deceased."⁷³ Feldman cites poetry by his friend that he had set twenty years before. He supplants his own desire to pursue abstraction and instead accepts the gorgeous music redolent of O'Hara's singularity. Unlike the music for *String Quartet 2*, the music of *Three Voices* refuses to disintegrate or be transformed by Feldman's memory. It insists on being what it is, in all its alterity. In letting it remain *other*, Feldman eschews mastery and lets his loss remain raw and inconsolable.

Informed by La Barbara's compositional aesthetics, her unique vocal timbre, and Feldman's deployment of both, *Three Voices* shows itself to be an intermundane performance of posthumous collaboration. In 1962, O'Hara had wished for himself, Feldman, and Guston to come together again as they had a few years earlier for Feldman's *New Directions in Music*. Through La Barbara's mediumship, O'Hara's hope for collaboration was realized, even after the death of two of the collaborators. But in the end, is this séance successful? As I hear it, three of the four voices supposedly present in *Three Voices* come through: Feldman, La Barbara, and O'Hara. But what of Guston? My reading of *Three Voices* has largely avoided the question of whether or not the work is a suitable memorial for him. It is my wager that despite Feldman's insistence on Guston's presence, his necromantic elegy fails to conjure his friend. Philip remains silent in the tomb. As will become clear in the next chapter, Feldman's mourning of Guston is *always* deferred. In La Barbara's séance, Feldman seems unable to recognize Guston's voice. It is there, it is quiet—hidden behind the camp glamour of O'Hara's. What provoked such difficulties of recognition, and how Feldman finally attempted to overcome them, is the topic to which I now turn.

Notes

1 Robert Motherwell, quoted in Robert Goodnough, ed., "Artists Sessions at Studio 33," in *Reading Abstract Expressionism: Context and Critique*, ed. Ellen G. Landau (New Haven, CT: Yale University Press, 2005), 159.
2 Frank O'Hara, *The Collected Poems of Frank O'Hara*, ed. Donald Allen (Berkeley, CA: University of California Press, 1995), 141.
3 See Ryan Dohoney, *Saving Abstraction: Morton Feldman, the de Menils and the Rothko Chapel* (New York: Oxford University Press, 2019), 48–52.

4 John Cage and Morton Feldman, *Radio Happenings: Conversations/Gespräche, 1966-1967,* ed. Gisela Gronenmeyer and Reinhard Oehlschlägel (Köln: MusikTexte, 2015), 143.

5 Gillian Rose, "Walter Benjamin—Out of the Sources of Modern Judaism," in *Judaism and Modernity: Philosophical Essays* (New York: Verso, 2017), 181.

6 Mark Silverberg has argued that a poetics of process serves as a collective ideal of the New York School *The New York School of Poets and the Neo-Avant-Garde* (Burlington, VT: Ashgate, 2010). While I agree that a poetics and aesthetics of process was a shared interest among poets, composers, and painters, it's important to note that Feldman was, by 1963, ambivalent about "process," saying in an interview with Robert Ashley that "it's not about process, it's about sound" (Morton Feldman and Robert Ashley, "Around Morton Feldman," Morton Feldman Collection, Paul Sacher Foundation, 1963, n.p., 31). Feldman's intensified relationship with "sound itself" in 1963 also led to a deeper engagement with the formalist vocabulary of Clement Greenberg, especially his focus on the notion of surface flatness as an aesthetic value.

7 Will Montgomery, "'In Fatal Winds': Frank O'Hara and Morton Feldman," in *Frank O'Hara Now: New Essays on the New York Poet,* ed. Robert Hampson and Will Montgomery (Liverpool: Liverpool University Press, 2010), 195–210.

8 Lytle Shaw, *Frank O'Hara: The Poetics of Coterie* (Iowa City: Iowa University Press, 2006).

9 Morton Feldman, "Frank O'Hara: Lost Times and Future Hopes," in *Give My Regards to Eighth Street: Collected Writings of Morton Feldman,* ed. B. H. Friedman (Cambridge, MA: Exact Change, 2000), 103.

10 Bruno Latour, *Reassembling the Social: An Introduction to Actor-Network-Theory* (New York: Oxford University Press, 2005), 27–42.

11 Morton Feldman, "Sketchbook 5," 1952, Morton Feldman Collection, Paul Sacher Foundation.

12 Frank O'Hara to Morton Feldman, January 2, 1954, Morton Feldman Collection, Paul Sacher Foundation.

13 Frank O'Hara, "New Directions in Music," in Feldman, *Give My Regards to Eighth Street,* 211–17.

14 *Morton Feldman—New Directions in Music 2.* Columbia Masterworks—MS6090, vinyl. The LP featured performances of numerous Feldman compositions including: *Piece for 4 Pianos, Intersection 3, Projection 4, Two Pieces for Two Pianos, Extensions 1, Structures,* and *Three Pieces for String Quartet.* See also Chapter 1.

15 O'Hara, "New Directions in Music," 211–17. Feldman's recording was reissued on compact disc in 2007 as *John Cage—Music For Keyboard, 1935–1948 / Morton Feldman—The Early Years*, New World Records, 80664-2.
16 Frank O'Hara, *Jackson Pollock* (New York: Braziller, 1959).
17 O'Hara, *The Collected Poems of Frank O'Hara*, 269. For a reading of *The O'Hara Songs*, see Montgomery, "In Fatal Winds," 199–207.
18 Frank O'Hara to Morton Feldman, November 23, 1962, Morton Feldman Collection, Paul Sacher Foundation.
19 Frank O'Hara, *Poems Retrieved*, ed. Donald Allen (San Francisco: Grey Fox Press, 1996), 160.
20 O'Hara to Feldman, November 23, 1962. O'Hara dates the poem December 20, 1956. Feldman's copy varies from the version printed in *Poems Retrieved* in stanzas one and four; the first stanza is markedly different: "How far away and gentle it seems / now the morning misery (s) of childhood / and its raining calm (s) over the schools." Compare with *Poems Retrieved*, 160.
21 I am grateful to David Cline for providing me with a recording of Feldman reading his lecture at the Studio School. Morton Feldman, "Frank O'Hara: Lost Times and Future Hopes" was first published in *Art in America* 60, no. 2 (1972), 52–55.
22 Feldman, "Frank O'Hara," 103.
23 Ibid., 105.
24 O'Hara, *The Collected Poems of Frank O'Hara*, 325.
25 Morton Feldman, Slee Lecture, 1972, Morton Feldman Collection, Paul Sacher Foundation, n.p., 1.
26 On Phillips and *Rothko Chapel* see Chapter 4 in Dohoney, *Saving Abstraction*.
27 Morton Feldman, *Three Clarinets, Cello, and Piano*, compositional sketches, 1972. Morton Feldman Collection, Paul Sacher Foundation, n.p.
28 Morton Feldman, "Give My Regards to Eighth Street," in Feldman, *Give My Regards to Eighth Street*, 196.
29 Franz Kline had died in 1962, and *For Franz Kline* was the first of several pieces by Feldman with such a dedication as the title.
30 For readings of the poem, see Marjorie Perloff, *Frank O'Hara: Poet Among Painters* (New York: Braziller, 1977), 141–46, Nick Selby, "Memory Pieces: Collage, Memorial and the Poetics of Intimacy in Joe Brainard, Jasper Johns and Frank O'Hara," in *Frank O'Hara Now: New Essays on the New York Poet*, eds. Robert Hampson and Will Montgomery (Liverpool: Liverpool University Press, 2010), 229–46; and Shaw, *Frank O'Hara*, 89–98.

31 O'Hara, *The Collected Poems of Frank O'Hara*, 252.
32 Ibid., 253.
33 Selby, "Memory Pieces," 231–43.
34 All my comments here refer to the performance by the Composers Ensemble with Paul Zukofsky conducting. The performers on the recording are Mark van de Wiel, Duncan Prescott, Robert Ault, clarinets; Zoe Martlew, cello; and Catherine Edwards, piano. See *Milton Babbitt: Septet but Equal; Fourplay; Morton Feldman: Instruments 1; Three Clarinets, Cello and Piano*, Composers Ensemble, conducted by Paul Zukofsky, recorded July 20 and 22, 1997, CP²/111, 2003, compact disc.
35 Catherine Costello Hirata, "Analyzing the Music of Morton Feldman," PhD diss., Columbia University, 2003.
36 Morton Feldman, "Studio International Interview," by Fred Orton and Gavin Bryars, in *Morton Feldman Says*, 69.
37 Feldman, "Frank O'Hara," 107.
38 O'Hara, *The Collected Poems of Frank O'Hara*, 201.
39 Feldman, "Frank O'Hara," 106.
40 On *The O'Hara Songs* and Feldman's mournful aesthetics, see Chapter 1 of Dohoney, *Saving Abstraction*.
41 Ben Anderson, "Affective Atmospheres," *Emotion, Space and Society* 2 (2009): 77–81.
42 Morton Feldman, *Morton Feldman in Middelburg: Words on Music, Lectures and Conversations Volume 1*, ed. Raoul Mörchen (Cologne: Musiktexte, 2008), 104.
43 Mikel Dufrenne, *The Phenomenology of Aesthetic Experience*, trans. Edward Casey (Evanston, IL: Northwestern University Press, 1973).
44 Anderson, "Affective Atmospheres," 80. See also Dufrenne, *The Phenomenology of Aesthetic Experience*.
45 D. H. Lawrence, *Studies in Classic American Literature*, eds. Ezra Greenspan, Lindeth Vasey, and John Worthen (1923; Cambridge: Cambridge University Press, 2003).
46 Ibid., 102.
47 Ibid.
48 Jonathan Sterne, *The Audible Past: The Culture Origins of Sound Reproduction* (Durham, NC: Duke University Press, 2002), 287–334.
49 I am grateful to Olivia Cacchione for this insight.
50 Lawrence, *Studies in Classic American Literature*, 102–3.

51 Benjamin Piekut and Jason Stanyek, "Deadness: Technologies of the Intermundane," *TDR: The Dance Review* 54, no. 1 (2010): 20.
52 Scott Klein, "For Frank O'Hara: Morton Feldman's *Three Voices* as Interpretation and Elegy," *Modernist Cultures* 8, no. 1 (Summer 2013): 127. Klein's essay appeared the same year as an earlier version of this chapter. Independent of one another, we each seized upon Feldman's attention to O'Hara's poetics of *sudden death*. He explored it in relation to *Three Voices* while I examined what I've called "posthumous collaborations" in the archival record. My extension of these thoughts to *Three Voices* in this final section is indebted to his insights.
53 Morton Feldman, quoted in Joan La Barbara, "Voice Is the Original Instrument," *Contemporary Music Review* 21, no. 2 (2002): 35.
54 Piekut and Stanyek, "Deadness."
55 Morton Feldman, *Three Voices*. Manuscript. 1982. Paul Sacher Foundation. n.p.
56 Sterne, *The Audible Past*, 290.
57 La Barbara describes the commissioning project in La Barbara, "Voice Is the Original Instrument," 44–45.
58 Joan La Barbara, "Letter to Morton Feldman, May 23, 1981," Morton Feldman Collection, Paul Sacher Foundation.
59 La Barbara, "Voice Is the Original Instrument," 43–44.
60 Ibid., 43.
61 On Electronic Voice Phenomena see Joshua Hudelson, "Spectral Sound: A Cultural History of the Frequency Domain," PhD diss., New York University, 2018, and Anthony Enns, "Voices of the Dead: Transmission/translation/transgression," *Culture, Theory, and Critique* 46, no.1 (2005): 11–27.
62 La Barbara, "Voice Is the Original Instrument," 42–3.
63 Mark Rothko and Adolf Gottlieb, "Rothko and Gottlieb's letter to the editor, 1943," in Mark Rothko, *Writings on Art*, ed. Miguel López-Rimero (New Haven, CT: Yale University Press, 2006), 36.
64 For Feldman's writings on surface, see his "Between Categories," in *Give My Regards to Eighth Street*, 83–89.
65 Morton Feldman, "Toronto Lecture, April 1982," in *Morton Feldman Says*, ed. Chris Villars (London: Hyphen, 2006), 144–5.
66 Feldman, "Toronto Lecture, April 1982," 145.
67 Ibid., 145.

68 John Cage, "July 18, 1992/Cage, Retallack, and Bach," in *Musicage: Cage Muses on Word, Art, Music*, ed. Joan Rettalack (Hanover, NH: University of New Hampshire Press, 1996), 279.
69 Frank O'Hara, "Wind," in *The Collected Poems of Frank O'Hara*, ed. Donald Allen (Berkeley, CA: University of California Press, 1995), 269.
70 Joseph Dubiel, "Uncertainty, Disorientation, and Loss as Responses to Musical Structure," in *Beyond Structural Listening? Postmodern Modes of Hearing*, ed. by Andrew Dell'Antonio (Berkeley, CA: University of California Press, 2004), 173–200.
71 Morton Feldman, John Cage, Bunita Marcus, and Francesco Pellizzi, "Conversation with Morton Feldman (Bunita Marcus and Francesco Pellizzi)," *Res* 6 (Autumn 1983): 129.
72 Tamara Levitz, *Modernist Mysteries: Perséphone* (New York: Oxford University Press, 2012), 480.
73 Ibid., 480–81.

4

"We broke up because of style"

For Hans Thomalla

Friends as ghosts.—If we greatly transform ourselves, those friends of ours who have not been transformed become ghosts of our past: their voice comes across to us like the voice of a shade—as though we were hearing ourself, only younger, more severe, less mature.[1]

Friedrich Nietzsche

We're going to start lifting tables in a minute. A séance.[2]

Philip Guston

In Chapter 1, I held up Guston and Feldman's friendship as a heuristic model for thinking about the broader meaning of friendship in New York School modernism. What revised account of the 1950s, I asked, might emerge from thinking of these artists not as solitary, rugged individuals, but as interdependent intimates, living with and through the work of others? While much of the work of painters, musicians, and writers is in fact solitary—I write these words alone at 5:12 a.m.—there remains the problem of how one sustains the spiritual discipline of creativity outside of working hours. It is obvious by now that my answer to this question is friendship. In this final chapter, I return in greater detail to the friendship of Feldman and Guston—truly one of the greatest and most fraught friendships in modernism—and in doing so draw together the themes explored in the preceding chapters. In the background of this chapter are matters of friendship, anxiety, and mourning that I explored in my book *Saving Abstraction*. There, I focused on Feldman's friendship with and creative empowerment by Mark Rothko. Here, I want to show the relevance of those themes when explored via an in-depth reconstruction of Guston and

Feldman's friendship. Their reciprocal offering of creative sustenance became increasingly unbalanced as their friendship transformed over the years.

I move chronologically, first exploring Feldman's and Guston's entangled lives in the 1950s and 1960s, then tracing the work of mourning each attempted after their friendship ended—including Guston's absorbing of Feldman's image and memory into his new figurative style (see Figure 4.1). I then turn to Feldman's memorialization of Guston after the painter's death in the 1980s to show how Feldman struggled to reconcile himself to his lost friend. In essays, talks, and the five-hour *For Philip Guston*, Feldman continually deferred mourning. Whereas his mourning of Frank O'Hara was *resistant*, Feldman's mourning of Guston was *resisted*—even as he realized that, with his own late style, he was changing as just Guston was changing. I took the first steps in documenting Feldman's attempt at reconciliation in the previous chapter wherein I noted Feldman's failure to conjure Guston in *Three Voices*. There, reconciliation was refracted through Feldman's

Figure 4.1 Renate Ponsold. Morton Feldman and Philip Guston, 1965. Courtesy of the Estate of Philip Guston.

prolonged mourning of the poet-critic Frank O'Hara, a friendship that was never troubled as Feldman and Guston's was. Here, I want to engage the longer *durée* of the relationship between painter and musician to show yet again how mourning friendship is a central—perhaps *the* central—concern of Feldman's musical abstraction.

Feldman met Guston through the mediation of others. His studies with Stefan Wolpe brought him into friendship with John Cage. Cage, with his wide-ranging social network, introduced Feldman to the downtown New York art world, where he made many of his closest artist friends, including Rothko, O'Hara, and numerous others. Before meeting Feldman, Guston was already close to Cage and together they attended D. T. Suzuki's lectures on Zen. Cage brokered their introduction. Feldman recalls seeing Guston's *Red Painting* at the Museum of Modern Art and being wowed by it:

> I'd just met John Cage, and he took me to a fabulous show. It was the first big show of the Abstract Expressionists that Dorothy Miller and Bob [Goodnough] put on. It was an absolutely incredible evening, I was just new to the whole art scene, and one of the few things I still remember—it was 1950 [really, 1951], and I even remember where I was standing. And I remember the first time I saw a painting by Guston. He was the quintessence of what Kierkegaard would define as an artist. Someone who was always in one mood and then another.[3]

Their friendship was one of the great partnerships of modernism—until it wasn't. In the mid-1980s, Feldman remembered (somewhat inaccurately) its end:

> he was ... my closest friend in art. I was in Europe for a year and he was at the Academy of Rome for a year, then I came back and he had a big show. I went down and I was just confronted with a completely new type of work. Before that I was always very supportive—almost to a fault. It was a big show and a glamorous gallery—the Marlborough Gallery—and the place was jammed. I was looking at a picture, he comes over and says, "What do you think?" And I said,
>
> "Well, let me just look at it for another minute." And with that, our friendship was over. We had no contact at all and then I got a call from his daughter ... he died and had a heart attack and on his death bed, I mean, to

make matters worse, he wanted me to come and say Kaddish. So, it's a sad story. What makes it extremely sad is that we broke up because of style. I mean, to me abstract painting and abstract type of music—that was it. There wasn't anything else. In other words, I was the student in advanced middle age, who was just thinking stylistically.[4]

The style Feldman refers to is Guston's late figurative style, which has recently garnered new interest because of its evocation and condemnation of white supremacist violence.[5] For Feldman, who was fully committed to what he called "abstract experience," this return to reference—visual and historical—was too much to bear. It was a betrayal of what they spent the 1950s fighting for. Yet in the 1950s, Guston and Feldman's friendship provided each with mutual support that made their work possible.

Let us return to Guston's words quoted near the opening of Chapter 1: "Would Van Gogh have painted if he'd been all alone, if he had nobody to support him? And I answered that he couldn't have done. He had to have Theo, his brother. . . . So I had Morty. . . . I need Feldman to tell me I'm not insane."[6] Feldman remembered, "We were together all the time in those days. I was around his studio all the time. We'd talk, he'd paint, we'd go to the deli, he'd come back to paint, I'd watch."[7] Feldman's keen observation of Guston's work brought out their shared sensibility. "His real gift was touch," Feldman would note. "He was so careful about how much paint he put on the brush and how much pressure he applied when he put it to the canvas. I loved watching him do it."[8] Statements like these capture the deep intimacy between the two men and highlight Feldman's generosity as a sustaining presence—a presence he would offer Guston for nearly two decades.

Their friendship in the 1950s was conducted in the privacy of the studio or among friends at the Cedar Tavern. There is little contemporary evidence of their conversations and what we do have is filtered through at least a decade of memory. But some traces survive, and these bear witness to the entanglement of their art and life. Dedications are one example—such as Guston's early dedication of an untitled drawing from 1952 inscribed "to Morty". Feldman, who did his own work alone at the piano in his home, inscribed works to Guston as well. Feldman was without a music publisher in the 1950s and his dedications to Guston are found on manuscripts gifted to the painter and preserved by his estate. The earliest extant dedication, on *Extensions 4 for Three Pianos* (1953), is from May 21, 1953. It reads: "This copy for Philip—whose work I love as much as him."[9] He gifted another manuscript in 1956—a movement titled "For String Quartet," which would appear in print as the last movement of *Three Pieces for String Quartet* (1954–6). At the work's conclusion we find, "This composition is dedicated to Philip Guston whose love and respect without which this work would not be possible."[10] We find yet another dedication from 1958 adorning a gift of the ultimately unpublished work "Extensions for Orchestra" (1951), which was inscribed, "To Philip—For himself—his paintings—and his friendship."[11] As these dedications make clear, Guston was not alone in emphasizing intimacy's role in sustaining artistic practice. Moreover, the dedications reveal a marked similarity to Feldman's appreciation of Cage's friendship, for example, "I sometimes wonder how my music would have turned out if John had not given me those early permissions to have confidence in my instincts."[12] Friendship did the important work of helping these men become more themselves by being together. But these processes of self-actualization lead to divergences. Guston recalled of Cage, Feldman, and himself that "in the early fifties we were kind of a trio for a while. . . . John used to come to the studio and talk. Anyway, in the early fifties, John was enthusiastic about my painting."[13] Cage, as is well known, eventually cooled on the work of the Abstract Expressionists. Guston, in turn, took an increasingly harsh view of Cage, whom he found to be "didactic."[14]

That dedication should prove an important genre for Feldman should come as little surprise to us. Feldman made dedication the very substance of composition titles, such as *For Franz Kline*, *For Frank O'Hara*, and *For John Cage*—each gives the dedicatory act pride of place and signals Feldman's participation within a community of artists. Feldman thus continued a practice that has been in place since the emergence of a capitalist market for musical scores and musical performance in the early nineteenth century. As Emily Green has beautifully argued, dedications on published music serve important functions, one of which is the publicizing of the composer's network of relationships. There is no doubt that Feldman's dedicatory titles do this publicity work after 1962, when he received a publishing contract with Edition Peters, and continued when he moved to Universal Edition in 1970.

Green writes of the early nineteenth century that

> dedications were, like late eighteenth-century and early nineteenth-century biography, a way to publicize private relationships and thus contribute to a new model of bourgeois exteriority.... After all, if biographies emphasized the value of sociability to a composer's development and reputation, dedications cemented it. By broadcasting the relationships between composers and others—so-named "friends" in particular—through the meaningful act of the public gift, dedications reduced the self-writing of biographies to a single moment of generosity and friendship.[15]

And it's easy to see something similar in Feldman's titular dedications. Few musicians were as invested in maintaining the boundary of a community and asserting one's privileged position within it as Feldman, who policed the borders of the New York School and celebrated its singularity. Feldman and Guston did not only dedicate works to one another, however. At times, their work came to share titles related to personal references, as in *Last Piece* (1958) by Guston (see Figure. 4.2) and *Last Pieces* (1959) by Feldman. In other instances, records became occasions for interdisciplinary collaborations, as in Feldman's first LP recording, *New Directions in Music 2*, which featured liner notes by Frank O'Hara and Guston's *Head–Double View* as its cover art. (See Chapter 1 for further discussion.) What changed for Guston and Feldman's collaborations after 1970 (after their "break up") was that their works were no longer *for* or *with* the other, but were instead *about* the other—that is, they each become subject matter for artistic practice.

The release of Feldman's first LP marked a significant shift in his public status going into the 1960s. While the 1950s for Guston and Feldman had been about mutual support and the circulation of intimate dedications, the 1960s was a time of celebrating that relationship, publicizing it, and consolidating the gains of the New York School. For Feldman, this meant widening the circulation of his music on recording as well as increasing the availability of his scores through a publication contract for his scores with Edition Peters. The contract was mediated by Cage, who suggested both Feldman and Christian Wolff to Walter Hinrichsen after he had secured a contract for himself.[16] Starting in 1962, Feldman's scores would become widely available—no longer merely traded from musician to musician or personally requested from Feldman by post. Once the

"We broke up because of style" 149

Figure 4.2 Philip Guston, *Last Piece*, 1958. Gouache on board, 22 × 30". Museum of Modern Art. Gift of Edward R. Broida. © The Museum of Modern Art / Licensed by SCALA / Art Resource, NY. © The Estate of Philip Guston, courtesy Hauser & Wirth.

New York Schools of painting, poetry, and music were vindicated by art markets, international music festivals, and college curricula, one's association with it became something to be celebrated and nurtured as valuable cultural capital. And with this newly won publicness, Feldman worked hard to announce his ties. Among the earliest pieces published under his contract with Edition Peters were *For Franz Kline*, *Piano Piece (to Philip Guston)* and *De Kooning*—each bearing witness to private friendships largely invisible to his audiences in the 1950s.

In the 1960s, Feldman also began lecturing widely on music and painting, publishing his writings, and curating shows. Toward the end of the decade, he took on an institutional role as dean of Mercedes Matter's New York Studio School, which brought in Guston as a member of the faculty. The Studio School became an important site for the public performance of Guston and Feldman's friendship—indeed, Guston's statement on his need for Feldman quoted earlier was made in a talk at the Studio School.

Their private conversations continued and we see a change in the dynamic of Guston and Feldman's relationship as the latter takes on a public role in

Figure 4.3 Philip Guston, *Attar*, 1953. Oil on canvas 48½ x 46 in. Private collection. © The Estate of Philip Guston, courtesy Hauser & Wirth.

supporting the former. Guston's need for Feldman's friendship does not diminish—rather, it intensifies as the painter undergoes a radical period of self-doubt and fundamental transformation. We can track these struggles in Guston's letters to and conversations with Feldman throughout the 1960s. For example, Guston wrote to Feldman a week before the opening of "American Abstract Impressionists and Imagists," mounted at the Guggenheim Museum between October 13 and December 31, 1961. "I did some paintings I like, finally," he wrote. "Three or four. One went to the Guggenheim show opening next week. Everything but what is relevant has been cut out of the new work. The figures are all above now, dumb, and the stage is very bare."[17] We can infer from Guston's comments that he is referring to the austere abstractions of the early 1960s, in which black forms come to inhabit gray fields. Also of interest is the theatrical language of action and acting Guston shared with his friend

Harold Rosenberg. As Guston stated in 1959, "I think of painting more in terms of the drama of this process than I do of 'natural forces.'"[18] In Rosenberg's terms, Guston's paintings are "Dramas As If," which Robert Slifkin describes in nuanced terms (see Figure 4.3):

> As metaphors for a living situation ("Dramas As If"), action paintings had the potential for social or political agency, perhaps even the power to affect life and break down the aesthetic boundary between the theatrical canvas and the empathetic viewer. . . . This dramatic understanding of action painting, in which artifice and performance rather than physical gesticulation and psychological disclosure motivate the final image in the work of art, challenges the simplified misunderstanding of Rosenberg's concept as purely physical and improvisatory, and invites the recognition of a work like *Attar* [which Feldman owned], and all the works Guston made between 1955 and 1966 as action paintings—which is how Rosenberg understood them.[19]

Guston's impulse in the early 1960s is toward a reduction of means in order to intensify the relational dynamic of his paintings—between painter and canvas, as well as between canvas and viewer. This was something that Feldman perceptively noted about Guston's work, that they "perform" and "engulf"—that is to say, *they act*.[20] His experience of viewing *Attar* is a case in point:

> As I write, *Attar* is hanging on the other side of my room. I have the feeling that if I moved it to another wall, it would be an entirely different painting. It seems to be reflecting rather than ordinating phenomena. As the tones vibrate, they recede beneath the pigment and return, but with another bowing. In music we would say the sound was sourceless due to the minimum of attack. This explains the painting's complete absence of weight. But the sensation of what you see not coming from what is seen is characteristic of all Guston's work.[21]

Feldman went on to link Guston's liquidating methods to his personality: "Very little pleased him. Very little satisfied him. Very little was art. Always aware in his own work of the rhetorical nature of the complication, Guston reduces, reduces, building his own Tower of Babel and then destroying it."[22] Yet, this pleasure in a newly intensified theatricality provides little protection against the intergroup agonism Guston felt for his friends. Again writing to

Feldman, Guston turns against their mutual friends and himself in the days following the show's opening:

> Dear Morty—
>
> I am writing you this so you won't waste money on a phone call—when I came home here I broke down with anger, disgust and frustration about everything in N.Y. Got sick and am nursing myself in bed. I've got to come in Friday or Saturday and settle matter once and for all with Janis and the Guggenheim. I feel like a cripple in the midst of all that slick, inhuman elegance the boys are grinding out, including de Kooning and Kline, etc and I have to separate myself from it. It's silly to burden you with all this I know, but I wanted to let you know that I am in this state and I must do something about it, if I want to continue working. Also I have to start on my loft. I'll see you soon.
>
> Love. Philip[23]

In his rejection of de Kooning and Kline's "slick inhuman elegance" we can hear an early expression of Guston's rejection of *purity*—his oft-repeated rationale for turning to figuration in 1968. Such criticism of the *inhuman* in art reiterates the importance he placed on intersubjectivity and drama. But it also recognizes the fragility of these qualities when art is put into circulation. In response to his friends "grinding out" one canvas after another, Guston retreated and unburdened his heart to Morty. Even as their coterie became more public and their art found success, the mutual support that allowed each to do their work in the 1950s remained essential, especially as Guston began to estrange himself from the New York School.

As their private colloquies continued in person and by post, Feldman took on a pronounced role as spokesman for his friends. Guston shows up regularly in the musician's major writings from the 1960s—in liner notes to his split LP with Earle Brown, in the existential manifesto "Vertical Thoughts," in the anti-system polemic "Predeterminate/Indeterminate," in the nuanced appreciation "Philip Guston: The Last Painter," as well as in "Some Elementary Questions" and the major historiographical intervention "After Modernism." Feldman, as I noted earlier, was a keen interpreter of Guston's work, recognizing its dramatic, even public qualities of narration. But he also charged it with metaphysical import as he does in "Vertical Thoughts":

> For Guston art at its inception is synonymous with an all-powerful dynamic in nature rather than a man-made history disguised as nature. His sole problem is not in relating man to art, but art to man. With Guston, then, art must have its fall. Like an ancient Talmudist he endeavors to find out within his conscience the why of its perpetual undoing.[24]

Guston's Jewish heritage becomes a key interpretive guide for Feldman as he articulates both the spirituality of the painter's practice ("like an ancient Talmudist") as well as Guston's relationship to history. We can see the tack he takes toward the latter in "Philip Guston: The Last Painter" from 1966:

> Guston is of the Renaissance. Instead of being allowed to study with Giorgione, he observed it all from the ghetto in the marshes outside of Venice where the old iron works were. I know he was there. Due to circumstance, he brought that art into the diaspora with him. That is why Guston's painting is the most peculiar history lesson we have ever had.[25]

Feldman seems to mark Guston as a Wandering Jew—an archetype that Dore Ashton would apply to Feldman himself—moving across time and space, from Renaissance Venice to modernist New York.[26] The migration has not left "that art" of the Early Modern unchanged, but has rather made it an individual idiom saturated with history and mediated by personal technique. The personal gesture, and its ability to capture—in Feldman's terms, borrowing from Kierkegaard—"the Instant," is observable in the work of Guston's beloved Piero della Francesca. Feldman writes that Piero's work

> has never lost its intense focus on the particular moment. It hasn't grown old and finally dropped dead of culture. At the exact moment, probably before it was seen or heard by anyone else, the artist in some mysterious way embalmed it. When della Francesca painted the cross in the background, it had nothing to do with subjectivity, or objectivity—it was *memory*.[27]

This curious quality of deep historical memory—a reservoir of transhistorical experience—is what Feldman also finds in Guston's ingrained experiences of Jewish ghetto life. This historical sense is sedimented in painterly technique. Feldman made this point more clearly when contrasting Guston with Picasso:

> On yet another level, Guston's conflict is between the personal, which is anti-process, and the impersonal, which is process. Where he differs from a painter like Picasso is that with Guston the historical is not an analysis of history, but a sort of distillation of hundreds of years of seeing, touching, observing, watching, waiting, deciding. Where Picasso analyzes, Guston continues. Where Picasso is saturated in a history lesson, Guston is saturated in history.[28]

History is stripped down, reduced, and even *embalmed*. This mortuary interpretation returns us to the themes of the previous chapter wherein we see Feldman valuing art inasmuch as it is *like death*. As he did with Frank O'Hara, Feldman finds the spirituality of Guston's work precisely in its morbidity:

> Guston tells us he does not finish a painting but "abandons it." At what point does he abandon it? Is it perhaps at the moment when it might become a "painting"? After all, it's not a "painting" that the artist really wanted. There is a strange propaganda that because someone composes or paints, what he necessarily wants is music or a picture. Completion is not in tying things up, not in "giving one's feelings," or "telling a truth." Completion is simply the perennial death of the artist. Isn't any masterpiece a death scene? Isn't that why we want to remember it, because the artist is looking back on something when it's too late, when it's all over, when we see it finally, as something we have lost?[29]

Feldman, as he does throughout his authorship, emphasizes loss in his experiences with art. He poetically referred to this affect as "the departing landscape"—that tendency of true artistic (i.e., *abstract*) experience to recede from us.[30] He described Guston's art in just such terms: "the paintings often 'perform' only as the viewer begins to leave them."[31] The question of a painting's completion dogged Guston, and his comments from the 1960s resonate with Feldman's subsequent interpretations, though he did not share Feldman's focus on death. Yet we do find him expressing a concern with historical feeling. In a talk at the Philadelphia Museum School of Art in 1960 (subsequently published in the abstract expressionist journal *It is.*), Guston linked the matter of finishing with a painting's historical sense: "The pressing thing for me in painting is 'When are you through?' I would like to think a picture is finished when it feels not new but old. As if its forms had lived a long time in you, even though until it appears you did not know what it would look like."³² In a brief essay in *Art News Annual* from 1965/66, Guston returns to the question of completion but makes its deferral a condition of living: "When do you stop? Or rather, why stop at all? But you have to rest somewhere. Of course, you can stay on one surface all your life, like Balzac's Frenhofer. And all your life's work can be seen as one picture—but that is merely 'true.' There *are* places where you pause."³³ Feldman's essay "Philip Guston: The Last Painter" appeared in the same issue of *Art News Annual* and expressed the continuity of life and work similarly, though described through the metaphor of (Talmudic?) exegesis:

> Each of Guston's paintings is a sentence, neither negating the last, nor redeeming the next. At what point do we break into this discourse? At what point can we withdraw, at the risk of missing any part of the fevered commentary? Willem de Kooning once said it is his final stroke that makes the picture. With Guston's final painting, all his work will be at rest.³⁴

Guston's painterly furor will end only with his death. The pairing of Guston's and Feldman's essays within *Art News Annual* provided a very public display of the friends' private conversations, debates, and interpretations. It also authorized Feldman to speak on Guston's behalf and legitimized his views on his friend's work. Guston himself published only two brief essays in the 1960s, both written in 1965: "Faith, Hope, and Impossibility" (quoted earlier) and "Piero della Francesca: The Impossibility of Painting."³⁵ His voice was otherwise heard in published interviews with trusted friends such as Bill Berkson and Harold Rosenberg. In taking on the role of spokesman, Feldman produced a shift in the dynamics of their relationship—one that transformed his private emotional support into public boosterism. Guston, however, did not comment on Feldman's music in print, nor, as far as I have seen, anywhere else. It is an open question how much of Feldman's music Guston heard and what he made of it. In a late interview, when asked if Guston was interested in his music, Feldman was equivocal, "He said he was, but who knows."³⁶

Instituting the New York School: Mercedes Matter, Feldman, Guston, and the Studio School

Despite such uncertainties, Feldman continued his support for Guston as their careers prospered in the 1960s. I've described this process thus far as a matter of increased *publicness*—that is, what was a private world of conversation, art, and music was commodified, circulated, and promoted by galleries, magazines, publishing houses, and record companies. Another institution that brought Feldman and Guston's friendship into public view was the New York Studio School. Feldman and Guston both served on the faculty and their lectures and conversations offered up their support of one another as a pedagogical model for young artists. This served the larger project of the Studio School, which made the working methods and artistic practices of the New York School painters into a curriculum—one that valued painterly furor and friendly conversation.

Feldman's role at the Studio School has been occasionally mentioned but rarely elaborated upon. Because of its relative absence from discussions of his (and Guston's) life, it merits some historical commentary. This scene of Feldman's teaching was (and remains today) one of the more remarkable arts institutions in the nation. The New York Studio School to this day proudly associates with Feldman, noting his importance both as a regular lecturer in the 1960s and as dean from 1968 to 1971. His longtime friend Mercedes Matter—whose husband Herbert Matter we met back in Chapter 2—founded the school with a group of disaffected art students from the Pratt Institute. These students were frustrated with the academic requirements that kept them out of the studio. In Feldman's terms, we might understand these students as desiring to pursue the anxiety of art. With an emphasis on studio practice, Matter formalized a curriculum that eschewed conceptual and critical frameworks that are today commonplaces of art education.[37] This emphasis on immersion in creative action is no doubt a legacy of Matter's and Feldman's vitalist and existentialist commitments, stretching back to Matter's own training with Hans Hofmann in the 1930s.

Matter laid out her pedagogical ideals in a 1963 manifesto titled "What's Wrong with U.S. Arts Schools?" She critiqued at least two aspects of art education in the university. Based on her own experience teaching at the Pratt

Institute in Brooklyn, she described the scene as a kind of enforced technical and stylistic pluralism beholden to modernist teleology: "The extraordinary kaleidoscope of events of the twentieth century, of movements following so closely one upon another, of extremes absurd and great, of ideas canceling each other out and of recurrent Dada and anti-art, all this breaks at [the artist's] feet in waves of cynicism, jaded feeling and no-belief."[38] Art is a matter of faith and value for Matter. She advocated, as Feldman later did, for art education to care for one's artistic self. She highlights ascetic aspects of the training once available at the academy:

> The atmosphere was one of silence, remote from the world. A dim cold light filtered down from the skylights high above, gently illuminating the lifeless surfaces of the casts and the immobile figure of the model; dust gathered on the still-lifes softly harmonizing their colors; times seemed to stand still. All of this, of course, has been swept away to fit the pace of the times. The new art school upholds the Tradition of the New—it dare not slip a moment behind the avant-garde.[39]

Central to her critique is her diagnosis of the horizontal expansion of pedagogy: "Learning is thus spread out on an ever-widening thin surface, sacrificing depth to breadth not of experience, since this is precisely what it excludes, but of activity." In its stead, Matter advocates for a new vertical pedagogy—training that affords silence and is attentive to "the central motivation which is the experience of an individual and the necessity this gives rise to, in him, to understand his means of expression." There is in Matter's critique an anti-conceptualism that resonates powerfully with Feldman (of a piece with the vitalism discussed in Chapter 2). In place of concepts, Matter emphasizes expression: "not the intellectual's pure curiosity for knowledge but a more focused pursuit of a particular scent born of his necessity at the time."[40] The "exacting labor of self-confronting" is what an art school should make possible for young artists: "Conditions should allow the student to develop the self-generating vitality that comes from the quality of the work being done."[41] In this final statement, Matter makes clear her continued investment in vitalist metaphysics. Feldman himself would translate this ascetic rigor into a pedagogical pursuit of anxiety.

Matter's manifesto provided the core tenets of the Studio School's curriculum: long hours of unimpeded studio time, affirmative contact with artists (such as

Feldman and Guston) who would reflect on their own creative practices, and regular lectures in art history offered by Meyer Shapiro (who articulated the powerful relationship between friendship and creative spontaneity discussed in Chapter 1). Matter and a handful of her students left Pratt in 1964 and inhabited a "drab, downtown loft" before later moving into the old Whitney Museum on 8th Street in 1965.[42] During the transition to the Whitney building, the board of the Studio School, led by Matter, made an appeal to the Ford Foundation that crystalized the school's values: the school was "one small but determined effort—amidst the vulgarization and dehumanization of modern life—to preserve art as a precious value and influence which remains incorruptible, inviolate."[43] This language trades in familiar tropes of cultural patrimony and protectionism, but maintains an oppositional stance resonant with the New York School's politics, especially resistance to the dehumanization and deadening of sensation fomented by modern capitalist culture. Naturally, as a document requesting much-needed support for a fledgling project, it was in the board's interests to make their case as starkly as possible; though it is apparent that the high-temperature, existential rhetoric and cultural critique of the Eighth Street Artists Club required little change to make an urgent case for funding from one of the major Cold War-era philanthropic organizations promoting US values. Matter had put this in starker anticapitalist terms in her manifesto where she railed against education "tak[ing] on the familiar, unctuous voice of America selling people what they do not need."[44] Matter argues that ascetic repetition—the kind valued by both Feldman and Guston—was an antidote: "To foster [the student's intrinsic growth], the daily life of the school is kept very simple, even monotonous, in the continuation of the same work. The aim is to avoid the alienation of self brought about by fragmentation."[45] Such fragmentation was the effect of training received elsewhere.

Feldman's association with the school began in 1965 when he delivered "The Anxiety of Art." He gave regular lectures at least through 1969 and organized concerts as well. He also participated in conversations with other artists, including long discussions with Guston. Feldman's talks—which included "Frank O'Hara: Lost Times and Future Hopes," "Give My Regards to Eighth Street," the aforementioned "The Anxiety of Art," and a series of lectures titled "New York Style"—emphasized the importance of anxiety in artistic work.

These talks helped shape the metaphysical tenor of the school, infusing its creative vitalism with a fraught existentialism.

As dean, Feldman continued to lecture and took on the role of fundraiser, making appeals to the Ford and Rockefeller Foundations as well as leveraging his warm relationship with John de Menil to secure the latter's place on the board of the Studio School. De Menil took the role seriously and served from 1969 until his death in 1973.[46] Feldman's time at the Studio School marked his emergence as a more public artist. A Guggenheim Fellowship in 1967 meant that he could be a composer full-time; his deanship, beginning in 1968, meant that he could work with artists and friends; and the rest of his career was comprised of high-profile grants and teaching positions at the University of Buffalo and Cal Arts. But of these opportunities, the Studio School alone mediated between the intimacies of the 1950s and the public demands made of him and his friends in the 1960s. To succeed in its mission, the Studio School depended upon Feldman and Guston making their friendship public for students and strangers, thus serving as a model of how to live as anxious artists.

Two recordings held in the library of the Studio School—later transcribed for Guston's collected writings—document how the pair's friendship figured in the life of the school beyond their role as faculty. The earlier recording, from 1967, is a brief commentary on Feldman offered by Guston (addressed in Chapter 1). In it, Guston expresses his "need" for Feldman "to tell me I'm not insane. He has a way of seeing which always more than fascinates me. I mean, it really involves me, how he sees."[47] Guston went on to recount a recent trip to Florida and an artistic crisis that ensued:

> And this winter Feldman was in Texas and I was in Florida, and again I'm going through some kind of changes and so on. I was doing a lot of drawings and I was really distressed. I was down to a line, a couple of lines. And he called from Texas and said, "I'd like to come and visit you." And I said, "Oh, I'm going crazy, I'm down to one line." He said, "Hold that line. I'll be right there." He was in Houston and he was on the way home, but he came to seem me down there on the Gulf of Mexico. I picked him up at the airport, and all these drawings were on the walls and he didn't say anything. After dinner we went walking along the seashore in the Florida moonlight. And I said,

"What do you think of these new things?" And he said, "You know the last trick of Houdini was that he locked himself in a trunk, they threw away the key and then threw the trunk off the Brooklyn Bridge, and he got out." And then there was a long pause. We walked another five minutes and he said, "But you haven't thrown away the key."

So you can tell what I feel about Feldman. He's a remarkable man.[48]

The 1960s brought crisis after crisis for Guston. We saw above his disgust with de Kooning and Kline at the beginning of the decade and his period of social estrangement. (He would also separate from his wife, Musa, for much of the 1960s). The path of reduction—down to a bare stage leaving him making single lines—commenced in 1961. And again he turns to Feldman. The foregoing episode leaves out the details of why Feldman was in Houston: he had just completed a residency at the University of St. Thomas sponsored by John and Dominique de Menil. There, with Dominique, he curated *Six Painters*, which featured a number of Guston's works (including his untitled drawing from 1952 dedicated "to Morty"). Feldman also spoke extensively on Guston's work in his lectures there, including his major statement on Mondrian, Rothko, and Guston, "After Modernism."[49] These events further confirm Feldman's dedicated support of Guston in public and private.

The Florida meeting remained on their minds in their 1968 conversation at the Studio School attended by Mercedes Matter and students.[50] Feldman brought it up, recalling that when looking at the new line drawings, Guston had said, "It's all rhetoric. . . . You see that line? And you see that line a little bit on top of it? Well, that line on top of it is talking into the ear of that bottom line, telling him its troubles."[51] Their conversation circles around such questions of rhetoric, reference, and visuality. Guston saw these problems as fundamental to the work of the Studio School and charged the collective artistic enterprise with the work of "bearing witness": "I always say that unless you want to dedicate your life to bearing witness, which is really what it's about, if you know what I mean, you're in the wrong art school. You'd just as well go to a place where you can work with company personnel."[52] Just *how* one should bear witness, however, becomes a point of disagreement between Feldman and Guston. While the painter frames his art as a self-revelatory poetics and communication, the musician rejects predetermined modes of communication—that is, musical language *as such*:

> Well, if I tell him [pointing to a student] to make a sound and him [pointing to another student] to make a sound, any sounds to be presented in an audible reality, that immediately becomes the language, you see. Then immediately I'm involved with history. In relation to that language, I cannot escape both the reality of the sound I hear and the reality of the history, the audible history which it comes from. That is I can't make my sound the way you [Guston] would go with your charcoal.[53]

Somewhat exasperated, Guston asks him, "What do you want?" to which Feldman responds, "I want a kind of insanity. I want to go like this and I want you to hear something not coming from your references, coming over from fifteen hundred years of goddamned references."[54] Feldman wants insanity, but also the impossible. Though he aspires to make immediate marks as Guston does with his charcoal, Guston himself aruges that such marks are always rhetorical, intersubjective, and freighted with meanings inherent or applied. Guston throughout the talk is conciliatory, but he is resolute in his loss of faith in abstraction:

> I feel I find total recognition in what you say, because I finally reached the point in these "essences," these "abstractions," that were of such essence that it drove me crazy. There was nothing to do with it. So it's as if then I have to immerse myself again, you might say, in the multitudinousness of forms. . . . But the abstract experience you've written about, Morty . . . It's a very nerve-wracking thing. It's to be pursued. It's the only thing you pursue but it's ineffable. . . . It eludes and eludes and eludes. It's a very difficult thing to work with, because there's nothing to work with. Or everything to work with, of course. I mean, it's always on the brink.[55]

Guston rejects abstract experience, likening it to a pursuit of essences—those markers of the "slick inhuman elegance" produced by his New York School coterie. In the remainder of the conversation with Feldman he details his experiments in figuration and symbolism, saying of his drawings, "I put one up. It looks like a pyramid! It looks like the Parthenon and a pyramid."[56] What these moments suggests—as Feldman's near-silence for the remainder of the conversation also does—is that the seeds of their friendship's destruction were planted already in 1968, perhaps at the very moment when Guston rejected abstract experience. In response to Guston's revelations, Feldman simply says, "in music it comes out kind of like a kitsch."[57] Regardless, Guston goes into such detail about what he does—his sketches of paint cans, his "drawing like a primitive," his "toilet drawings"—that Feldman had to know what was happening. Guston had given up the pursuit of anxiety.

Perhaps sensing a need for reparation, Guston wrote Feldman shortly after their conversation,

> I am still contemplating your whole idea of Surface—I find so much recognition in what you are saying. Now that I've said all this, I think about the piece on Frank [O'Hara]—your thoughts on creation and death (towards the end of the piece) and I could easily feel that I am more moved by this piece! What I really want to tell you is that it is my great ~~good~~ fortune that you exist and continue to carry the burden of that which is life itself to the artist. I am grateful and inspired.[58]

Guston reiterates his gratitude—and indeed his need—for Feldman's friendship as well as for the continued inspiration of his ideas of surface and the importance of death to artistic work. Yet no mention is made of Guston's current work. For knowledge of that, Feldman would have to wait until his friend's next big show—his first at the Marlborough Gallery—in 1970.

Guston's Mourning of Feldman

After the collapse of their friendship, Guston told stories about it. Obliquely refracted through a repertoire of personal references, he kept Feldman in mind. This keeping-in-mind was done on Guston's terms and mediated through his vivid late style. In the aphorism that serves as this chapter's first epigraph, Nietzsche writes, "If we greatly transform ourselves, those friends of ours who have not been transformed become ghosts of our past: their voice comes across to us like the voice of a shade—as though we were hearing ourself, only younger, more severe, less mature."[59] Guston indeed greatly transformed himself, and Feldman, with his unyielding commitment to abstraction, becomes a shadowy

"We broke up because of style" 163

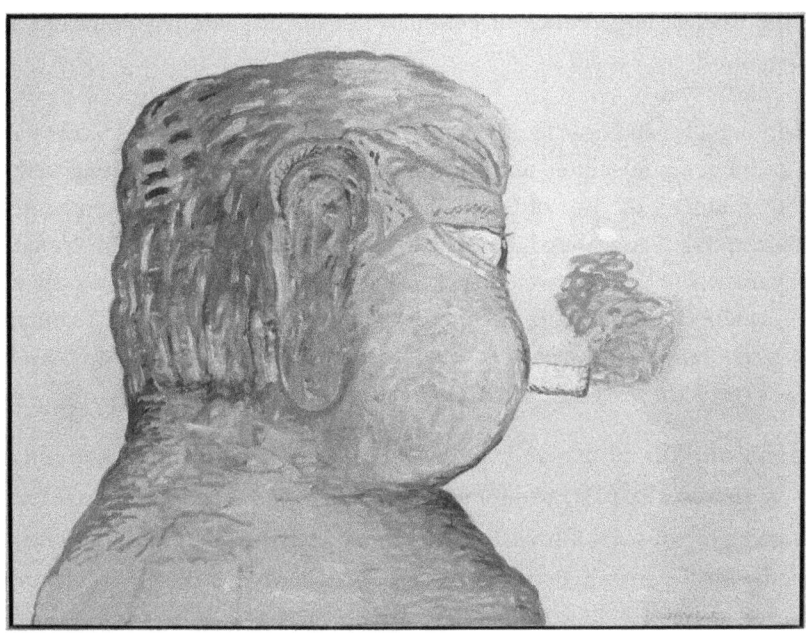

Figure 4.4 Philip Guston, *Friend—To M.F.*, 1978. Oil on canvas; 68 × 88". Purchased with funds from the Nathan Emory Coffin Collection of the Des Moines Art Center, 1991.48. Photo Credit: Rich Sanders. © The Estate of Philip Guston, courtesy Hauser & Wirth.

ghost of Guston's past. Yet Guston couldn't forget him. Feldman, or at least his image, stayed with him.

Beginning in the mid-1970s, Feldman begins to appear as a spectral presence in Guston's art—first in Guston's *Allegory* (1975) and most explicitly in *Friend—To M.F.* (see Figure 4.4) from 1978. Guston's friend Ross Feld described *Friend* as "a picture composed out of pain plus a startling concentration of simple adult resignation."[60] Its color palette calls back to *Attar*—the painting Feldman owned—with its oranges and pinks. Feld elaborated: "As still and frozen as a Piero in its way, the remarkable, almost helmet-like Feldman hair is captured in the front while the back of the head begins looking very mineral indeed, that solidified-blood-look that Guston used so effectively."[61] Ironic, then, that a work documenting personal trauma in a style Feldman rejected has graced so many album covers as well as the covers of Feldman's collected writings. Yet, it is neither the only nor the earliest appearance of Feldman in Guston's late paintings. As Feld remembered:

> Paintings of coats began to appear [in the middle 1970s]. Feldman's father was a garment manufacturer, and Guston delightedly used to tell of long walks with Feldman, the two of them talking about Valéry but being eminently interruptible when they happened to go by the old S. Klein's-on-Union-Square, where Feldman would duck inside to handle a sleeve, to comment on a garment's workmanship. These coat paintings were paintings of Feldman as well—Feldman as *schneider*, the Jewish artist, tailor of the goods. And, like *Friend*, they were done during the men's long estrangement.[62]

Guston's work to mourn and preserve Feldman's friendship was predicated on a return to the past, to memories of the 1950s when they would walk, talk, go to movies, eat Chinese food—those activities that restored Guston's capacity for intense artistic work. The image of the coat, as Feld notes, takes on particular significance as a figure of memory. It is a synecdoche not only of Feldman's presence but also of their spontaneous, life-giving conversations so essential to Guston's creative practice. A conjuration trick, Guston's painting—through the figuration of Feldman's overcoat (which we can see in Renate Ponsold's photograph of Feldman in Figure 4.1)—attempts to recapture their time together even as it mourns the impossibility of its recovery. Feldman is there as a ghost—his jacket appears on the canvas as if animated in a furtive séance.

Reflecting on one of these paintings, Guston's *The Coat II* (see Figure 4.5), I'm struck by the emotional importance of clothes within New York School modernism. Guston's coats resonate with the poem "Joe's Jacket" by O'Hara. In it, O'Hara apostrophizes the seersucker coat of his lover/roommate/friend Joe LeSueur:

> I borrow Joe's seersucker jacket though he is still asleep I start out
> when I last borrowed it I was leaving there it was on my Spanish plaza back
> and hid my shoulders from San Marco's pigeons was jostled on the Kurfürstendamm
> and sat opposite Ashes in an enormous leather chair in the Continental
> it is all enormity and life it has protected me and kept me here on
> many occasions as a symbol does when the heart is full and risks no speech

Figure 4.5 Philip Guston, *The Coat II*, 1977. Anderson Collection at Stanford University, Gift of Harry W. and Mary Margaret Anderson, and Mary Patricia Anderson Pence, 2014.1.047. Collection of Harry W. and Mary Margaret Anderson. © The Estate of Philip Guston, courtesy Hauser & Wirth.

> a precaution I loathe as the pheasant loathes the season and is preserved
> it will not be need, it will be just what it is and just what happens[63]

Joe's jacket is for O'Hara a reservoir of memory as well as armor with which to face the humdrum workday which contrasts so starkly with the exuberant, boozy weekend in Southampton with friends that preceded it. As Marjorie Perloff argues it, Joe's jacket is "the talisman that protects Frank from daily misfortunes; as a synecdoche, it stands, of course, for Joe's love. But Frank also resents its protection ('a precaution I loathe'), and in a second, ironic sense, Joe's jacket is his straitjacket. . . . The jacket is, then, an ordering principle which the poet alternately needs and resents."[64] Given the emergence of the coat as a figure in Guston's work from 1977 until his death, he, like his friend O'Hara, treated it as a synecdoche for an absent presence reactivated by memory. Guston's paintings *The Coat*, *The Coat II*, and *Room and Sea* (1978) form an imaginary triptych in which we are presented with a garment that recalls not only Feldman's penchant for natty clothes but also his and Guston's long walks through the city.

With Feld's insight into the coat as figure for Feldman, we have ample evidence to look further into Guston's late oeuvre and suss out other places where Feldman may reside. In *Back View* (see Figure 4.6) and *Back View II*, both from 1977, the coat now covers a human figure, who is likely Feldman himself. In both *Back View* paintings we find the "solidified-blood-look" back of the head that appears in *Friend—To M.F.*

Looking at *Back View*, I am reminded of a line Feldman used in relation to Guston's abstract work and its association with Jewish esotericism: "God exists, but is turned away from us."[65] Guston seems to be taking up the theme of abandonment—but with friendship as his subject. Here, the coat is no longer a nostalgic sign of better times, but instead covers the body of a departing friend. In these paintings Guston carries over a profound theme from his abstract work: our relationship to the other is fragile and constantly at risk of estrangement. With our biographical knowledge of both Feldman and Guston, *Back View* feels like a condemnation of Feldman's perceived rejection. But as

Figure 4.6 Philip Guston, *Back View*, 1977. Oil on canvas; 69 × 94". San Francisco Museum of Modern Art, Gift of the artist. © The Estate of Philip Guston, courtesy Hauser & Wirth.

part of Guston's allegorical storytelling, there is more going on than simple personal score-settling.

For instance, what of the feet caught beneath the coat-clad figures arms? I get the disconcerting feeling that this figure—*Feldman*—is dragging bodies toward the viewer through a red sea—a common figure in late Guston that is the site of suffering and violence. The presence of massed bodies (hinted at in the stacked feet and blood-dappled legs) uncomfortably entangles Feldman within the broader ethical and (self-)critical mythos of Guston's paintings in the 1970s. If this is indeed Feldman, then we see that their friendship—its memorialization and failure—saturate the stories Guston was telling in his late work, where ethical ambivalence and radical potential for self-loss to fascism always looms. Thus the need to constantly bear witness to that ambivalence and keep everyone (including oneself) on the hook. Feldman himself becomes entangled in masses of bodies. In the paintings *Pink Sea* (1978) and *Group in Sea* (1979), no longer the violent actor, Feldman himself is subjected to violence, his head piled up with other heads.[66]

This series, stretching from *The Coat* to *Group in Sea*, shows us how completely Feldman was absorbed into Guston's new world. Where Guston had drawn upon Feldman's ideas of abstract experience to nurture his art and had depended upon his companionship to sustain his creative spontaneity, after the 1970s Feldman's memory remains a necessary other that helps Guston do his work. Understood as such, these paintings enact a tragic reconciliation in which Guston comes to terms with the past. This reconciliation does not paper over the rupture of Feldman and Guston's friendship, but it allows for a reconfigured relationship between them, moving from the personal to the allegorical. In doing so, the absent friend is absorbed into the new idiolect, the "style" that the other developed. Feldman and Guston's tensions resonant with Maurice Blanchot's agonistic figuration of friendship: "friendship of the one for the other, as passage and as affirmation of a continuity that takes off from the necessary discontinuity."[67] It is the necessary discontinuity—Feldman's prolonged silence at the Marlborough show—that set into motion the tragic continuities we find in Guston's paintings of his last decade. Feldman is resurrected, condemned, and mourned.

Feldman's Mourning and Melancholia

Feldman and Guston spoke rarely, if at all, after the Marlborough show. Despite this near-silence, Guston continued their decades-long intellectual exchange. In a public talk on "survival" from 1974, he spoke of his affection for Feldman in the present tense:

> I can't explain Morty's music, other than that I'm involved with it and have been for a long time. . . . I'm devoted to his music, as I'm devoted to his mind. I'm fond of him personally. And of course he's one of the two or three people who respond to my work. That seem related to me or to how it feels to myself. And also on whom I depend a great deal.[68]

This devotion was spectral, however, and as I have argued earlier, Guston depended upon Feldman as a figure in his image repertoire. In private, to his friend Clark Coolidge, Guston was more forthcoming about his frustration with Feldman.

> Guston: My painting of the object has to do with the frustration of not being able to paint the object . . . I would say that the frustration is a crucial ingredient here. . . . It's the resistance. It's the frustration of the desire to not paint altogether. That is to say, art is the frustration of the desire *not* to make art, you know? . . . And the trouble with that . . . I've had my lonely winter nights worrying about that, those two lines . . .
> Coolidge: That *is* the desire to make art.
> Guston: That's right. And that's why I had to give it up. That makes art too available to me. And that's where my fight with Feldman is, and he knows it and that's why he won't call me. He wants me to do *that*.
> Coolidge: Well, that's what I meant. He loved that, right?
> Guston: That's right. And he wants art.
> Coolidge: You were in hell, and he was loving that.
> Guston: He was loving it. And he wants art. And I don't want to be an artist really. But I am and I'm going to be and I want to make these forms.[69]

This conversation turns on a matter raised in Feldman and Guston's conversation at the Studio School. There Guston detailed his new interest in "the multitudinousness of forms," and his rejection of "abstract experience"—that mode of artistic creation Feldman defined as being grounded in anxiety and risk (being "in hell"). Guston has clearly had enough of such existentialist claptrap and instead began to work in productive tension with the world and its objects. Seeping through Guston's reflections is the vitriol we find in *Back View* through *Group in Sea*.

In the 1970s, Feldman spoke of Guston's importance to his past but was less reluctant to go on record with their difficulties. He gave an account of their break-up to Fred Orton and Gavin Bryars:

> I don't see Guston any more, things kind of cooled off. You know there is a great line of Frank O'Hara's where he says "I'm the most reasonable of men: all I want is unbounded love," some fabulous remark like that. And Guston was always like that in my life. He was very reasonable but, boy, was he demanding. When his work started going into this new period I saw it the first time in his studio. I looked at it a long time and just couldn't say anything about it. He was a little upset that I didn't give him this instant enthusiasm.[70]

Guston and Feldman frame the matter differently: for Guston, the matter is one of intellectual disagreement; for Feldman, Guston at last demanded too much from him. It is possible to sympathize with Feldman, given the sheer range of support he offered his friend over the years, from his encouraging presence in the studio to his enthusiastic public pronouncements on the work to his willingness to come when called. The balance of the friendship and its demands titled in Guston's favor—or at least that is how Feldman interpreted it in the 1970s.

Guston would make one last demand on Feldman when he suffered a debilitating heart attack in 1979. During his recovery, Guston took a yellow note pad and made a number of requests in the event of his death. One of these was that Feldman—along with Ross Feld and the novelist Philip Roth—say Kaddish over his grave. Feldman granted this last wish and came down from Buffalo for the funeral in 1980.

Feld's memoir records the awkwardness with which Guston's family and friends reintegrated Feldman into their world. It was to repair their personal estrangement, but Feldman took the opportunity to reconcile himself to Guston's late work. Feld recalled that:

> [Feldman] kept glancing over all these tacked-up sheets [in Guston's studio] but was understandably constrained, being in a group of friends and family that full well knew the cause of the chill between the two men years back. Finally, however, he had to go over and look at them (and be seen looking at them), which he did quickly, repeatedly, lightning raids each time. On his first return from them he exclaimed to no one in particular, yet somehow to everyone: "*Now* I understand what he was getting at!" . . . "I see the rhythm of the images. I see how he arranged them, which ones repeat, the *pattern*. Now I *see* it!"[71]

Feld was horrified and likened Feldman's performed epiphany to an "existential splinter the philosopher Emmanuel Levinas analogizes insomnia to: hearing and seeing what you don't want to hear and see, the intimate hollowness, the seemingly endless vertigo of time coming at you in waves."[72] Musa, Guston's widow, was equally distraught, and Feld recalls her shyly saying, "Oh, Morty, that Morty. I put those pictures up myself today. Ingie [Guston's daughter, Musa Mayer] helped me. They're just where we decided to put them."[73] Feld gently contradicts Musa, saying that Guston's daughter and David McKee insisted that the painter himself had arranged the pictures.

This moment of Feldman's belated recognition was predicated on a number of changes he had undergone in the intervening years. He had grown less opposed to the inclusion of recognizable references in his music—such as a tune from his youth grafted onto the conclusion of *Rothko Chapel* (1971), or a 12-tone row of Webern's lifted wholesale and inserted into *Violin and Orchestra* (1979). Speaking in an interview in 1980, he noted that these borrowings worked for him like "old torn photographs."[74] He likened them to Robert Rauschenberg's photomontages: "At that time I would use a tune just the way Bob would put a photo on a canvas. But now I feel that in music it doesn't work the same way."[75] What *did* seem to work the same way, in both music and painting, if Feld's memory serves, was pattern and repetition. Feldman recognized in Guston's serial deployment of his personal vocabulary of images a similar approach that he was adapting from his study of Anatolian and Coptic rugs. Pattern, crippled symmetry, and developmental variation became key concepts in his music from the 1980s, and it provided at last a feasible musico-visual link between his work and Guston's post-1970 oeuvre.

This work of mourning continued beyond Guston's funeral and Feldman quickly resumed his role as Guston's spokesperson. He was commissioned to write an essay for a show of final works mounted at the Phillips Collection in 1981. His comments elaborate on the links he saw between his interests and Guston's:

> In recent years I have become preoccupied with oriental rugs, discovering quite soon that what I was looking for had little to do with either the study or the collecting of rugs. I am mostly drawn to special examples of the nomadic Yoruk rugs from Anatolia. What the choice nineteenth-century Yoruk has that is unique is mood. This mood is closer to Jasper Johns than to Mark Rothko, tips over to Van Gogh rather than Piero. Kierkegaard both has it and writes about it. You rarely come across it in music.
>
> The mood I'm trying to describe, like a fingerprint, is in all of Guston's work. One might argue that the figurative painting of the seventies is a more appropriate language for it. Yet whereas the enigma in the earlier paintings was how this mood coexisted with abstract shapes, the same distance between mood-object is now present with an identifiable mythology of images.[76]

Feldman continues to steady himself on the bedrock of his and Guston's friendship—along with their shared love of Kierkegaard and the primacy of mood. He is cagey, however, about just what that mood is. He is loath to name it and thus suggest to us that he can yet locate abstract experience—"an emotion the philosophers have failed to categorize"—in the work.[77] Despite Guston's rejection of abstract experience, Feldman continues to insist upon it, and in doing so willfully misreads the late paintings.

Or does Feldman even read them at all? Despite recognizing shared concerns with repetition and pattern between them, Feldman refuses to comment on any work specifically—to hazard any guess as to their meaning. He's left wondering "Where did these images come from?"[78] Despite finding an abiding concern with mood across Guston's authorship, Feldman ends his reflection with a contradiction: "There is no attempt in these last paintings towards any aspect of reconciliation with his past concerns. It was a new life, in which his past *skills* helped him survive on the new ground he immigrated to."[79] Reading "Philip

Guston: 1980" is a bewildering experience. Its metaphors—which once had been hermetic and evocative in reference to Guston—are obtuse and confused. He avoids any serious engagement with the work and defers to other, more pressing interests, such as rugs and the music of Schoenberg and Stravinsky. Feldman attempts a reconciliation in good faith, but seems unable to achieve it. His struggle to reconcile himself to Guston continued into the following year, when he tried to conjure him in *Three Voices*. As argued in the previous chapter, this séance fails to bring him through—deferring yet again the sort of aesthetic mourning that Guston undertook in paintings such as *Friend—To M.F.* Feldman's deferrals suggest his inability to inaugurate his mourning for Guston. His displacements and sideways paths around their disagreement evinces Feldman's melancholic relationship to Guston. Whereas he was able to resistantly mourn O'Hara—first in *For Frank O'Hara* and again in *Three Voices*—Feldman's melancholy suffuses those works nominally about Guston: his essay for the Phillips Collection and the great late work *For Philip Guston* (1983).

For Philip Guston is a glacial trio written for flutist, percussionist, and keyboardist (doubling piano and celesta). Its title recalls Feldman's previous dedications from the 1950s and 1960s. With its explicit reference to the painter, he reestablished a relationship between his music and Guston, though it is shaded by the ambivalence of his essay "Philip Guston: 1980." Like the essay, Feldman again defers. *For Philip Guston* is more "for" the painter than it is "of" or "about" him. As such, it is distinct from the work of mourning accomplished by *Three Voices*; its deferrals—of history, reference, and emotion—mark it as a work of abject melancholy.

Tamara Levitz notes the difference between musical mourning and melancholy: a mourner provides a coherent story that clearly articulates memories of the lost object. They maintain a strong degree of authorial agency and control the narrative of their grieving. A melancholic, on the other hand, "struggles and finds it impossible to articulate memories and feelings of grief in a clear fashion. S/he will be overwhelmed by affect and unable to control the intrusion of . . . memories from the past. The melancholic narrative is characterized by discontinuity, lack of direct voice, masked expression, temporal disjunction, and the use of quotation."[80] Though she marks these as salient aspects of interwar neoclassicism, they are of a general enough character that we might productively apply them to Feldman's music and explore how they enact his deferred reconciliation with Guston.

For Philip Guston is marked by radical discontinuity and temporal disjunction as material appears and vanishes over several hours. There is little sense of implication or causality as one section of music moves to the next. The sound world is ruminative and stripped down to brief melodic segments. The music of each instrumental part is predominantly notated in different time signatures and these parts are superimposed on one another. This rhythmic non-alignment gives the piece an unsettled, anxious affect throughout—one all the more pronounced when contrasted with the moments of rhythmic alignment that do occur. There is no explicit teleology, only a recursive sense of musical memories irrupting for a moment only to be submerged again.

In fine melancholic fashion, *For Philip Guston* begins with quotation: a four-note melody taken from Feldman's *Trio* (1980). In *Trio*, it is written F, C, C-sharp, A-flat and it is shared by the violinist, cellist, and pianist in a brief, rhythmically unaligned passage. As Feldman notes, "I remembered very little [music] in the trio of Aki [Takahashi] and it's amazing: there's material there, which I used for [*For*] *Philip Guston* and I didn't know that I took it from there, that I went back five or six years, and I took this material."[81] In the heterophonic opening of *For Philip Guston*, Feldman transposed the material to C, G, A-flat, E-flat. Recontextuallized in the later work, the music of *Trio* is an instance in which a memory intrudes unexpectedly, beyond the composer's awareness. Feldman's transposition of the melody reveals another potential personal reference, one that provides the source material for the story Feldman tells about *For Philip Guston*.

Speaking to an audience at CalArts in 1985, Feldman identified the meaning of the opening motive: "And it begins with Cage. C–A–G–E [actually, C–G–A-flat–E-flat]. One of the oldest devices in music. When I came across it I wondered, 'What's going to happen with this C–A–G–E thing throughout the piece?'"[82] At the outset of the piece, we are already led away from Guston to Cage. But Cage becomes a guide back into history and Feldman's autobiography:

> We start our trip in 1950 at the Museum of Modern Art. I'd just met John Cage, and he took me to a fabulous show. It was the first big show of the

Abstract Expressionists that Dorothy Miller and Bob [Goodnough] put on. It was an absolutely incredible evening. I was just new to the whole art scene, and one of the few things I still remember—it was 1950 [actually, 1951], and I even remember where I was standing. And I remember the first time I saw a painting by Guston. He was the quintessence of what Kierkegaard would define as an artist. Someone who was always in one mood and then another as opposed to the religious man that only has one mood. But at the same time these moods are very, very important.[83]

Moods, as we've seen, are indeed important—important for Feldman's sense of Guston, who was capable of sustaining a unified mood across his work even as he veered from one mood to the next. Feldman took up the question of mood and its relationship to grief and mourning in his glosses on his musical elegy for Guston.

The stories Feldman tells about *For Philip Guston* are consistent: in his talks at CalArts as well as at the Middelburg Festival in 1985 he repeats his stories about the CAGE motive, its role in the piece, as well as the historical narrative it tells about retreating to the memory of the 1950s. These stories suggest that the mood Feldman hoped to recapture was of the untroubled early days of his friendships with both Guston and Cage. Reconciliation with the difficult later years was deferred. Examining Feldman's manuscript for *For Philip Guston* reveals other details that get at the mood he was in while writing it and the ways in which grief as a demonstrable mood was realized within the work. In Chapter 3 I argued that Feldman was particularly interested in the idea of atmosphere. Drawing on the work of D. H. Lawrence, he likened his music to having a particular spectral atmosphere that was definable as a consistent affect. The particular morbidity of this atmosphere is something we find in *Three Voices*, with its evocation of gravestones and the mediumship of Joan La Barbara in conjuring the presence of Frank O'Hara. In that same passage, Feldman continues, noting the relationship between atmosphere and mood:

> If you feel that music should not or doesn't have atmosphere, then you don't believe that it is an art form, that is my point of view. Schubert is a terrific example. Let's take . . . [sings opening melody to the F-minor Fantasy]. It's going along and even though I know what key it is and even though I know

where it is on the piano it is as if he discovered a place, and I'm saying, "Where the hell is that?" And where it is, is creating that atmosphere. Now that could be the reason why they use certain keys. It might be true. He is using the same key as everybody else but they haven't got that atmosphere! Why does he have it? Why does his major sound like minor music? Don't expect to hear anything just because I walked over here! [Plays Schubert's Sonata in A major, D.959] Don't tell me he is playing so much with the relative minor, because that is not that much. It is definitely in A major and the harmony is not out of context. Why does it sound so sad? Do you agree that it sounds sad? Don't you feel sad when you hear that A major? Let's take another piece in A major. [Mozart's Piano Concerto in A, K.488] That doesn't sound sad, does it? And the more major Schubert gets the sadder you get. It's just: "Stop it, I can't take it anymore, it is too sad!" That's what I mean by the atmosphere of a certain composer.[84]

In *For Philip Guston*, Feldman realizes his own version of major-key sadness, that atmosphere he so cherishes in Schubert. The first of these moments occurs about two hours into the piece, on page 52, systems 3 and 4. Feldman desaturates the chromaticism that has prevailed to this point and moves to an entirely diatonic "white-note" collection played by a rhythmically aligned ensemble. This embrace of unabashed consonance coincides with the emergence of the most luxurious melody we've heard so far in the piece, an aching six-note arc in the glockenspiel, which begins on A, rises to G, and then descends to F, E, C, and B. But it vanishes as quickly as it appeared, and we are back in the sound world of Feldman's typical fragmented late-style chromaticism. Hours go by, and then, on page 98, Feldman moves again to a desaturated white-note music. The glockenspiel melody returns, though this time the first note is transposed up an octave. The melody loses its arc and becomes a single descending line repeated no fewer than forty times over the next several minutes. The combined musical factors—consonance, melodic gesture, and repetition—produce an overwhelming sense of grief, as though Feldman's melancholic music has finally transitioned to a resistant mourning. The association of this melodic material with mourning is strengthened when we look at Feldman's working manuscript, where we find inscribed below varied transpositions of the descending melody this necrology: "Mom, Philip, Frank, Mark, Jackson, Franz, Stefan."[85] The names are those most important to his art—all dead: his mother, Frances Feldman, Guston, Frank O'Hara, Mark Rothko, Jackson Pollock, Franz Kline, and Stefan Wolpe. This litany of losses does not undermine the story Feldman told about the piece later—but it points to the fact that Feldman was reticent to disclose everything in public.

Heinz-Klaus Metzger succeeded more than most to get him to open up on the matter of mourning by suggesting that "For many years now, you are writing these soft pieces. Sometimes I think, they are a kind of mourning epilogue to murdered Jiddishkeit in Europe and dying Jiddishkeit in America, especially in New York. Is there something true about it?" Feldman responded:

> It's not true, but at the same time I think that's an aspect of my attitude about being a composer that is mourning. Say, for example, the death of art. . . . I do in a sense mourn something that has to do with, say Schubert leaving me. Also, I really don't feel that it's all necessary any more. And so what I tried to bring into my music, are just very few essential things that I need. So I at least keep it going for a little while more. I must say you did bring up something that I particularly don't want to talk about publicly, but I do talk privately.[86]

The mourning music of *For Philip Guston* and its juxtaposition with the names of lost loved ones and friends is the private ground from which Feldman cultivated the peculiar affects of loss projected across his career. It returns us to further reflection on the ethical value of writing a music that is, somehow, like death. Guston recognized himself in Feldman's equation of creativity and death formulated in his obituary for O'Hara. And, in a sense, death provided the only common ground upon which he might reconcile himself to his lost friends. This reconciliation meant coming to a new self-understanding, one that he explained toward the end of his life:

> So in thinking about how we're committed to aesthetic considerations, as if the Shiites and the Jews and the Sunnis and the Catholics and the Protestants. . . . It's the same thing in art. So I was no different than any kind of fanatic. I felt that only an abstract kind of art could exist; only an art like [Guston's] earlier work, which I thought was sublime, more like Rothko or Pollock. I thought that no other work could exist. And I noticed that I myself was changing the way he was changing. Not completely the way he was changing

but at least enough to make me see what he was going through. And it wasn't just the times. It wasn't the fact that the times were changing but that *I* had to change.[87]

Derrida writes that, "surviving is at once the essence, the origin and the possibility, the condition of possibility of friendship; it is the grieved act of loving. This time of surviving thus gives the time of friendship."[88] Feldman, by surviving Guston, responded with grieved acts of melancholic deferral as well as mournful reconciliation that point up a basic truth: we're not going to be here very long and we're going to need our friends.

Notes

1 Friedrich Nietzsche, *Human, All Too Human*, trans. R. J. Hollingdale (Cambridge: Cambridge University Press, 1986), 274.
2 Philip Guston and Morton Feldman, "Conversation with Morton Feldman," in *Philip Guston: Collected Writings, Lectures, and Conversations*, ed. Clark Coolidge (Berkley: University of California Press, 2012), 104.
3 Morton Feldman, "For Philip Guston," in *Give My Regards to Eighth Street*, 199.
4 Ibid., 198.
5 For details of the controversy over the postponement of a multi-museum Guston retrospective, see Susan Tallman, "Philip Guston's Discomfort Zone," *New York Review of Books*, January 14, 2021. https://www-nybooks-com/articles/2021/01/14/philip-gustons-discomfort-zone/, accessed April 15, 2021.
6 Philip Guston, "On Morton Feldman," in *Philip Guston: Collected Writings, Lectures, and Conversations*, ed. Clark Coolidge (Berkeley: University of California Press, 2011), 76.
7 Morton Feldman, "Touch," in Michael Auping, *30 Years: Interviews and Outtakes* (Fort Worth, TX: Prestel, 2007), 141.
8 Ibid.
9 The title page of *Extensions 4* is reproduced in Douglas Dreishpoon, *Nothing and Everything: Seven Artists, 1947–1962* (New York: Hauser & Wirth, 2017), 10.
10 The three pages of the manuscript are reproduced in facsimile in Dreishpoon, *Nothing and Everything*, 58–59. Dedication on 59.
11 Feldman wrote the dedication on February 13, 1958. A facsimile of the manuscript pages is published in Dreishpoon, *Nothing and Everything*, 54–57, dedication on 54.

12 Morton Feldman, "Liner Notes," in *Give My Regards to Eighth Street*, 5.
13 Philip Guston, "On Morton Feldman," in *Guston: Collected Writings*, 77–78.
14 Philip Guston, "Interview with Jan Butterfield," in *Guston: Collected Writings*, 293.
15 Emily H. Green, *Dedicating Music, 1785–1850* (Rochester, NY: University of Rochester Press, 2019), 120.
16 Kenneth Silverman, *Begin Again: A Biography of John Cage* (New York: Knopf, 2010), 173.
17 Philip Guston, Letter to Morton Feldman, October 5, 1961. Morton Feldman Collection, PSS.
18 Robert Slifkin, *Out of Time: Philip Guston and the Refiguration of Postwar American Art* (Berkley, CA: University of California Press, 2013), 147.
19 Ibid., 146–47.
20 Morton Feldman, "Philip Guston: The Last Painter," in *Give My Regards to Eighth Street*; "perform" on 38, "engulf" on 39.
21 Ibid.
22 Morton Feldman, "Give My Regards to Eighth Street," in *Give My Regards to Eighth Street*, 99.
23 Philip Guston, Letter to Morton Feldman, October 24, 1961. Morton Feldman Collection, PSS.
24 Morton Feldman, "Vertical Thoughts," in *Give My Regards to Eighth Street*, 13. For further discussion of this in relation to Feldman's ideas of "verticality," see Chapter 1 in Ryan Dohoney, *Saving Abstraction* (New York: Oxford, 2019).
25 Morton Feldman, "Philip Guston: The Last Painter," 39.
26 Dore Ashton, "No Way to be Mortified," in *Vertical Thoughts: Morton Feldman and the Visual Arts*, ed. Seán Kissane (Dublin: Irish Museum of Modern Art, 2010), 85.
27 Morton Feldman, "Conversations without Stravinsky," in *Give My Regards to Eighth Street*, 58.
28 Morton Feldman, "Some Elementary Questions," in *Give My Regards to Eighth Street*, 65.
29 Morton Feldman, "After Modernism," in *Give My Regards to Eighth Street*, 78.
30 Morton Feldman, "The Anxiety of Art," in *Give My Regards to Eighth Street*, 25.
31 Morton Feldman, "Philip Guston: The Last Painter," 39.
32 Philip Guston, "From Panel at the Philadelphia Museum School of Art," in *Guston: Collected Writings*, 29.
33 Philip Guston, "Faith, Hope, and Impossibility," in *Guston: Collected Writings*, 53.

34 Feldman, "Philip Guston: The Last Painter," 38.
35 In his Piero essay, Guston takes up the theme of artistic anxiety so powerfully developed in Feldman's essay "The Anxiety of Art," also from 1965. See Feldman, "The Anxiety of Art." See also Chapter 1 of Dohoney, *Saving Abstraction* for a discussion of Feldman and anxiety. Philip Guston, "Faith, Hope, and Impossibility," in *Guston: Collected Writings*, 53–55 and "Piero della Francesca: The Impossibility of Painting," also in *Guston: Collected Writings*, 41.
36 Feldman, "Touch," 142.
37 Grace Glueck, "New Art School Stresses Essentials," *New York Times*, January 11, 1965, 31.
38 Mercedes Matter, "What's Wrong with U.S. Art Schools?" *Art News* 62, no. 5 (1963): 57, 40.
39 Ibid., 57.
40 Ibid.
41 Ibid., 58.
42 Glueck, "New Art School Stresses Essentials."
43 "Presentation of the New York Studio School to the Ford Foundation." n.d. [c.1964–65]. 17–18. New York Studio School Papers.
44 Matter, "What's Wrong with U.S. Art Schools?" 57.
45 "Presentation of the New York Studio School," 7.
46 The somewhat rough record-keeping of the school from its early days in the 1960s makes the dating of John de Menil's joining of the board—a position that likely ended with his death in 1973—unclear. Yet his presence on it shows the intertwining of the various historical processes that entangled Feldman, the de Menils, and New York School modernism and calls back to my previous work, *Saving Abstraction*. John's support for the anxious pedagogy the school offered, made intelligible by his formation in interwar Parisian modernism, and his support of it financially, documents in miniature the larger convergence of modernist ascetic practices, the spiritual work on self figured by Feldman as "tragic verticality" and by de Menil as a continuation of the avant-garde values of the *renouveau catholique*. John de Menil's own financial and political commitments come through in a letter to Feldman on October 31, 1969. Faced with Feldman's question about the constitution of the board, de Menil replied:

"I would exclude faculty from the board because in a studio school the students should be the pace setters. I envisage a board made of students and patrons who would represent the budget imperatives and explain them. Faced with their responsibilities the students would understand them. They would become conscious partners instead of feeling prisoners of a loft business point of view."

De Menil's dismissal of the faculty from any role in self-governance was a radical gesture at the time—though in the days of the corporate university in the early twenty-first century, it feels quite familiar. But de Menil's simultaneously naive and imperious tone is striking for its good-faith effort to empower students (in the heyday of late-1960s student movements) and blind to the impossibility of equitable relationships between students and patrons like himself, much less major philanthropic organizations such as the Ford Foundation, whose grants helped sustain the School during Feldman's years as dean and beyond. Indeed, the temporary presence of students on the board, rotating off it as they completed their studies, guaranteed that the patrons of the school would have immense power over its operations and direction. At the time of de Menil's writing, he and Dominique were in the process of divesting from the University of St. Thomas—a small Catholic liberal arts college in Houston run by priests from the Order of St. Basil. What the de Menils had intended for the school—that it be a laboratory for the ascetic and artistic practices extending the work of the *renouveau catholique* in both avant-garde aesthetics and ecumenical spirit—chafed against the reticence of the Basilian fathers and the slower pace of change they were comfortable with. Though we can glean from his letter to Feldman something of de Menil's patronage style and intention to consolidate power in the hands of benevolent patrons who, it would seem, just simply *know better* than the faculty charged with running the institution day to day.

De Menil saw no value in the Studio School's "present master/disciple relationship": "Our students must live in the seventies and become part of it, otherwise our school is at the level of Pratt or Rhode Island and this is not the purpose." Striking in this excerpt—and in the letter as a whole—is de Menil's use of the first person plural ("our," "we") that indicates a level of personal and financial investment in the school that belies his brief time as one of its patrons. Such a sense of ownership, as well as his warm relationship with Feldman, gave him license to speak of a new plan that would radically diminish the power of the faculty in day-to-day operations. In a fashion exemplary of his broader approach to artists, de Menil envisioned this alternative: "The faculty should be at the service of the students, and its authority founded on personal prestige. We are not teaching how to hold a pencil or a brush. We are offering the students the possibility to develop their vocation and their style." The de Menils had long premised their patronage at least in part on the work of identifying "remarkables," as Pamela G. Smart has put it in her ethnography of the Menil Collection, and John's emphasis on authority being properly derived from prestige is of a piece with this. Such an attitude is congruent with the school's mission—that each student be given time, space, and encouragement in their own sensibility as artists and be inspired by greatness, not instructed in technique, in how to proceed. De Menil continued in a vein aligned with Matter's own, though, in a typically expansive gesture for the patron, de Menil wanted to make it even grander:

"The stimulation they need would come through visits on the pattern of the Buckminster Fuller seminar of last summer, and visitors shouldn't be limited to artists and architects, but include writers, philosophers, seers from all horizons. Think of the impact a Baudelaire of today could have on young people 'fighting with the Angel.' The present faculty could well provide some of those visiting stimulants."

The model event to which de Menil refers was Buckminister Fuller's *World Game*. But beyond this, John gives subtle hints as to the spiritual dimensions in which he conceives artistic practice: the visiting faculty should be "seers" representing an ecumenical array of inspirational thought. In keeping with his own *renouveau* commitments, de Menil expressed an attitude toward modernity that embraced it while resisting the nostalgia of the past: this is not an "off-modern" position, as Smart insists the de Menils held, but an actualization of Maritain's hylomorphic imaginary, in which spiritual truth exists in the present moment embodied in materials and concepts of that moment. This is, nevertheless, a spiritual struggle as de Menil likens the attempt to create authentically as an artist to the biblical narrative of Jacob wrestling with the angel of the lord recounted in Genesis 32. The metaphor also captures well Feldman's pedagogical sense of anxiety as that which, like the unrelenting struggle with the angel, will leave one victorious but not unscathed. Recall that the price Jacob paid was a wounded hip that left him debilitated for the rest of his life.

47 Philip Guston, "On Morton Feldman," in *Collected Writings*, 76.
48 Ibid., 77.
49 For a full account of this exhibition and Feldman's role, see Chapter 3 of Dohoney, *Saving Abstraction*.

50 Though it is not included in the transcript, Guston mentions Matter by name and she briefly participates in the conversation. "Conversation with Morton Feldman," cassette tape. New York Studio School Library. I am grateful to David Cline for allowing me to hear the recording of this conversation.
51 Feldman and Guston, "Conversation with Morton Feldman," 89.
52 Ibid., 81.
53 Ibid., 87.
54 Ibid., 88.
55 Ibid., 103–4.
56 Ibid., 105.
57 Ibid., 106.
58 Philip Guston, Letter to Morton Feldman, November 12, 1968. Morton Feldman Collection, Paul Sacher Stiftung.
59 Nietzsche, *Human, All Too Human*, 274.
60 Ross Feld, *Guston in Time: Remembering Philip Guston* (New York: Counterpoint, 2003), 71.
61 Ibid.
62 Ibid.
63 Frank O'Hara, "Joe's Jacket," in *The Collected Poems of Frank O'Hara*, ed. Donal Allen (Berkley: University of California Press, 1995), 330.
64 Marjorie Perloff, *Frank O'Hara: Poet Among Painters* (New York: George Braziller, 1977), 152.
65 Feldman, "After Modernism," 74.
66 Images for *Room and Sea*, *Pink Sea*, and *Group in Sea* can all be found in Guston's online catalogue raisonné: https://www.gustoncrllc.org/home/catalogue_raisonne, accessed October 7, 2021.
67 Quoted in Jacques Derrida, *The Politics of Friendship*, trans. George Collins (New York, Verso 2005), 47 n15.
68 Philip Guston, "On Survival," in *Guston: Collected Writings*, 252.
69 Philip Guston, "Conversation with Clark Coolidge, 1972," in *Guston: Collected Writings*, 208–9.
70 Morton Feldman, "Studio International Interview," in *Morton Feldman Says*, 67. The line of poetry Feldman recalls is "I Am the Least Difficult of Men. All I Want Is Boundless Love." "Meditations in an Emergency" in O'Hara, *The Collected Poems*, 197.
71 Feld, *Guston in Time*, 72.

72 Ibid.
73 Ibid.
74 Morton Feldman, "*Soundpieces* Interview," in *Morton Feldman Says*, 93.
75 Ibid., 91.
76 Morton Feldman, "Philip Guston: 1980/The Last Works," in *Give My Regards to Eighth Street*, 130.
77 Feldman, "After Modernism."
78 Feldman, "Philip Guston: 1980," 131.
79 Ibid., 132.
80 Tamara Levitz, *Modernist Mysteries: Perséphone* (New York: Oxford, 2012), 480.
81 Feldman, *Words on Music*, 464.
82 Feldman, "For Philip Guston," 199.
83 Ibid.
84 Feldman, *Words on Music*, 104, 106.
85 Morton Feldman, *For Philip Guston*, Morton Feldman Collection, Paul Sacher Stiftung. MF 438-0518.
86 Morton Feldman, "Prolog: About Jiddishkeit," in *Essays*, ed. Walter Zimmerman (Kerpen: Beginner Press, 1985), 7.
87 Feldman, *Words and Music*, 158.
88 Derrida, *The Politics of Friendship*, 74.

Conclusion

Friendship's Silence

Silence may be a much more interesting way of having a relationship with people.[1]

Michel Foucault

To end my account of Feldman's friendships, I return to the analytical insight that has guided the work as a whole: that friendship is no safe haven from unequal power relations. Friendship is not always a positive force—it is sometimes an underdetermined name for remarkably varied attachments. Friendships are impinged upon by all sorts of forces and yet they sustain human flourishing. While in the first chapter I drew upon the work of religious historian Brenna Moore in my assessment of Feldman's friendships, I want to close by placing them under the sign of *tragic friendship*, which I have developed through the work of Hannah Arendt. Friendship is a near-constant theme in her work and it vividly exemplifies her pluralist ontology as well as her political vision of "the web of human relationships and entangled stories."[2] Arendt is no arbitrary choice. She was entangled within Feldman's community of artists. She spoke at the Eighth Street Artists Club, where it was possible—even likely—that Feldman, Guston, and others heard her lecture on "The European Intellectual."[3] She was friends with Christian Wolff as well as his parents, the publishers of Pantheon Books.[4] She was also close with Guston's friend Harold Rosenberg. Like Arendt, Rosenberg reflected on the categories of *action* and *acting* as political forces and strenuously argued that artistic praxis modeled a particularly potent form of both. Her relationship with Rosenberg, however, was not untroubled. And though she understood friendship to be a necessary and sustaining force, Arendt herself knew the fragility of these fraught intimacies—first through her life as a stateless person in the 1930s, and again with the controversy erupting from the publication of *Eichmann in Jerusalem* in the 1960s. The latter nearly ended her friendship with Rosenberg and succeeded in terminating others, including her long friendship with Gershom Scholem.

Arendt had much to say about such matters of friendship, tragedy, and reconciliation. In her seminal essay, "Humanity in Dark Times," she explores the political value of friendship for world-making, the need for tragic reconciliation, and the power of aesthetic and expressive practices to accomplish both. She approaches these topics in her essayistic and elliptical style, circling around the themes of friendship, tragedy, reconciliation, poetics, history, and politics.

Arendt conceptualizes friendship via Gotthold Ephraim Lessing and, to a lesser extent, Jean-Jacques Rousseau, finding in the former a political sense of friendship figured as mutual world-building—political precisely because it sustains pluralistic action and relationality. Rousseau's interest in fraternity and compassion led him to think of it as "the fulfilment of humanity."[5] Arendt is careful to distinguish fraternity from friendship not on the grounds of affect, but rather on the grounds of worldliness. Fraternity is generated particularly strongly among what Arendt call "pariah peoples"—those like the Jews of eighteenth-century Europe, who were largely excluded from participation in the work of politics. Fraternity is felt, as Lessing put it, as "philanthropic feelings"—"brotherly attachment to other human beings which springs from hatred of the world in which men are treated 'inhumanly.'"[6] Such warm brotherhood comes at a cost, Arendt notes: "it is often accompanied by so radical a loss of the world, so fearful an atrophy of all the organs that we respond to it—starting with the common sense with which we orient ourselves in a world common to ourselves and others." She concludes this elaboration noting that "worldlessness, alas, is always a form of barbarism."[7]

Friendship, in contradistinction to fraternity, cannot help but be worldly. Its affections are not bound to sameness of identity/identification (whether self-identified or oppressively forced into a group identity one did not choose) but rather transcend those categories to form a pluralistic conception of humanity. According to Arendt, in Lessing's play *Nathan the Wise*, a broad-minded, non-identitarian conception of friendship is felt in its theme ("It suffices to be a man"): "The appeal: 'Be my friend,' which runs like a leitmotif through the whole play, corresponds to that theme."⁸ The worldly character of Lessing's conception of friendship puts it in stark contrast to that of Rousseau:

> We are so wont to see friendship solely as a phenomenon of intimacy, in which the friends open their hearts to each other unmolested by the world and its demands. . . . Thus it is hard for us to understand the political relevance of friendship. . . . [T]hat humanity is exemplified not in fraternity but in friendship; that friendship is not intimately personal but makes political demands and preserves reference to the world—all this seems to us so exclusively characteristic of classical antiquity that it rather perplexes us when we find quite kindred features in *Nathan the Wise*—which, modern as it is, might with some justice be called the classical drama of friendship.⁹

Arendt notes that "Nathan's wisdom consists solely in his readiness to sacrifice truth to friendship." This, in Lessing's broader authorship, means never making dogma, identity, or *sameness* the condition for attachment:

> He, who was polemical to the point of contentiousness, could no more endure loneliness than the excessive closeness of a brotherliness that obliterated all distinctions. He was never eager really to fall out with someone with whom he had entered into a dispute; he was concerned solely with humanizing the world by incessant and continual discourse about its affairs and the things in it. He wanted to be the friend of many men, but no man's brother.¹⁰

Arendt's model of friendship, resonating with her thoughts about Lessing, gives us a hermeneutic through which to approach both Feldman and Guston's friendship and its dissolution. As transcripts and recordings of their conversations in the late 1960s make clear, they were concerned with humanizing the world, with "bearing witness" (in Guston's words), and with engaging in "continual discourse about its affairs" (in Arendt's). Guston's recognition of what Feldman's friendship gave him, discussed in Chapter 1 and again in Chapter 4, testifies to the world-expanding possibilities of their relationship in which creative action was energized through it and enabled by it. Guston and Feldman's friendship was woven from talk. A torrent of words, ideas, metaphors, analogies, and memories sustained their friendship for nearly two decades. And then it didn't. Feldman was silent when Guston asked him what he thought about the Marlborough paintings, and that silence ended something. It cut the rope bridge of words that had been carefully woven by them. We think of Feldman's music as a kind of silence—sounds that project the semblance of silence. But here, Feldman's silence—as a friend—was real. And it was hard to hear. Actual silence in front of *those* paintings became the absence of relation and a failure of recognition.

Silence, though, can also *save* friendship. Nietzsche tells us a bit more about how such quiet salvation is possible, first by recognizing the sheer variety of opinions and perspectives—what Arendt would call *doxa*—held by our friends: "Only reflect to yourself how various are the feelings, how divided the opinions, even among your closest acquaintances, how even the same opinions are of a quite different rank of intensity in the heads of your friends than they are in yours; how manifold are the occasions for misunderstanding, for hostility and rupture."[11] Glossing Nietzsche, Derrida attests that "Friendship does not keep silence, it is preserved by silence."[12] This preservation, Nietzsche notes, is dependent upon a double realization: that our "alliances and friendships" are built on "uncertain ground" and "the opinions of one's fellow men . . . are just as necessary and unaccountable as their actions."[13] Instead of giving into bitterness and terror ("Friends, there are no friends!"), we must cultivate a proper attitude to silence:

> One will, rather, avow to oneself: yes, there are friends, but it is error and deception regarding yourself that led them to you; and they must have learned how to keep silent in order to remain your friend; for such human relationships almost always depend upon the fact that two or three things are never said or even so much as touched upon: if these little boulders do start to roll, however, friendship follows after them and shatters.[14]

For Arendt, *doxa* is not truth; truth is that which is worked out in common through compassion and understanding founded on plurality and the principle of substitutability—that is, being able to imagine yourself in the position of others and, in doing so, to think with and as another.[15] Mistaking one's *doxa* for truth is the problem of *Nathan the Wise*—one Lessing attempts to solve by, as Arendt notes, "sacrificing truth to friendship." Nietzsche, following Lessing and presaging Arendt, enjoins us to make a similar move: to keep silent and remain friends. To return to Arendt's biography (and her close proximity to New York School modernism), we can see her practicing this ethics of silence in the aftermath of the Eichmann affair. Elisabeth Young-Bruehl recounts how Harold Rosenberg,

> whom Arendt had known since the early 1950s, visited Arendt in Chicago and spent several hours telling her about his strenuous objections to *Eichmann in Jerusalem*, reiterating the stance he had taken in a 1961 article for Commentary, "Guilt to the Vanishing Point." She did not give Rosenberg a poem; she simply listened in uncomfortable silence, made not one attempt to defend herself, and then, when Rosenberg had finished, asked him to pour them both a drink so they could relax like good friends. He was startled, but understood that she had decided that she would not sacrifice their friendship to her work and the insights she had struggled for, and that she expected him to realize that their friendship should withstand their disagreements. . . . Harold Rosenberg was impressed; he refrained from engaging publicly in the controversy and often told this story of Arendt's *humanitas*, both to praise her and to defend her from personal attacks.[16]

Young-Bruehl interprets this through Arendt's conception of "true humanism," derived from Cicero, in which the being among others, having relations and friendships with others (*inter homine esse*), is to be valued more highly than overzealous commitments to abstract notions of truth and beauty. We also might see this as an instance of tragic friendship as I have derived it from "Humanity in Dark Times." Arendt silently echoes the theme of *Nathan the Wise* simply by asking Rosenberg to pour her a drink. Her gesture quietly insists, "Be my friend" by refusing to contradict him and, instead, reconciling herself to their disagreement.

We can gain further insight into Arendt's choice of friendship over truth—that is, truth figured as an abstract concept to which we overly-commit ourselves—by turning to her difficulties with Gershom Scholem, occasioned as they were by the same controversy that upset Rosenberg: the Eichmann trial and *Eichmann in Jerusalem*. Scholem was angered by the tone of *Eichmann*—its bitter, tragic irony, of the kind we find in the writings Arendt produced in her years of statelessness and soon after her arrival in the United States. "We Refugees" is exemplary in this regard.[17] Scholem, however, found the tone of *Eichmann* "heartless" and "downright malicious." He was troubled by what he felt was an absence of "what the Jews call *ahavath Israel*, or love for the Jewish people." He elaborated: "With you, my dear Hannah, as with so many intellectuals coming from the German left, there is no trace of it."[18] Arendt's response homes in on this matter and she devotes much of the letter responding to it. After dismissing Scholem's claim that her origins are in the German left, she writes,

> Let's get to the real issue. Tying in with what I just said, I'll begin with *ahavath Israel* (by the way, I would be extraordinarily grateful to you if you could tell me when this expression began to play a role in the Hebrew language and literature, when it appeared for the first time, and so on). How right you are that I have no such love, and for two reasons: first, I have never in my life "loved" some nation or collective—not the German, French, or American nation, or the working class, or whatever else there might be in this price range of loyalties. The fact is that I love only my friends and am quite incapable of any other sort of love.[19]

Arendt accepts what she calls the "brute facts" of belonging to a collective in some form, but she can have no *love* for impersonal collectives—be they nations, religions, or classes. To do so would, following Whitehead, commit a fallacy of misplaced concreteness by accepting a conceptual abstraction for a real entity.[20] Furthermore, it would contradict the foundational importance placed on both the plurality and uniqueness of existents in her thought. To love is to love individuals in their singularity and specificity, to love them in all partiality as one's friend. Arendt insists that she simply cannot love abstractions; as concepts they require fearless interrogation and frequent revision. Our friends cannot be treated as we treat matters such as "truth"—Arendt's response to Rosenberg has shown us this. Thus friendship *has* a concreteness. This particularity is what we should love.

Let us then return to the scene of the Marlborough Gallery in October of 1970. Feldman's silence does seem like a Nietzschean or Arendtian attempt to save friendship. He tried to carve out a space for thought—half a minute, as he remembered it—to come to grips with what might be said so that silence would not overtake their friendship and end it. Guston—Philip—didn't give him time. He needed Morty's opinion instantly, to feel Morty's affection and understanding to keep going. And he didn't get it in time. The "truth of abstraction" proved stronger for Feldman than friendship itself. Therein lies the tragedy.

Tragedy is an effect arising from a growing awareness of a failure of recognition—that is, the awareness of the fundamental incapacity of humans to have full knowledge of the consequences of their actions. The process of recognition tracks a reversal through which the hero becomes the sufferer: "The tragic hero becomes knowledgeable by re-experiencing what has been done in the way of suffering and in this *pathos*, in resuffering the past, the network of individual acts is transformed into an event, a significant whole."[21] In their post-1970 work, both Feldman and Guston adopted a strategy of retrospection realized through aesthetic transformation and, following Arendt, I argue that their work can be allied, if not through style, at least through a poetics of tragic reconciliation. We find in both authorships an exploration of the genre of lament. Each mourns the personal and world-historical, and as such, they resonate with Arendt's own concept of lament, which affords second reflection on past events. It is a specific "suffering by memory operating retrospectively and perceptively."[22] But going further, the work of lamentation and its repetition (through, for instance, musical performance) memorializes but cannot undo the past: "We can no more master the past than we can undo it. But we can reconcile ourselves to it. The form for this is the lament, which arises out of all recollection."[23] To think of the past, to recollect, is always to lament that what *has happened* and cannot be undone. This is where the role of friend and poet complement one another. Friendship and the dialog of friends in public create a space for action and world-building. The poet then, along with the historian, has the responsibility of reconciling us to what has happened, to give events their meaning. I quote Arendt at length:

> The tragic impact of this repetition in lamentation affects one of the key elements of all action; it establishes its meaning and that permanent significance which then enters into history. In contradistinction to other elements peculiar to action—above all to the preconceived goals, the impelling motives, and the guiding principles, all of which become visible in the course of action—the meaning of a committed act is revealed only when the action itself has come to an end and become a story susceptible to

narration.... The poet in a very special general sense and the historian in a very special sense have the task of setting this process of narration in motion and of involving us in it.²⁴

A work exemplifying Arendt's tragic aesthetics is William Faulkner's *A Fable* from 1954 and her description of it provides some helpful concepts with which to approach Guston and Feldman's own attempts at reconciliation:

> After the First World War we experienced the "mastering of the past" in a spate of descriptions of the war that varied enormously in kind and quality; naturally this happened not only in Germany, but in all the affected countries. Nevertheless, nearly thirty years were to pass before a work of art appeared which so transparently displayed the inner truth of the event that it became possible to say: Yes, this is how it was. And in this novel, William Faulkner's *A Fable*, very little is described, still less explained, and nothing at all "mastered"; its end is tears which the reader also weeps, and what remains beyond that is the "tragic effect" or the "tragic pleasure," the shattering emotion which makes one able to accept the fact that something like this war could have happened at all. I deliberately mention tragedy because it more than the other literary forms represents a process of recognition.²⁵

What I find compelling in Arendt's description of *A Fable* is her profound investment in the work art does to reconcile and reveal inner truth through tragedy. Arendt here is talking about world-historical tragedy, but she, more than most, knew that the political was indeed personal. Moreover, she—as Cecilia Sjöholm has brilliantly argued—understood the role art played in sustaining human relationships by appealing to *common sense* and collective judgment.²⁶

In all cases—Arendt, Rosenberg, Scholem, Guston, Feldman—intimacy was threatened by attachment to an ideal, concept, or abstraction external to the friendship. For Arendt, Scholem, and Rosenberg, intimacy was predicated in part upon a shared feeling of being "pariah people"—exiles in the case of Arendt and Scholem, and Jewish intellectuals in the case of all three. Feldman and Guston shared a similar identification as Jewish intellectuals, though unlike Arendt's ruptures, their friendship did not dissolve because of conflicts over ethnic and intellectual identification. It dissolved over aesthetics—namely, it ended because of Guston's perceived loss of faith in abstraction (what he called "all that purity") and Feldman's dogged insistence upon its primacy.

Herein lies the tragic element: Feldman, more than Guston, did not recognize his friend *until it was too late*. Exacerbating this tragedy is the matter that Feldman's late recognition was, perhaps inevitably, misrecognition, and a retreat to the memory of the 1950s—to the Guston he could accept. To some extent, Feldman understood the tragic character of the breakdown and the weakness of his attempt at reconciliation. He noted near the end his life that the whole affair was sad, but, with his posthumous encomiums for his friend, tentatively stated that "I think I made it up to him."[27] Guston's death offered the possibility of reconciliation. Indeed, Guston in death *insisted* upon reconciliation—recall that he has requested that Feldman say Kaddish at his funeral. But as a conflict over matters of aesthetics and style, both Feldman and Guston reconciled themselves through *poeisis*, the very shoal upon which their relationship had run aground.

Notes

1. Michel Foucault, "An interview by Stephen Riggins," in *The Essential Works of Michel Foucault, Vol. 1: Ethics, Subjectivity, and Truth*, ed. Paul Rabinow (New York: New Press, 1997), 122.
2. Hannah Arendt, *The Human Condition* (Chicago, IL: University of Chicago Press, 1998 [1958]), 181–88. For a trenchant development of Arentian plurality in the life and work of Feldman's composition teacher Stefan Wolpe, see Brigid Cohen, *Stefan Wolpe and the Avant-Garde Diaspora* (Cambridge: Cambridge University Press, 2012).
3. Ryan Dohoney, *Saving Abstraction: Morton Feldman, the de Menils, and the Rothko Chapel* (New York: Oxford University Press, 2019), 66, 69–70.
4. Christian Wolff, interview with the author, January 18, 2018.
5. Hannah Arendt, "Humanity in Dark Times," in *Men in Dark Times* (New York: Harcourt Brace, 1968), 3–32, 12.
6. Ibid., 12–13.
7. Ibid., 13.
8. Ibid., 12.
9. Ibid., 25.

10 Ibid., 30.
11 Friedrich Nietzsche, *Human, All Too Human*, trans. R. J. Hollingdale (Cambridge: Cambridge University Press, 1996), 148.
12 Jacques Derrida, *The Politics of Friendship*, trans. George Collins (New York: Verso, 2005), 53.
13 Nietzsche, *Human, All Too Human*, 148.
14 Ibid.
15 On this notion of objectivity, see Hannah Arendt, "The Concept of History: Ancient and Modern," in *Between Past and Future* (New York: Penguin, 2006), 51.
16 Elisabeth Young-Bruehl, *Hannah Arendt: For Love of the World* (New Haven, CT: Yale University Press, 1982), 352.
17 Hannah Arendt, "We Refugees," in *The Jewish Writings*, ed. Jerome Kohn and Ron H. Feldman (New York: Schoken, 2007), 264–74.
18 Gershom Scholem, "Letter 132," June 23, 1963, in *The Correspondence of Hannah Arendt and Gershom Scholem*, ed. Marie Luise Knott, trans. Anthony David (Chicago, IL: University of Chicago Press, 2017), 202.
19 Hannah Arendt, "Letter 133," July 20, 1963 in *The Correspondence of Hannah Arendt and Gershom Scholem*. 206.
20 Alfred North Whitehead, *Process and Reality* (New York: Free Press, 1978), 7–8.
21 Arendt, "Humanity in Dark Times," 20.
22 Ibid.
23 Ibid., 21.
24 Ibid.
25 Ibid., 20.
26 Cecilia Sjöholm, *Doing Aesthetics with Arendt: How to See Things* (New York: Columbia University Press, 2014).
27 Morton Feldman, "For Philip Guston," 198.

Acknowledgments

Nietzsche wrote in *Human, All Too Human* that "A good writer possesses not only his own spirit but also the spirit of his friends." While I leave it for the reader to judge the quality of my work, there is no doubt that this book bears the traces of many long friendships. It is a joy to thank the following people.

Thanks first and foremost to Leah Babb-Rosenfeld, my commissioning editor at Bloomsbury. I'm grateful for her patience as I completed the project under the less-than-ideal conditions of a global pandemic. Josh Rutner again provided excellent editing and indexing. Simon Nugent provided expert bibliographic assistance. Special thanks to Barbara Monk-Feldman for help with permissions as well as her interest in my work. Joan La Barbara kindly fielded my questions about her collaboration with Morton Feldman and granted me permission to reproduce her correspondence. The fine folks at Hauser and Wirth and the Estate of Philip Guston were generous with permissions and images. Renate Ponsold kindly allowed me to use her amazing photo of Feldman in Guston's studio for the book's cover. Thanks also to the Kaplan Institute for the Humanities at Northwestern University for a generous subvention.

This work would not have been possible without the wonderful scholars and librarians at the Paul Sacher Stiftung. Thanks to Dr. Felix Meyer, the director of the Sacher, for his encouragement as well as help with reproductions. I had the distinct pleasure of working with Sabine Hänggi-Stampfli, now-retired librarian of the Feldman collection, for more than a decade. Her knowledge of Feldman's papers was invaluable and she provided a wealth of insights over the years. Chapter 2 is dedicated to her.

Many of the ideas in the book have their misty origins in my dissertation research at Columbia University. I'm grateful to Lytle Shaw, Caroline A. Jones, Branden Joseph, Ellie Hisama, Joseph Dubiel, Marion Guck, and George E. Lewis for their early (and ongoing) intellectual support.

My colleagues in Northwestern's libraries have again been terrific collaborators. Thanks as always to Sigrid Perry, Nick Munagian, Jason Nargis, Greg MacAyal, and D. J. Hoek. Scott Krafft went above and beyond the call of duty. He was instrumental in securing photo permissions and knew what I needed before I even thought to ask for it. The Intermission is dedicated to him.

My scholarly community at Northwestern has given me some of the best friendships of my life. Penelope Deutscher remains a wise and trusted mentor. Lydia Barnett kept me sane with regular walks along the lakefront. Mary Weismantel improved ideas found in Chapters 1 and 2. J. Michelle Molina gave trenchant feedback on Chapters 1 and 3. She inspires me with her intellectual and emotional generosity. Chapter 1 is dedicated to her.

At the Bienen School of Music, I'm lucky to work with the best minds in the music business. Among them, a few deserve special mention. Mark Butler, Alex Mincek, Inna Naroditskaya, and Jesse Rosenberg are reliable sources of intellectual energy. As is Andrew Talle, who talked through Guston's paintings and helped me see what was actually going on in them. Kyle Kaplan, Olivia Cacchione, and Kirsten Carithers each impacted this work with their fierce vigilance of thought. Olga Loevski was an enormous help throughout the publication process, kindly chasing down invoices and following up on requests so that my mind could stay on writing. My dean, Toni-Marie Montgomery, continues to make the Bienen School an ideal scholarly home. Hans Thomalla provides warm camaraderie and boundless enthusiasm. Chapter 4 is dedicated to him.

My friends outside Northwestern have been instrumental in the completion of this book. Martin Iddon, Phillip Thomas, Emily Payne, and Laura Emmery provided forums for me to develop Chapter 2. Audiences at the University of Bern offered trenchant thoughts on Chapter 4 and helped me work out the Arendtian reflections in the conclusion. Special thanks to Marc Kilchenmann and Prof. Dr. Michaela Schäuble for that invitation. Matthew Honegger read Chapter 2 and the conclusion and provided terrific feedback. Ana Alonso-Minutti, Andrea Bohlman, Seth Brodsky, Mark Burford, Joy Calico, Brigid Cohen, Tamara Levitz, David Novak, Peter Schmelz, and Benjamin Steege kept me going with the vibrancy of their minds. Fumi Okiji is the kind of thinker

I eventually hope to be. I'm grateful for Sianne Ngai's faith in me. Chapter 3 is dedicated to her.

My practice of friendship has been strengthened by Antoine Beuger, Max Bober, Bryan Eubanks, Jürg Frey, Eva-Maria Houben, Irene Kurka, Catherine Lamb, Rebecca Lane, André O. Möller, Marianne Schuppe, Stefan Thut, Deborah Walker, and Emmanuelle Waeckerle. Here's to another summer in Düsseldorf.

Boundless love and endless thanks to Frank Dohoney, my dad, and Bryan Markovitz, my husband. Each sustained this work in their own essential way. Whatever insights I've had into friendship have been made possible by all these people, but none more so than Sheila Hall—my oldest and dearest friend. I humbly dedicate this book to her.

Portions of this book have appeared elsewhere in earlier versions. Chapter 1 was published as "Spontaneity, Intimacy, and Friendship in Morton Feldman's Music of the 1950s" in *Modernism/Modernity* Print Plus, 2/3 (Fall 2017). Parts of Chapter 2 appeared as "*Élan vital* ... and how to fake it: Morton Feldman and Merle Marsicano's Vernacular Metaphysics" in *Contemporary Music Review*, 38/3 (2019): 229–46. The Intermission appeared as "Charlotte Moorman's Experimental Performance Practice" in *Charlotte Moorman and the Avant-Garde, 1960-1980,* edited by Lisa Corine Graziose and Corinne Granoff (Evanston, IL: Block Museum of Art/Northwestern University Press, 2016), 19–27. Portions of Chapter 3 appeared as "Mourning Coterie: Morton Feldman and Frank O'Hara's Posthumous Collaborations" in *New York School Collaborations: The Color of Vowels,* edited by Mark Silverberg (New York: Palgrave MacMillan, 2013), 183–197.

Bibliography

Archive

Morton Feldman Collection, Paul Sacher Stiftung, Basel Switzerland.

Published Sources

Adorno, Theodor. "On Some Relations Between Music and Painting." *The Musical Quarterly* 79, no. 1 (Spring 1995): 66–79.
Adorno, Theodor. *Philosophy of New Music*. Translated by Robert Hullot-Kentor. Minneapolis, MN: University of Minnesota Press, 2006.
Anderson, Ben. "Affective Atmospheres." *Emotion, Space and Society* 2, no. 2 (December 2009): 77–81.
Arendt, Hannah. *Between Past and Future*. New York: Penguin, 2006.
Arendt, Hannah. "Letter 133, July 20, 1963." In *The Correspondence of Hannah Arendt and Gershom Scholem*, edited by Marie Louise Knott, translated by Anthony David, 206. Chicago, IL: University of Chicago Press, 2017.
Arendt, Hannah. *Men in Dark Times*. New York: Harcourt Brace, 1968.
Arendt, Hannah. *The Human Condition*. Chicago, IL: University of Chicago Press, 1998.
Arendt, Hannah. "We Refugees." In *The Jewish Writings*, edited by Jerome Kohn and Ron H. Feldman, 264–74. New York: Schoken, 2007.
Aston, Dore. "No Way to be Mortified." In *Vertical Thoughts: Morton Feldman and the Visual Arts*, edited by Seán Kissane, 80–5. Dublin: Irish Museum of Modern Art, 2010.
Aston, Dore. *Philip Guston*. New York: Grove Press, 1960.
Auping, Michael and Morton Feldman. "Touch." In *30 Years: Interviews and Outtakes*, edited by Michael Auping, 140–4. Fort Worth, TX: Modern Art Museum of Fort Worth, 2007.
Beal, Amy. "An Interview with Earle Brown." *Contemporary Music Review* 26, no. 3 (2007): 341–56.

Belgrad, Daniel. *The Culture of Spontaneity: Improvisation and the Arts in Postwar America*. Chicago, IL: University of Chicago Press, 1998.

Berger, Arthur. "Music Notes: Jeritza Back, 'Dybbuk' Off; Chance Games." *New York Herald Tribune*, January 28, 1951. D8.

Bergson, Henri. *Creative Evolution*. Translated by Arthur Mitchell. Mineola, NY: Dover, 1998. First published 1911 by Henry Holt & Co. (New York).

Bergson, Henri. *The Creative Mind: An Introduction to Metaphysics*. Translated by Mabelle L. Andison. Mineola, NY: Dover, 2007. First published 1946 by Citadel Press (New York).

Bergson, Henri. *Time and Free Will: An Essay on the Immediate Data of Consciousness*. Translated by Arthur Mitchell. Mineola, NY: Dover, 1998. First published 1911 by George Allen and Unwin (London).

Berkson, Bill and Frank O'Hara. *Hymns of St. Bridget and Other Writings*. Woodacre, CA: The Owl Press, 2001.

Bernard, Jonathan. "Feldman's Painters." In *The New York Schools of Music and Visual Arts*, edited by Steven Johnson, 173–216. New York: Routledge, 2002.

Bernas, Richard and Adrian Jack. "The Brink of Silence." In *Morton Feldman Says: Selected Interviews and Lectures 1964–1987*, edited by Chris Villars, 43–4. London: Hyphen Press, 2006.

Berry, Paul. *Brahms Among Friends: Listening, Performance, and the Rhetoric of Allusion*. New York: Oxford University Press, 2014.

Boutwell, Brett. "Morton Feldman's Graphic Notation: *Projections* and Trajectories." *Journal of the Society for American Music* 6, no. 4 (2012): 457–82.

Broekman, David. "Music in the Making May Make Jobs for Musicians." *International Music* (February 1953): 10–11.

Brown, Richard H. *Through the Looking Glass: John Cage and Avant-Garde Film*. New York: Oxford University Press, 2019.

Cadieu, Martine. "Morton Feldman—Waiting." In *Morton Feldman Says: Selected Interviews and Lectures 1964–1987*, edited by Chris Villars, 38–40. London: Hyphen Press, 2006.

Caffi, Andrea. "On Mythology." *Possibilities* 1 (Winter 1947–1948): 87–92.

Cage, John. *Musicage: Cage Muses on Word, Art, Music*. Edited by Joan Rettalack. Hanover, NH: University of New Hampshire Press, 1996.

Cage, John. *Silence: Lectures and Writings*. Middleton, CT: Wesleyan University Press, 1961.

Cage, John and Morton Feldman. *Radio Happenings: Conversations/Gespräche, 1966–1967*. Edited by Gisela Gronenmeyer and Reinhard Oehlschlägel. Köln: MusikTexte, 2015.

Cavarero, Adriana. *Relating Narratives: Storytelling and Selfhood.* Translated and with an introduction by Paul A. Kottman. New York: Routledge, 2000.

Claren, Sebastian. *Neither: Die Musik Morton Feldman.* Hofheim m Taunus: Wolke Verlag, 2000.

Cline, David. *The Graph Music of Morton Feldman.* Cambridge: Cambridge University Press, 2016.

Cohen, Brigid. "Enigmas of the Third Space: Mingus and Varèse at Greenwich House, 1957." *Journal of the American Musicological Society.* 70, no. 1 (2018): 155–211.

Cohen, Brigid. "Ono in Opera: A Politics of Art and Action." *ASCAP/Journal* 3, no. 1 (2018): 41–66.

Cohen, Brigid. *Stefan Wolpe and the Avant-Garde Diaspora.* Cambridge: Cambridge University Press, 2012.

Cowell, Henry. "Current Chronicle." *Musical Quarterly* 38, no. 1 (1952): 132–43.

Craft, Catherine. *An Audience of Artists: Dada, Neo-Dada, and the Emergence of Abstract Expressionism.* Chicago, IL: University of Chicago Press, 2012.

Craven, David. *Abstract Expressionism as Cultural Critique: Dissent During the McCarthy Period.* Cambridge: Cambridge University Press, 1998.

Cronan, Todd. *Against Affective Formalism: Matisse, Bergson, Modernism.* Minneapolis, MN: University of Minnesota Press, 2013.

de Certeau, Michel. *The Writing of History.* Translated by Tom Cooley. New York: Columbia University Press, 1988.

Deleuze, Gilles. *Bergonism.* Translated by Hugh Tomlinson and Barbara Habberjam. New York: Zone, 1988; First published 1966 by Presses universitaires de France (Paris).

Derrida, Jacques. *The Politics of Friendship.* Translated by George Collins. New York: Verso, 2005.

Dohoney, Ryan. *Saving Abstraction: Morton Feldman, the de Menils, and the Rothko Chapel.* New York: Oxford University Press, 2019.

Dreishpoon, Douglas. *Nothing and Everything: Seven Artists, 1947–1962.* New York: Hauser & Wirth, 2017.

Dubiel, Joseph. "Uncertainty, Disorientation, and Loss as Response to Musical Structure." In *Beyond Structural Listening? Postmodern Modes of Hearing,* edited by Andrew Dell'Antonio, 173–200. Berkeley, CA: University of California Press, 2004.

Dufrenne, Mikel. *The Phenomenology of Aesthetic Experience.* Translated by Edward Casey. Evanston, IL: Northwestern University Press, 1973.

Enns, Anthony. "Voices of the Dead: Transmission/translation/transgression," *Culture, Theory, and Critique* 46, no. 1 (2005): 11–27.

Epstein, Andrew. *Beautiful Enemies: Friendship and Postwar American Poetry*. New York: Oxford University Press, 2006.

Feld, Ross. *Guston in Time: Remembering Philip Guston*. New York: Counterpoint, 2003.

Feldman, Morton. "Brushed Off For Years, Avant Garde Music Finally Gaining Recognition." *Variety*. February 21, 1962. 53.

Feldman, Morton. *Essays*. Edited by Walter Zimmerman. Kerpen: Beginner Press, 1985.

Feldman, Morton. "Frank O'Hara: Lost Times and Future Hopes." *Art in America* 60, no. 2 (1972): 52–5.

Feldman, Morton. *Give My Regards to Eighth Street: Collected Writings of Morton Feldman*. Edited by B. H. Friedman. Cambridge, MA: Exact Change, 2000.

Feldman, Morton. "Marginal Intersection, Intersection II, Intermission VI." *Kulchur* 3, no. 11 (Autumn 1963): 33.

Feldman, Morton. *Morton Feldman in Middelburg: Words on Music, Lectures and Conversations Volume 1*. Edited by Raoul Mörchen. Cologne: Musiktexte, 2008.

Feldman, Morton. *Morton Feldman Says: Collected Interviews and Lectures 1964–1987*. Edited by Chris Villars. London: Hyphen, 2006.

Feldman, Morton. "Parrēsia." Translated by Graham Burchell. *Critical Inquiry* 41, no. 2 (2015): 219–53.

Feldman, Morton, John Cage, Pierre Boulez, and Christian Wolff. "4 Musicians at Work." *Trans/Formation: Arts, Communications, Environment* 1, no. 3 (1952): 168–72.

Feldman, Morton, John Cage, Bunita Marcus, and Francesco Pellizzi. "Conservation with Morton Feldman." *Res* 6 (Autumn 1983): 112–35.

Foss, Lukas. "The Changing Composer-Performer Relationship: A Monologue and a Dialogue." *Perspectives of New Music* 1, no. 2 (1963): 45–53.

Foucault, Michel. "An interview by Stephen Riggins." In *The Essential Works of Michel Foucault, Vol. 1: Ethics, Subjectivity, and Truth*, ed. Paul Rabinow. 121–34. New York: New Press, 1997.

"Four Artists in a 'Mansion.'" *Harper's Bazaar*, July 1952. 79.

Glanville-Hicks, Peggy. "Music in the Making at Cooper Union." *International Musician* (March 1953): 13, 35.

Glass, Loren. *Counterculture Colophon: Grove Press, the Evergreen Review, and the Incorporation of the Avant-Garde*. Stanford: Stanford University Press, 2013.

Glueck, Grace. "New Art School Stresses Essentials." *New York Times*, January 11, 1965.

Goldberg, Albert. "Record Reviews." *Los Angeles Times*, September 18, 1960. F7.

Goodman, Paul. "Advance-Guard Writing: 1900–1950." *Kenyon Review* 13, no. 3 (1951): 375–6.

Goodnough, Robert, ed. "Artists Sessions at Studio 35." In *Reading Abstract Expressionism: Context and Critique*, edited by Ellen G. Landau, 159–64. New Haven, CT: Yale University Press, 2005.

Green, Emily. *Dedicating Music, 1785–1850*. Rochester, NY: University of Rochester Press, 2019.

Greenberg, Clement. *The Collected Essays and Criticism, Volume 2: Arrogant Purpose, 1945–1949*. Edited by John O'Brian. Chicago, IL: University of Chicago Press, 1986.

Greenberg, Clement. *The Collected Essays and Criticism, Volume 4: Modernism with a Vengeance, 1957–1969*. Edited by John O'Brian. Chicago, IL: University of Chicago Press, 1995.

Gunter, Peter A.Y. "Bergson and Proust: A Question of Influence." In *Understanding Bergson, Understanding Modernism*, edited by P. Ardoin, S.E. Gontarski, and L. Mattison, 157–76. New York and London: Bloomsburg, 2013.

Guston, Philip. *Philip Guston: Collected Writings, Lectures, and Conversations*. Edited by Clark Coolidge, 290–7. Berkeley, CA: University of California Press, 2011.

Harris, Ellen T. *George Frideric Handel: A Life with Friends*. New York: Norton, 2014.

Hellstein, Valerie. "The Cage-iness of Abstract Expressionism." *American Art* 28, no. 1 (2014): 56–77.

Hennion, Antoine. "The History of Art—Lessons in Mediation." *Réseaux* 3, no. 2 (1995): 233–62.

Hirata, Catherine Costello. "Analyzing the Music of Morton Feldman." PhD diss., Columbia University, 2003.

Holzapfel, John. "David Tudor and the Performance of American Experimental Music, 1950–1959." PhD diss., City University of New York, 1994.

Holzapfel, John. "Painting by Numbers." In *New York Schools of Music and Visual Art*, edited by Stephen Johnson, 159–72. New York: Routledge, 2002.

Holzapfel, John. "The *Intersections* of Morton Feldman and David Tudor." In *The New York Schools of Music and Visual Art*, edited by Stephen Johnson, 159–72. New York: Routledge, 2002.

Hudelson, Joshua. "Spectral Sound: A Cultural History of the Frequency Domain." PhD diss., New York University, 2018.

Hunter, Sam. *Modern American Painting and Sculpture*. New York: Dell, 1959.

Iddon, Martin. *John Cage and David Tudor: Correspondence on Interpretation and Performance*. Cambridge: Cambridge University Press, 2013.

Iddon, Martin and Philip Thomas. *John Cage's Concert for Piano and Orchestra*. New York: Oxford, 2020.

"Jackson Pollock Film to be Shown at Museum of Modern Art." January 11, 1957. Museum of Modern Art Archives. https://www.moma.org/docs/press_archives/2145/releases/MOMA_1957_0003.pdf?2010, accessed October 8, 2021.

Jones, Caroline A. "Finishing School: John Cage and the Abstract Expressionist Ego." *Critical Inquiry* 19, no. 4 (1993): 628–55.

Jones, Caroline A. *Machine in the Studio: Constructing the Postwar American Artist*. Chicago, IL: University of Chicago Press, 1996.

Joseph, Branden W. *Beyond the Dream Syndicate: Tony Conrad and the Arts After Cage*. New York: Zone, 2008.

Joseph, Branden W. *Experimentations: John Cage on Music, Art, and Architecture*. New York and London: Bloomsbury, 2016.

Joseph, Branden W. *Random Order: Robert Rauschenberg and the Neo-Avant-Garde*. Cambridge, MA: The MIT Press, 2003.

Kanovitz, Howard. "Prefatory Note." In *Kurt Weill: Alabama Song, Arranged for Ensemble and Voice ad lib*, edited by Morton Feldman (1984). London: Universal Edition, 2004.

Katz, Jonathan. "Jackson Pollock's Vitalism: Herbert Matter and the Vitalist Tradition." In *Pollock/Matters*, edited by Ellen G. Landau, 59–72. Boston: McMullen Museum of Art.

Kim, Rebecca Y. "John Cage in Separate Togetherness with Jazz." *Contemporary Music Review* 31, no. 1 (2012): 63–89.

Klein, Scott. "For Frank O'Hara: Morton Feldman's *Three Voices* as Interpretation and Elegy," *Modernist Cultures* 8, no. 1 (Summer 2013): 120–37.

Klorman, Edward. *Mozart's Music of Friends: Social Interplay in the Chamber Works*. Cambridge: Cambridge University Press, 2016.

Kotz, Liz. *Words to Be Looked At: Language in 1960s Art*. Cambridge, MA: The MIT Press, 2007.

La Barbara, Joan. "The Voice is the Original Instrument," *Contemporary Music Review* 21, no. 2 (2002): 35–48.

Landau, Ellen G. "Action/Re-Action: The Artistic Friendship of Herbert Matter and Jackson Pollock." In *Pollock/Matters*, edited by Ellen G. Landau, 9–58. Boston: McMullen Museum of Art, 2007.

Langer, Susanne K. *Feelings and Form: A Theory of Art*. New York: Scribner, 1953.

Latour, Bruno. *Reassembling the Social: An Introduction to Actor-Network-Theory*. New York: Oxford University Press, 2005.

Lawrence, D. H. *Studies in Classic American Literature*. Edited by Ezra Greenspan, Lindeth Vasey, and John Worthen. Cambridge: Cambridge University Press, 2003. First published 1923 by Thomas Seltzer, Inc. (New York).

Lee, Benjamin. "Avant-Garde Poetry as Subcultural Practice: Mailer and Di Prima's Hipster." *New Literary History* 41, no. 4 (Autumn 2010): 775–94.

Levine-Packer, Renée. *This Life of Sounds: Evenings for New Music in Buffalo*. New York: Oxford University Press, 2010.

Levitz, Tamara. *Modernist Mysteries: Perséphone*. New York: Oxford University Press, 2012.

Levy, Benjamin R. "Vertical Thoughts: Feldman, Judaism, and the Open Aesthetic." *Contemporary Music Review* 32, no. 6 (2013): 571–88.

Lewis, George E. "Improvisation After 1950, Afrological and Eurological Perspectives." *Black Music Research Journal* 16, no. 1 (1996): 91–122.

Lippold, Richard. "Merle Marsicano." *Dance Observer* 21, no. 5 (May 1954): 71–2.

Lipton, Seymour. "Statement." In *12 Americans*, edited by Dorothy C. Miller, 72. New York: The Museum of Modern Art, 1956.

Louchheim, Aline B. "An Art Film Festival." *The New York Times*, September 9, 1951, X8.

Matter, Mercedes. "What's Wrong with U.S Art Schools?" *Art News* 62, no. 5 (1963): 40–1, 56–8.

Mattis, Olivia. "From Bebop to Poo-wip: Jazz Influences in Varèse's *Poème Électronique*." In *Edgard Varèse: Composer, Sound Sculptor, Visionary*, edited by Felix Meyer and Heidy Zimmermann, 309–17. Woodbridge: Boydell and Brewer, 2006.

Mattis, Olivia. "Morton Feldman: Music for the Film *Jackson Pollock* (1951)." In *Settling New Scores: Music Manuscripts from the Paul Sacher Foundation*, edited by Felix Meyer, 165–7. Mainz: Schott, 1998.

McDonagh, Donald. *The Complete Guide to Modern Dance*. New York: Doubleday, 1976.

Meyer, Stephen. *Irresistible Dictation: Gertrude Stein and the Correlations of Writing and Science*. Palo Alto: Stanford University Press, 2001.

Milz, Manfred. "Essay in Honor of Robert Motherwell's Centenary: 'temporalized form': Mediating Romanticism and American Expressionism—Robert Motherwell, Henri Bergson, and the Ontological Origins of Abstraction Around 1800." *Journal of Aesthetics and Culture* 8 (2016): 1–22.

Montgomery, Will. "'In Fatal Winds': Frank O'Hara and Morton Feldman." In *Frank O'Hara Now: New Essays on the New York Poet*, edited by Robert Hampson and Will Montgomery, 195–210. Liverpool: Liverpool University Press, 2010.

Moore, Brenna. "Friendship and the Cultivation of Religious Sensibilities." *Journal of the American Academy of Religion* 83, no. 2 (2015): 437–63.

Ngai, Sianne. "Theory of the Gimmick." *Critical Inquiry* 43, no. 2 (2017): 466–505.

Nickels, Joel. *The Poetry of the Possible: Spontaneity, Modernism, and the Multitude*. Minneapolis, MN: University of Minnesota Press, 2012.

Nietzsche, Friedrich. *Human, All Too Human*. Translated by R. J. Hollingdale. Cambridge: Cambridge University Press, 1986.

Nixon, Jon. *Hannah Arendt and the Politics of Friendship*. New York: Bloomsbury, 2015.

Nobel, Alastair. *Composing Ambiguity: The Early Music of Morton Feldman*. Burlington, VT: Ashgate, 2013.

O'Hara, Frank. *Art Chronicles 1954–1966*. New York: Braziller, 1975.

O'Hara, Frank. *Jackson Pollock*. New York: Braziller, 1959.

O'Hara, Frank. "New Directions in Music: Morton Feldman." In *Give My Regards to Eighth Street: Collected Writings of Morton Feldman*, edited by B. H. Friedman, 211–17. Cambridge, MA: Exact Change, 2000.

O'Hara, Frank. *Poems Retrieved*. Edited by Donald Allen. San Francisco: Grey Fox Press, 1996.

O'Hara, Frank. *The Collected Poems of Frank O'Hara*. Edited by Donald Allen. Berkeley, CA: University of California Press, 1955.

Ono, Yoko. "Word of a Fabricator." In *From Postwar to Postmodern: Art in Japan 1945–1989: Primary Documents*, edited by Doryun Chong, Michio Hayashi, Fumihiko Sumitomo, and Kenji Kajiya, 136–8. New York: Museum of Modern Art, 2012.

Pavia, Philip. *Club Without Walls: Selections from the Journals of Philip Pavia*. Edited by Natalie Edgar. New York: Midmarch Arts Press, 2007.

Pellizzi, Francesco. "Morton Feldman and the Arts: A Recollection." In *Vertical Thoughts: Morton Feldman and the Visual Arts*, edited by Sean Kissane, 115–23. Dublin: Irish Museum of Modern Art, 2010.

Perloff, Marjorie. *Frank O'Hara: Poet Among Painters*. New York: Brazillers, 1977.

Piekut, Benjamin. "Chance and Certainty: John Cage's Politics of Nature." *Cultural Critique* 84 (Spring 2013): 134–63.

Piekut, Benjamin. *Experimentalism Otherwise: The Avant-Garde and Its Limits*. Berkeley, CA: University of California Press, 2011.

Piekut, Benjamin. *Henry Cow: The World Is a Problem*. Durham, NC: Duke University Press, 2019.

Piekut, Benjamin and Jason Stanyek. "Deadness: Technologies of the Intermundane." *TDR: The Dance Review* 54, no. 1 (2010): 14–38.

Pollock, Jackson. "My Painting." *Possibilities* 1 (Winter 1947–1948): 79.

"Presentation of the New York Studio School to the Ford Foundation." New York Studio School Papers, n.d [c. 1964–1965].

Quirk, Tom. *Bergson in American Culture: The Worlds of Willa Cather and Wallace Stevens*. Chapel Hill: University of North Carolina Press, 1990.

Rose, Gillian. *Judaism and Modernity: Philosophical Essays*. New York: Verso, 2017.

Rosenberg, Harold. "The American Action Painters." In *The Tradition of the New*, 23–39. New York: McGraw Hill, 1959.

Rosenholtz-Witt, Jason. "Beyond the Score: Charlotte Moorman and John Cage's 26'1.1499 for a String Player." In *A Feast of Astonishments: Charlotte Moorman and the Avant-Garde, 1960s–1980s*, edited by Lisa Graziose Corrin and Corinne Granof, 29–41 Evanston, IL: Northwestern University Press, 2016.

Rothfuss, Joan. *Topless Cellist: The Improbably Life of Charlotte Moorman*. Cambridge, MA: The MIT Press, 2014.

Rothko, Mark. "The Romantics Were Prompted." *Possibilities* 1 (Winter 1947–48): 87–92. Reprinted in Rothko, Mark. *Writings on Art*. New Haven, CT: Yale University Press, 2006.

Rothko, Mark. *Writings on Art*, edited by Miguel López-Rimero. New Haven, CT: Yale University Press, 2006.

Schapiro, Meyer. "The Liberating Quality of Avant-Garde Art." In *Reading Abstract Expressionism: Context and Critique*, edited by Ellen G. Landau, 215–20. New Haven, CT: Yale University Press, 2005.

Scholem, Gershom. "Letter 132, June 23, 1963." In *The Correspondence of Hannah Arendt and Gershom Scholem*, edited by Marie Louise Knott, translated by Anthony David, 202. Chicago: University of Chicago Press, 2017.

Selby, Nick. "Memory Pieces: Collage, Memorial and the Poetics of Intimacy in Joe Brainard, Jasper Johns and Frank O'Hara." In *Frank O'Hara Now: Essays on the New York Poet*, edited by Robert Hampson and Will Montgomery, 229–46. Liverpool: Liverpool University Press, 2010.

Shaw, Lytle. *Frank O'Hara: The Poetics of Coterie*. Iowa City: University of Iowa Press, 2006.

Silverberg, Mark. *The New York School of Poets and the Neo-Avant-Garde*. Burlington, VT: Ashgate, 2010.

Silverman, Kenneth. *Begin Again: A Biography of John Cage*. New York: Knopf, 2010.

Sjöholm, Cecilia. *Doing Aesthetics with Arendt: How to See Things*. New York: Columbia University Press, 2014.

Slifkin, Robert. *Out of Time: Philip Guston and the Refiguration of Postwar American Art*. Berkeley, CA: University of California Press, 2013.

Smart, Pamela. "Possession: Intimate Artifice at the Menil Collection." *Modernism/modernity* 13, no. 1 (2006): 765–85.

Sontag, Susan. "Notes on Camp." In *Against Interpretation*, 275–92. New York: Picador, 1966.

Stephenson Smith, S. "Good Programs Mean Jobs." *International Musician* (March 1953): 13.

Sterne, Jonathan. *The Audible Past: The Cultural Origins of Sound Reproduction*. Durham, NC: Durham University Press, 2002.

Stevens, Wallace. "The Man with the Blue Guitar." *Poetry* 50, no. 2 (1937): 61–9.

Streckler, Dorothy. "Oral History interview with Lee Krasner, 1964, Nov. 2–1968 Apr. 11." *Smithsonian Archives of American Art*. https://www.aaa.si.edu/download_pdf_transcript/ajax?record_id=edanmdm-AAADCD_oh_214115, accessed October 8, 2021.

Tallman, Susan. "Philip Guston's Discomfort Zone." *New York Review of Books*, January 14, 2021. https://www.nybooks.com/articles/2021/01/14/philip-gustons-discomfort-zone/, accessed October 8, 2021.

Trimble, Lester. "Music." *The Nation*. February 20, 1960. 175.

Verderame, Lori. *An American Sculptor: Seymour Lipton*. State College, PA: Palmer Museum of Art, 1999.

Volans, Kevin. "What Is Feldman?" *Tempo* 68, no. 270 (2014): 7–14.

Whitehead, Alfred North. *Process and Reality. An Essay in Cosmology. Gifford Lectures Delivered in the University of Edinburgh During the Session 1927–1928*. New York: The Free Press, 1978. First published 1928 by Macmillan (New York).

Whitehead, Alfred North. *The Concept of Nature*. Mineola, NY: Dover, 2004. First published 1920 by Cambridge University Press (Cambridge).

Williams, Jan. "An Interview with Morton Feldman." *Percussive Notes* (1983): 4–14. Reprinted in *Morton Feldman Says: Selected Interviews and Lectures 1964–1987*, edited by Chris Villars, 151–2. London: Hyphen Press, 2006.

Wolff, Christian. "New and Electronic Music." In *Writings about John Cage*, edited by Richard Kostelanetz, 85–92. Ann Arbor: University of Michigan Press, 1996.

Young-Bruehl, Elisabeth. *Hannah Arendt For Love of the World*. New Haven, CT: Yale University Press, 1982.

Discography

Feldman, Morton. *Morton Feldman: New Directions in Music 2*. Columbia Masterworks, MS6090, 1959, vinyl.

Feldman, Morton. *Morton Feldman: Rothko Chapel / For Frank O'Hara*. Center for the Creative and Performing Arts, conducted by Gregg Smith and Jan Williams. Odyssey Y34138, 1976, vinyl.

Feldman, Morton. *The Early Years*. Columbia Odyssey 32160302, 1968, vinyl.

Feldman, Morton. *The Viola in My Life*. CRI SD 276, 1971, vinyl.

Feldman, Morton and Earle Brown. *Morton Feldman / Earle Brown*. Time Records, 58007/S8007, 1962, vinyl.

Feldman, Morton and John Cage. *John Cage: Music for Keyboard, 1935–1948 / Morton Feldman: The Early Years*. New World Records, 80664, 2007, compact disc.

Moorman, Charlotte, cellist. *Cello Anthology*. Alga Marghen, 2006, 4 compact discs.

Zukofsky, Paul, conductor. *Milton Babbitt: Septet but Equal; Fourplay; Morton Feldman: Instruments 1; Three Clarinets, Cello and Piano*. Composers Ensemble, recorded July 20 and 22, 1997. CP2/111, 2003, compact disc.

Filmography

Boxer, Nathan, dir. *Sculpture by Lipton*. New York: Image Films, 1954.

Matter, Herbert, dir. *Works for Calder*. New York: New World Film Productions for the Museum of Modern Art, 1950.

Namuth, Hans, dir. *Jackson Pollock 51*. New York: Museum at Large, 1951.

Index

abstraction
    and dance   66
    Feldman's desire for   32, 132, 145–6, 161–2, 171, 176, 193
    Guston's frustration with   152, 160–2, 168–9, 171, 192–3
    vs. improvisation   94
    and love   190
    and nature   71–2
    politics of   132
acceptance
    Cage's   32, 35–7, 44
    and discipline   38
    Feldman's   29, 31, 37–8, 42, 128, 135
    and spontaneity   31
agency. *See also* necessary others
    of the artwork   21, 29
    human   74
    of mourners   172
    of movement itself   64
    of performers/artists   25, 29, 34, 39, 43–4, 60, 67, 74, 93–104, 111
    and spontaneity   31
alienation
    overcoming   23, 30, 38, 44, 58, 60
Anderson, Ben. *See also* atmosphere
    on affective atmospheres   122–3
anxiety   118–19, 157–8, 173
Arendt, Hannah   28
    on aesthetics   7–8
    on doxa   188
    Eichmann in Jerusalem   186, 189–90
    and the Eighth Street Artists Club   7, 23, 185
    on friendship   7, 14, 185–93
    "Humanity in Dark Times"   186–9
    on human relations and narrative   11, 185
    on lament   191
    and the present moment   30
    and Rosenberg   7, 185–6, 189–90
    and Scholem   186, 189–90
    on spontaneous spaces of appearances   23
    and Wolff   7, 185
Aristophanes
    The Frogs   57
artist films   68–85. *See also Jackson Pollock 51* (Namuth); *Sculpture by Lipton* (Boxer); *Works of Calder* (Matter)
Ashbery, John
    and friendship   9
Ashley, Robert   45, 93–5, 97, 101
    on the imagery of personality   100
Ashton, Dore
    on Feldman   153
    on spontaneity in Guston's painting   20
atmosphere   118–20, 122–5, 132, 174–5
audience
    vs. friends   8, 10
    frustrated (by Feldman's quiet music)   114
    as "unfooled" (by Feldman's graph music)   38

Bach, Michael. *See also Three Voices* (Feldman)
    on *Three Voices*   133
Barab, Seymour
    and the "tradition of the new"   99
Baraka, Amiri   103
    and friendship   9
beauty   128, 131–6
    and language   134
    as problematic   133
Beckett, Samuel   125
    For Samuel Beckett (Feldman)   3
Belgrad, Daniel. *See also* spontaneity
    on spontaneity at midcentury   19

Berger, Arthur
  on Feldman's "gimmick" 26
Bergson, Henri 42, 55–62, 67–8, 71, 80, 83. *See also* vitalism
  on the artist 59
  on cinema 68
  Creative Evolution 54, 59
  and Feldman 53–4
  "The Perception of Change" 59
  Time and Free Will 54
Berkson, Bill
  and Guston 155
  "St. Bridget's Hymn to Philip Guston" 12. *See also* O'Hara, Frank
Bernard, Jonathan. *See also Jackson Pollock 51* (Namuth)
  on the gestural in Feldman's score to *Jackson Pollock 51* 77
Berry, Paul
  on resonances between musical works 11
Blanchot, Maurice
  on friendship 167
Boulez, Pierre 60
  on Feldman 17
  Feldman on 24, 53
Boutwell, Brett 32
Boxer, Nathan. *See also Sculpture by Lipton* (Boxer)
  Sculpture by Lipton 13, 57, 60, 68, 79–83
Britten, Benjamin. *See also* realization
  on realizations 96–7
Broekman, David
  and the "Music in the Making" series 37–8
Brown, Earle 60, 94, 96. *See also Works of Calder* (Matter)
  December 1952 101
  and Feldman 152
  Music for Cello and Piano 99
  Synergy 13, 100–2, 105 n.21
Brown, Richard H.
  on *Works of Calder* 69
Bryars, Gavin 139
Bussotti, Sylvano 96

Caffi, Andrea 28
Cage, John 5, 46, 60, 79, 84, 94–6, 100, 102. *See also Works of Calder* (Matter)
  4′33″ 31
  26′1.1499″ 99
  and Abstract Expressionism 13, 28, 56, 147
  and Bergson 54
  on the commodification of music 28
  and the Eighth Street Artists Club 7, 19, 26–8, 32, 79, 110
  and Feldman 6, 9, 12–13, 17–19, 22–9, 32–8, 44, 53, 57, 85, 108, 110, 145, 147–8, 173–4
  on Feldman's music 23–4, 27–39, 54
  and Guston 147
  Hymns and Variations 104 n.14
  and the *I Ching* 67
  Imaginary Landscape No. 3 33
  Imaginary Landscape No. 5 36
  For John Cage (Feldman) 3, 147
  and La Barbara 127–8
  "Lecture on Something" 26–32, 36–7, 40, 44
  and Marsicano 63
  on nature 69, 72, 74, 83–4
  and Pollock 73
  and *Possibilities* 28
  on Rauschenberg's *White Paintings* 31
  Silence 32
  Solo for Voice 45 128
  and technology 71
  on *Three Voices* (Feldman) 133
  and vitalism 58, 60
  and *Works of Calder* 68–9, 83
Calder, Alexander 68, 70, 73–4, 84. *See also Works of Calder* (Matter)
  Works of Calder 57, 60, 68–74, 78–9, 81–3, 110
Cavarero, Adriana. *See also* necessary others
  on friendship and narrative reciprocity 11
  on "necessary others" 101
  on the relationship between Stein and Toklas 102

Chatham, Rhys
  and La Barbara   127
Chiari, Giuseppe   100–1. *See also*
  Moorman, Charlotte
citation. *See also* mourning; quotation
  and mourning   135
Claren, Sebastian
  on Bergson's philosophy and Feldman's
    thinking   54
Cline, David
  on Feldman's feelings about
    performers' decisions   29
  on *Figure of Memory*   87 n.25
  on links between *Marginal Intersection*
    and Cage's early percussion
    pieces   33
clown
  as compliment   101
coats
  and Feldman   17, 34, 164–7
containment   40–3
Coolidge, Clark
  on Guston and Feldman's
    relationship   168
Cowell, Henry   57, 64, 87 n.25
Craft, Catherine
  on the moral aspect of critical
    judgement   37
Cunningham, Merce. *See also* dance
  and Feldman   17, 27, 63, 105 n.17
  and Marsicano   63

dance   62–7, 84. *See also* Cunningham,
    Merce; Marsicano, Merle
  and abstraction   66
  and Feldman   58, 87 n.25
  and painting   65–6
death. *See also* mediumship; mourning
  and beauty   133
  and friendship   12–13, 107–36
  and music/art (for Feldman)   12, 67,
    121, 154, 162
  and recorded sound   124–7, 130, 133,
    174
  speaking for the dead   3
  sudden (in O'Hara's poetry)   12,
    112–13, 116, 121, 140 n.52

de Certeau, Michel   3
dedications   146–8, 160, 172
  For Bunita Marcus   3
  For Christian Wolff   3
  Dance Suite for Merle Marsicano
    63
  For Franz Kline   3, 116, 123, 138 n.29,
    147, 149
  For Frank O'Hara   3, 113, 116–25,
    147, 172
  Friend—To M.F. (Guston)   163, 166,
    172
  For John Cage   3, 147
  For Philip Guston   3, 10, 14, 108, 122,
    144, 172–7
  Piano Piece (to Philip Guston)   45,
    104 n.7, 149
  For Samuel Beckett   3
  For Stefan Wolpe   3, 108
de Kooning, Willem   18, 66
  on completing a picture   155
  De Kooning   149
  as rejected by Guston   152,
    160–1
Deleuze, Gilles. *See also* Bergson, Henri
  Bergsonism   55
de Menil, Dominique
  and Feldman   4, 17, 160
  and Rothko   4
de Menil, John
  and Feldman   4, 159–60
  and Rothko   4
  and the Studio School   159, 179 n.46
Derrida, Jacques
  on friendship and silence   188, 190
  on friendship and surviving   177
  on mourning   135
Dewey, Anne
  on friendships   4
Dodge, Charles
  and La Barbara   127
Dohoney, Ryan
  Saving Abstraction   4, 14, 143,
    179 n.46
Dubiel, Joseph   135
Dufrenne, Mikel   122. *See also*
    abstraction

Eighth Street Artists Club   7, 19, 23, 26–9, 32, 58, 63, 65–6, 68, 79, 110, 158. *See also It is. A Magazine for Abstract Art*
and jazz   36
Epstein, Andrew. *See also* friendship
on friendship's role in aesthetic/cultural forms   8–9
Erdman, Jean. *See also* dance
and Feldman   58, 63, 87 n.25
and Marsicano   63

Faulkner, William. *See also* Arendt, Hannah
A Fable   192
Feld, Ross. *See also Jackson Pollock 51* (Namuth); *New Yorkers II, The* (Kanovitz); *Sculpture by Lipton* (Boxer)
on the awkwardness of Feldman's presence at Guston's funeral   169–70
on coats (as Feldman) in Guston's late paintings   164
on *Friend—To M.F.* (Guston)   163
Feldman, Morton
and abstraction   32, 132, 145–6, 161–2, 171, 176, 193
"After Modernism"   152, 160
and anxiety   118–19, 157–8, 173
and atmosphere   118–20, 122–5, 132, 174–5
on beauty   128, 131–6
and Brown   152
For Bunita Marcus   3
and Cage   6, 9, 12–13, 17–19, 22–9, 32–8, 44, 53, 57, 85, 108, 110, 145, 147–8, 173–4
Chorus and Instruments II   63
For Christian Wolff   3
Christian Wolff in Cambridge   63
and coats   17, 34, 164–7
and Cunningham   17, 27, 63, 105 n.17
Dance Suite for Merle Marsicano   63
and death   12–13, 67, 107–36, 154, 162, 176

De Kooning   149
Durations   54
The Early Years   1
on *élan vital*   53–4
Extensions 1   34–5, 54, 57
Extensions 3   34, 54, 57, 82
Extensions 4   34, 54, 57, 147
Figure of Memory   56–7, 62–7, 84
and film   73–9
"Four Lectures: New York Style"   53–4, 158–9
"Frank O'Hara: Lost Times and Future Hopes"   158
For Franz Kline   3, 116, 123, 138 n.29, 147, 149
For Frank O'Hara   3, 113, 116–25, 147, 172
"Give My Regards to Eighth Street"   9, 115–16, 158
hair of   163, 166
and the "illusion of feeling"   113–14, 116–18, 121
I Met Heine on the Rue Fürstenberg   113–14
Intermission 3   7
Intermission 6   34, 56–62, 82, 84
Intersection 1   29–32, 37
Intersection 2   32, 34, 99
Intersection 3   6–7, 42, 99
Ixion   17, 88 n.39, 105 n.17
on jazz   36, 50 n.71
For John Cage   3, 147
and Judaism   53–4, 123, 146, 153, 164, 166, 169, 176, 192–3
and Katz   1
and Kierkegaard   53, 84, 145, 153, 171
and La Barbara   125–36
Last Pieces   148
Madame Press Died Last Week at Ninety   113–14
Marginal Intersection   19, 29, 32–42, 57
and Marsicano   13, 56–7, 62–8, 84
and Moorman   93–103
New Directions in Music 2   1, 12, 19, 32, 41, 44–5, 51 n.101, 110–11, 136, 148

in *The New Yorkers II* (Kanovitz)   1–2
and the New York Studio School   149, 156–62, 168–9, 179 n.46
and O'Hara   1, 12–13, 19, 23, 39–44, 107–36, 145, 175–6
The O'Hara Songs   111, 114, 122
and pattern/rugs   170–2
"Philip Guston, The Last Painter"   152–5
"Philip Guston 1980"   171–2
For Philip Guston   3, 10, 14, 108, 122, 144, 172–7
Piano Piece (to Philip Guston)   45, 104 n.7, 149
Piece for 4 Pianos   43–4
on process   137 n.6
Projection 1   6, 13, 97–9, 101, 104 n.15
Projection 2   6, 25–8, 98
and/on publicity   8–10, 17–19, 23, 44, 116, 148–52, 175–6
and quietude   60, 114, 116, 118–20
on realization   96
and Rothko   4, 18, 23, 143, 145, 175–6
Rothko Chapel   4, 113–14, 170
For Samuel Beckett   3
Skizzenbuch 3   57–62, 87 n.25
For Stefan Wolpe   3, 108
String Quartet No. 2   122, 135–6
as subject in the art of others   144, 148, 162–8
Three Clarinets, Cello, and Piano   113–15, 117–24
Three Dances   63, 66
Three Pieces for String Quartet   147
Three Voices   10, 13, 122, 125–36, 140 n.52, 144, 172, 174
Trio   173
and Tudor   5–7, 23, 25, 32, 34, 42, 45, 62–3, 93–4, 96–7, 99, 104 n.7, 105 n.17
"The Unframed Frame"   31
and the University of Buffalo   1, 113, 128, 159
and verticality   83, 179 n.46
"Vertical Thoughts"   152–3

Vertical Thoughts 3   123
Vertical Thoughts 5   123
The Viola in My Life   113–14
Violin and Orchestra   170
and Wolpe   23–4, 110, 145, 175–6
Figure of Memory (Feldman)   56–7, 62–7, 84
film. *See* artist films
Finnegans Wake   135
and Feldman (for Cage)   29–30
flatness. *See also Three Voices* (Feldman)
and the Abstract Expressionists   125
as aesthetic value   137 n.6
and truth   131
Fluxus   100
Foss, Lukas
on the composer/performer relationship   102
Foucault, Michel. *See also parrēsia*; silence
on the *parrēsiatic* gesture   37
on silence and relationships   185
For Frank O'Hara (Feldman)   3, 113, 116–25, 147, 172. *See also* Feldman, Morton; O'Hara, Frank
Friedman, B. H. *See also New Yorkers II, The* (Kanovitz)
and Feldman   1
in *The New Yorkers II* (Kanovitz)   1–2
friendship   2–6. *See also* intimacy; silence
as an (almost) accidental social relation   2
and concreteness   190
and death   12–13, 107–36
vs. fraternity   186–7
and history   2
as non-existent   3
and pedagogy   156, 159
and permission   5–6
and silence   185–93
and subject-formation   5, 116–17
and surviving   177
and transformation   143–77
and truth   187–91
and understanding   45
and the world   186–7, 191

ghosts. *See also* death; mediumship
  as distraction   130
  friends as   143, 162–3
  as wills   124
gimmickry   26–7
Glanville-Hicks, Peggy
  on Feldman's graph music   38
Goodman, Paul. *See also* spontaneity
  "Advance-Guard Writing"   21–3, 45
Gottlieb, Adolf
  on flat forms   131
Graham, Martha. *See also* dance;
    Marsicano, Merle
  and Cowell   64
  and Marsicano   63
Green, Emily
  on dedications as publicizing private
    relationships   147–8
Greenberg, Clement   65
  on flatness   137
  formalism of   4
  on medium-specificity   68, 107
  on O'Hara's Pollock monograph   42
Guston (née McKim), Musa   160, 170.
    See also Guston, Philip
Guston, Philip   5, 131, 143–77, 187–93.
    See also New Directions in Music 2
    (Feldman); *Three Voices* (Feldman)
  and abstraction   152, 160–2, 168–9,
    171, 192–3
  Allegory   163
  Attar   111, 150–1, 163
  Back View   166, 169
  Back View II   166
  on bearing witness   160–1, 167, 187
  and Cage   147
  on Cage   31
  The Coat   165, 167
  The Coat II   164–5
  and death   154–5
  death of   144–6, 165, 169–70
  depiction of white supremacists   146,
    167
  and the Eighth Street Artists Club   7
  "Faith, Hope, and Impossibility"   155
  and Feldman   6, 9, 12–14, 18–21, 23,
    31, 45, 108, 125–7, 136, 143–77,
    187–93
  and the figural   12, 162–71
  Friend—To M.F.   163, 166, 172
  Group in Sea   167, 169
  Head-Double View   41, 111, 136, 148
  and history   153–5
  Last Piece   148–9
  and the New York Studio School   149,
    156–62, 168–9
  and O'Hara   12, 111
  Painting 1954   111
  For Philip Guston   3, 10, 14, 108, 122,
    144, 172–7
  Piano Piece (to Philip Guston)   45,
    104 n.7, 149
  "Piero della Francesca: The
    Impossibility of Painting"   155
  Pink Sea   167
  Red Painting   145
  and reduction   151, 154, 160
  Room and Sea   165
  and Rosenberg   150–1, 155, 185
  on the "slick inhuman elegance" of
    de Kooning and Kline, etc.   152,
    160–1

Harris, Ellen
  on Handel's friendship networks   10
Harrison, Lou   24
Hawthorne, Nathaniel
  The Blithedale Romance   122–4
Hellstein, Valerie. *See also* Cage, John
  on Cage as anti-expressive   22, 27–8
  on vitalism and the Eighth Street
    Artists Club   55–6
Hennion, Antoine
  on music as the art of mediation
    itself   22
Hirata, Catherine. *See also* Feldman,
    Morton; *For Frank O'Hara*
    (Feldman); O'Hara, Frank
  on *For Frank O'Hara*   119–20
history
  and the Annual Avant Garde
    Festival   95
  and friendship   2
  and Guston   153–5
  and (musical) language   161
  and narration   191–2

Hofmann, Hans 68, 72, 156
Holzaepfel, John 88 n.39
  on collaboration (between Feldman and Tudor) in *Intersection 3* 6–7
Hunter, Sam. *See also New Yorkers II, The* (Kanovitz)
  Modern American Painting and Sculpture 1
  in *The New Yorkers II* (Kanovitz) 1–2
Hymovitz, Edwin. *See also Intermission 6* (Feldman)
  and *Intermission 6* 63–5

Intermission 6 (Feldman) 34, 56–62. *See also* Feldman, Morton
Intersection 1 (Feldman) 29–31. *See also* Feldman, Morton
intimacy. *See also* friendship
  and spontaneity 3–4, 19–23, 44, 158, 167
  and understanding 45
intuition
  for Feldman 61–2
  for Marsicano 67, 84
It is. A Magazine for Abstract Art 32, 44

Jackson Pollock 51 (Namuth) 13, 18, 32, 34, 41, 57, 68, 71, 73–9, 81, 83. *See also* Namuth, Hans; Pollock, Jackson
James, William 58. *See also* vitalism
jazz
  and the New York School 1, 34–6, 50 n.71
Johnson, Ray 18
Jones, Caroline A.
  on artist films 18
  on Cagean indeterminacy 56
Joseph, Branden
  on Cage 54, 56, 83–4
  "minor history" 85
judgement
  of Feldman's work (as useless) 30

Kanovitz, Howard
  and Feldman's *The Early Years* 1
  The New Yorkers II 1–2, 5, 7, 12
  and Rivers 1

Kaprow, Alan 94
Katz, Alex. *See also New Yorkers II, The* (Kanovitz)
  and Feldman 1
  and O'Hara 1
  in *The New Yorkers II* (Kanovitz) 1–2
  and the New York Studio School 1
Katz, Jonathan
  on Pollock's vitalism and community 84
  on vitalism and the Eighth Street Artists Club 55–6
Kierkegaard, Søren
  Feldman and 53, 84, 145, 153, 171
  "the Instant" 153
Kim, Rebecca
  on Cage's *Imaginary Landscape No. 5* 36
Klee, Paul
  Hauptweg und Nebenweg 130–1
  Klee Alee (La Barbara) 129–31
Klein, Scott. *See also Three Voices* (Feldman)
  on *Three Voices* 125, 140 n.52
Kline, Franz 175–6
  death of 107, 138 n.29
  For Franz Kline 3, 116, 123, 138 n.29, 147, 149
  as rejected by Guston 152, 160–1
Klorman, Edward
  on friendship and musical expression 10–11
Krasner, Lee 77. *See also* Pollock, Jackson
  on Pollock's invocation of natural forces 71–3

La Barbara, Joan
  and Cage 127–8
  Cathing 128
  Circular Song 128
  Erin 129
  Ides of March 128
  Klee Alee 129–31
  as medium 108, 125–36, 174
  October Music 129
  Reluctant Gypsy 128
  ShadowSong 129–30
  Tapesongs 127–8

Thunder 127–8
Twelvesong 129
Vocal Extensions 128. See also
 mediumship; Three Voices
 (Feldman)
Landau, Ellen
 on Pollock and Matter 73
 on vitalism and the Eighth Street
 Artists Club 55–6
 on vitalism in Jackson Pollock 51 and
 Works of Calder 79
Langer, Susanne K.
 on Bergson as the artists'
 philosopher 59
La Touche, John. See also Works of Calder
 (Matter)
 as imagined Feldman
 collaborator 110
 and Works of Calder 69–73
Latour, Bruno
 on the instability of groups 109
Lawrence, D. H. See also atmosphere;
 mediumship
 on atmosphere and
 mediumship 123–5, 174
Lee, Benjamin
 on vernacular styles 55
Lessing, Gotthold Ephraim. See also
 Arendt, Hannah; friendship
 Nathan the Wise 186–9
LeSueur, Joe 164–5. See also O'Hara,
 Frank
 "Joe's Jacket"
Levitz, Tamara
 on mourning 135, 172
Lewis, George E.
 on jazz 36
limits
 of perception 33–4
 of spontaneity 39–44
Lippold, Richard 18. See also Marsicano,
 Merle
 on Marsicano 65–6
Lipton, Seymour 68, 79–85
 and the Eighth Street Artists
 Club 79–80
 Sanctuary 83

Sculpture by Lipton (Boxer) 13, 57,
 60, 68, 79–85
 and vitalism 58, 80, 83
Litz, Katherine. See also dance
 and Feldman 58, 87 n.25

McDonagh, Don. See also Figure of
 Memory (Feldman); Marsicano,
 Merle
 on Marsicano and Figure of
 Memory 64–6
McKee, David 170
Mac Low, Jackson 94
Marcus, Bunita
 For Bunita Marcus 3
Marginal Intersection (Feldman) 19,
 29, 32–42, 57. See also Cage, John;
 Feldman, Morton; jazz; limits;
 nationalism; quotation
Marsicano, Merle 62–7, 83–5. See also
 Figure of Memory (Feldman)
 on art 66
 and Cage 63
 on dance 63–4, 66, 84
 and the Eighth Street Artists Club 63,
 65–6
 and Feldman 13, 56–7, 62–8, 84
 Fragment for a Greek Tragedy 63
 Green Song 65–6
 Jet Pears 65–6
 and O'Hare 65
Marsicano, Nicholas. See also Eighth Street
 Artists Club; Marsicano, Merle
 and the Eighth Street Artists Club 63
Matter, Alexander "Pundy" 69–71, 82.
 See also Works of Calder (Matter)
Matter, Herbert 156. See also vitalism
 and the Eighth Street Artists Club 79
 and Pollock 73
 Works of Calder 57, 60, 68–74, 78–9,
 81–3, 110
Matter, Mercedes. See also New York
 Studio School
 and the New York Studio School 1,
 17, 149, 156–62
 "What's Wrong with U.S. Arts
 Schools?" 156–8

Mattis, Olivia. *See also Jackson Pollock 51* (Namuth)
   on the gestural in Feldman's score to *Jackson Pollock 51*   77
Mayer, Musa "Ingie"   170. *See also* Guston, Philip
mediumship   3, 108, 122–36. *See also* La Barbara, Joan
memory. *See also* Bergson, Henri; *Figure of Memory* (Feldman); history; Proust, Marcel; *Three Voices* (Feldman)
   of action (as opposed to action itself)   77
   coat as figure of   164–5
   and death   107–36
   and friendship   8–9, 113, 115, 135, 187
   and innocence   67
   and lament   191
   "In Memory of My Feelings" (O'Hara)   114–20
   vs. objectivity/subjectivity   153
   reliable   63
   unreliable   32, 145–6
Meredith, Burgess   69, 82. *See also Works of Calder* (Matter)
Metzger, Heinz-Klaus
   on mourning in Feldman's music   176
misunderstanding
   of "freeing sound"   98
Mitchell, Joan   40. *See also* O'Hara, Frank "Poem Read at Joan Mitchell's"
Montgomery, Will
   on the friendship of Feldman and O'Hara   40
mood. *See also* Kierkegaard, Søren
   and artists   145
   and atmosphere   174–5
   importance of   171, 174
Moore, Brenna
   on friendships   4–5, 23, 185
Moorman, Charlotte   5–6, 11, 13, 93–104 n.14. *See also Projection 1* (Feldman)
   Annual Avant Garde Festival   93, 95, 100–1, 104 n.12
   and *Projection 1* (Feldman)   13

   and *Synergy* (Brown)   13, 100–2, 105 n.21
   trial of   103
Motherwell, Robert
   on his community/peers   46, 107
   and *Possibilities*   28
   and Whitehead   56
mourning   14, 107–36. *See also* death; friendship
   and citation   135
   deferred   136, 143–77
   and melancholy   14, 118, 168–77
   resistant   136, 144, 175
Mumma, Gordon   94, 97

Namuth, Hans. *See also Jackson Pollock 51* (Namuth)
   Jackson Pollock 51   13, 18, 32, 34, 41, 57, 68, 71, 73–9, 81, 83
   photographs of Pollock   18
narrative
   and human relations   11, 185
   and reciprocity   11–12, 14
nationalism. *See also Marginal Intersection* (Feldman); quotation
   in *Marginal Intersection*   39, 43, 95
nature. *See also* vitalism
   and abstraction   71–2
   and art   69–84
   bifurcation of   68, 74
   and Guston   153
   and human nature (for Feldman)   74
   Pollock *as*   68, 71–3, 77
   and rhythm   70
necessary others   5–7, 20, 93–103, 108, 146, 149–50, 159, 162, 177, 190–1
New Directions in Music 2 (Feldman)   1, 12, 19, 32, 41, 44–5, 51 n.101, 110–11, 136, 148
New Yorkers II, The (Kanovitz)   1–2, 5, 7, 12. *See also* Kanovitz, Howard
New York Studio School   1, 17, 112, 149, 156–62, 179 n.46. *See also* Matter, Mercedes
Ngai, Sianne. *See also* gimmickry
   on the gimmick   26
Nickels, Joel   23

Nietzsche, Friedrich
  on friendship and silence   188–90
  on friendship and transformation   143, 162–3
Nixon, Jon. *See also* Arendt, Hannah
  on the hermeneutics of friendship in Arendt   8
Noble, Alistair. *See also Intermission 6* (Feldman)
  on *Intermission 6*   60

O'Hara, Frank   4, 39–44, 103, 107–36. *See also New Yorkers II, The* (Kanovitz); *Three Clarinets, Cello, and Piano* (Feldman); *Three Voices* (Feldman)
  "Augustus"   65
  "The Day Lady Died"   112, 118
  and death   12, 108, 112–13, 116, 121, 140 n.52, 154, 165
  death of   12–13, 107, 109–10, 112–13, 115, 118, 123, 176
  and the Eighth Street Artists Club   7, 110
  and Feldman   1, 12–13, 19, 23, 39–44, 107–36, 145, 175–6
  on Feldman's music   25, 40, 42–4, 110
  For Frank O'Hara (Feldman)   3, 113, 116–25, 147, 172
  and Goodman   22
  and Guston   12, 111
  "It seems far away and gentle now" (a.k.a., "To Philip Guston")   111, 138 n.20
  "Joe's Jacket"   164–5
  and Katz   1
  liner notes for *New Directions in Music 2* (Feldman)   1, 12, 19, 41, 44, 110–11, 136, 148
  and love   169, 182 n.70
  and Marsicano   65
  "Mayakovsky"   121
  "In Memory of My Feelings"   114–20
  in *The New Yorkers II* (Kanovitz)   1–2
  and names   9–10
  The O'Hara Songs (Feldman)   111, 114, 122

"Poem Read at Joan Mitchell's"   39–43
  on poetry and personal connection   7, 12, 22
  on Pollock   41–4, 111
  "Second Avenue"   1, 107
  "St. Bridget's Hymn to Philip Guston"   12
  "Wind"   111, 122, 129, 134
O'Hara Songs, The (Feldman)   111, 114, 122. *See also* Feldman, Morton; O'Hara, Frank
Ono, Yoko   94. *See also* Cage, John
  on Cage   72
Orton, Fred   169

Paik, Nam June
  and Moorman   102–3
  Opera Sextronique   103
  violence of (for Feldman)   95
parrēsia   37–8
Pavia, Philip. *See also It is. A Magazine for Abstract Art*
  and the Eighth Street Artists Club   79–80
  It is. A Magazine for Abstract Art   32
Perloff, Marjorie
  on O'Hara's "Joe's Jacket"   165
permission. *See also* agency
  and friendship   5–6
  to murder a piece (refused)   95
Petersen, Jerry   63
For Philip Guston (Feldman)   3, 10, 14, 108, 122, 144, 172–7. *See also* Feldman, Morton; Guston, Philip
Phillips, Karen   114. *See also* Feldman, Morton
  The Viola in My Life
phonograph
  in *Marginal Intersection*   33–5
Piekut, Benjamin. *See also* death; mediumship
  on actually existing experimentalism   94
  on "deadness"   125
  on musical performance and relationships   47 n.21
  on the vernacular avant-garde   55

Piero della Francesca 153, 163, 171. *See also* Guston, Philip
Pollock, Jackson 13, 18, 41–3, 66, 73–81, 84. *See also Jackson Pollock 51* (Namuth); *Works of Calder* (Matter)
    on the agency of the artwork 29
    Blue Poles 42–4
    death of 107
    and the Eighth Street Artists Club 79
    and Feldman 44, 175–6
    and jazz 36
    and Matter 73
    as nature 68, 71–3, 77
    and O'Hara 41–4, 111
    and vitalism 42, 58, 60, 80–1, 84
    and *Works of Calder* 68, 73
Ponsold, Renate 144, 164
Possibilities 28–9, 76, 80
posthumous collaborations 109, 136. *See also* death; *Three Clarinets, Cello, and Piano* (Feldman); *For Frank O'Hara* (Feldman)
Projection 1 (Feldman) 13, 97–9, 101, 104 n.15. *See also* Feldman, Morton; Moorman, Charlotte
Projection 2 (Feldman) 25–8, 98. *See also* Feldman, Morton
Proust, Marcel 135. *See also* vitalism
    In Search of Lost Time 58–9
publicity
    vs. privacy 8–10, 12, 17–19, 23, 27, 40, 44–6, 74–9, 116, 147–9, 152, 156–62, 176

quotation
    in Feldman's music 33–5, 95, 170, 173
    and history 161
    and melancholy 172–3. *See also* citation; nationalism

Rauschenberg, Robert
    photomontages of 170
    White Paintings 31
realization 96–102
repetition
    ascetic (as antidote to capitalism) 158

and the creation of classic works 37–8
    as enabled by notation 99
    and grief 175
    in Guston (according to Feldman) 170
    as impossible 111
    of lamentation 191
    and listening 43
    and stability 109
    of works on the same program 25–6, 98
Retallack, Joan. *See also Three Voices* (Feldman)
    on "oom-pah-pah" cultures 133
Reynolds, Roger
    and La Barbara 127
Rifkin, Libbie
    on friendships 4
Rivers, Larry. *See also New Yorkers II, The* (Kanovitz)
    and Kanovitz 1
    in *The New Yorkers II* (Kanovitz) 1–2
Roach, Tom
    on shared estrangement 12
Rose, Gillian
    on Walter Benjamin 108
Rosenberg, Harold 19, 21, 27, 58
    and Arendt 7, 185–6, 189–90
    on commodification 28
    and Guston 150–1, 155, 185
    on intimacy and understanding 45
    and *Possibilities* 28
Roth, Philip
    and Guston 169
Rothko, Mark 132, 171
    and communal art 28
    and the de Menils 4
    and Feldman 4, 18, 23, 143, 145, 175–6
    on flat forms 131
    and the present moment 30
Rothko Chapel 4. *See also* Feldman, Morton, *Rothko Chapel*
Rousseau, Jean-Jacques
    on fraternity and compassion 186

Schapiro, Meyer. *See also* spontaneity
"The Liberating Quality of Avant-Garde Art"   21–2, 30, 45
and the New York Studio School   158
Schoenberg, Arnold   24
Scholem, Gershom. *See also* Arendt, Hannah
and Arendt   186, 189–90
Schubert, Franz
for Feldman   174–6
Sculpture by Lipton (Boxer)   13, 57, 60, 68, 79–85. *See also* Lipton, Seymour
Selby, Nick
on subjectivity in O'Hara's "In Memory of My Feelings"   116–17
sensibility   14, 16
collective   110–13
and sound   58–9
sentimentality   6–7, 24, 126
shadow
life as a passing   123
painting   74, 77
Pollock's   77
ShadowSong (La Barbara)   129–30
sound as (for Feldman)   31
Shaw, Artie   35–6. *See also* jazz; *Marginal Intersection* (Feldman)
Shaw, Lytle
on the poetics of coterie   2, 9–10, 22, 40, 43, 109
silence   185–93
and Bergson   54
in Feldman's music   60, 118–19
as friendship-ender   145–6, 161–2, 167, 169, 187–8
as friendship-preserver   14, 30, 159, 188–90
and pedagogy   157
Silence (Cage)   32
and solitude (of modern life and art)   28
and temporality   190–1
Sjöholm, Cecilia
on art and the public sphere   8, 192
Slifkin, Robert
on action painting and drama   151

Smart, Pamela G. *See also* de Menil, Dominique; de Menil, John
on the de Menils   179 n.46
Smith, S. Stephenson. *See also* Broekman, David
on the "Music in the Making" series   38
Sontag, Susan. *See also* sensibility
on sensibility   14, 16
Soyer, David
and the "tradition of the new"   99
spontaneity
and acceptance   31
and chance music   23–32
and intimacy   3–4, 19–23, 44, 158, 167
and jazz   34
limits of   39–44
vs. predetermination   98–103
as undesirable   38
Stanyek, Jason. *See also* death; mediumship
on "deadness"   125
Stein, Gertrude. *See also* vitalism
Things As They Are   58
and Toklas   102
Stern, Daniel   35. *See also Jackson Pollock 51* (Namuth)
and Feldman   42, 74–5
Sterne, Jonathan
on the recording as resonant tomb   127
Stevens, Wallace. *See also* vitalism
and Bergson   58
"The Man with the Blue Guitar"   58
Stockhausen, Karlheinz   60
stroboscopic photography   71, 79. *See also* Matter, Herbert
Works of Calder
Studio School. *See* Matter, Mercedes; New York Studio School
Subotnick, Morton
and La Barbara   127
Synergy (Brown)   13, 100–2, 105 n.21. *See also* Brown, Earle; Moorman, Charlotte

Takahashi, Aki   173
taste
　escaping of   67, 84
　and jazz   36
　lapse of   134
　vs. truth   37
temporality
　and art   8, 30, 58–61
　and creation of the new   83
　and dance   65
　durée/duration   30, 54, 59–60, 64, 71, 83, 96, 98, 111, 134, 145
　and silence   190–1
　and tragedy   193
Tenney, James
　and La Barbara   127
Thomson, Virgil   24
Three Clarinets, Cello, and Piano (Feldman)   113–15, 117–24
Three Voices (Feldman)   10, 13, 122, 125–36, 140 n.52, 144, 172, 174. *See also* Feldman, Morton; La Barbara, Joan; mediumship
Trimble, Lester
　on Feldman's graph music   38
Tudor, David
　and Cage   34–5, 37, 96–7
　and Feldman   5–7, 23, 25, 32, 34, 42, 45, 62–3, 93–4, 96–7, 99, 104 n.7, 105 n.17

Varèse, Edgard   94
　as influence for Feldman's *Marginal Intersection*   33
　and jazz   36
verticality
　for Feldman   83, 179 n.46
　for Mercedes Matter   157
vision
　deferrals of   1–2. *See also* New Yorkers II, The (Kanovitz); of paintings   21
vitalism   13, 53–85. *See also* Bergson, Henri; nature
　and artist films   68–85

　and/of the Eighth Street Artists Club   22, 26–7, 53–85
　of Feldman   30, 53–62
　of Lipton   58, 80, 83
　of Marsicano   57–8, 63–7, 83–4
　of Mercedes Matter   157, 159
　of Pollock   42, 58, 60, 80–1, 84
Volans, Kevin
　on Feldman's musical practice (as anti-conceptual)   61

Weber, Ben   24
Webern, Anton
　as "father" of Feldman and Cage   24
　as quoted by Feldman in *Violin and Orchestra*   170
Whitehead, Alfred North. *See also* vitalism
　and Bergson   55–6, 58
　on the bifurcation of nature   68, 74
　on the fallacy of misplaced concreteness   190
Wolff, Christian   94–5
　and Arendt   7, 185
　and Cage   148
　For Christian Wolff   3
　Christian Wolff in Cambridge   63
Wolpe, Stefan   63, 94
　and Feldman   23–4, 110, 145, 175–6
　For Stefan Wolpe (Feldman)   3, 108
Works of Calder (Matter)   57, 60, 68–74, 78–9, 81–3, 110. *See also* Cage, John; vitalism

Young, La Monte   103
Young-Bruehl, Elisabeth. *See also* Arendt, Hannah; Rosenberg, Harold
　on Arendt and Rosenberg after the Eichmann affair   189

Zionism   53
Zukofsky, Paul. *See also Three Clarinets, Cello, and Piano* (Feldman)
　Composers Ensemble   139 n.34

www.ingramcontent.com/pod-product-compliance
Ingram Content Group UK Ltd.
Pitfield, Milton Keynes, MK11 3LW, UK
UKHW021857100326

468857UK00005B/909